Script Analysis
for Actors, Directors,
and Designers

Script Analysis for Actors, Directors, and Designers

James Thomas

Focal Press
Boston London

Focal Press is an imprint of Butterworth–Heinemann.

Recognizing the importance of preserving what has been written, it is the policy of Butterworth–Heinemann to have the books it publishes printed on acid-free paper, and we exert our best efforts to that end.

Library of Congress Cataloging-in-Publication Data

Thomas, James
    Script analysis for actors, directors, and designers / by James Thomas .
      p.   cm.
    Includes bibliographical references and index.
    ISBN 0-240-80129-6 (alk. paper)
    1. Drama—Explication. I. Title.
    PN1707.T46 1992
    808.2—dc20   91–45956
                                                    CIP

British Library Cataloguing in Publication Data

Thomas, James
    Script analysis for actors, directors, and designers.
    I. Title
    792.02

    ISBN 0-240-80129-6

Butterworth–Heinemann
80 Montvale Avenue
Stoneham, MA 02180

10 9 8 7 6 5 4 3 2 1

Printed in the United States of America

For my respected friends at the Moscow Art Theatre School–Studio who make a life in the theatre significant.

In fact it is the simplest things that are the most tricky to do well. To read, for example. To be able to read exactly what is written without omitting anything that is written and at the same time without adding anything of one's own. To be able to capture the exact context of the words one is reading. To be able to read!

Jean-Louis Barrault, *Reflections on the Theatre*

Contents

Preface

This book is the outcome of teaching and directing experience acquired in theatre programs with many different educational objectives. In all of them, I found that at some point in the curriculum teachers require that their students analyze plays in orderly fashion before the experience of acting, directing, or designing. At the Florida State University School of Theatre and at a growing number of other theatre programs, the faculty has determined that students should have a minimum of one course devoted entirely to this purpose. In the process of teaching these and related courses, I examined theatre textbooks concerned with the craftsmanship of performance and literature textbooks concerned with the scholarly aspects of drama. I did not find any current text dedicated to discussing the dramatic energies of a play in ways practical for actors, directors, and designers. In too many cases, I found otherwise talented students unable to use their talents to their best advantage because they did not know how to study plays from a theatrical point of view.

This book is designed to teach the serious theatre student the skills of script analysis using a formalist approach. By this, I mean first that it uses a standard system of classifications to study the written part of a play, excluding performance, scenery, and so forth. Formalist methodology also means that the book does not cover all the topics included in the usual literature textbooks. There is no extensive attention to dramatic forms or styles; no scrutiny of historical-critical theories or sociopolitical implications; no attention to the life, mind, or personality of the author; and no specific treatment of current trends in drama (although the book relates to all these matters). The approach is not new. We know how scientists adopt the practice of deliberately neglecting certain data outside their own spheres of interest. Likewise professional theatre artists tend to avoid outside details and turn instead to the play itself when they are looking for the key to their work. The scientist and artist know perfectly well that the neglected information exists all the time, but they act as if it didn't for the special purposes of their work. I admit that this kind of restricted approach can claim no scholarly pretensions. The aim is exclusively practical and intended mainly for the theatre.

Most of this book deals with play analysis, but since the acts of thinking and reading are intimately connected with this analysis, I have provided an Introduction I hope will make those processes a little better. It begins with a brief sketch of the heritage of formalist analysis and then offers general guidelines for reading and thinking about plays.

The largest portion of the book is involved with understanding the basic dramatic potential of a play. I have attempted to keep the design simple. Each of the first eight chapters treats one of the basic elements of drama originally described by Aristotle and later adopted by many other teachers, scholars, and theatre artists. Though all the elements, of course, depend strongly on each other, the method used is to select one as the essence of the play for the time being and to disregard the others. This is what I believe is unique and what will prove the most useful about the book. By narrowing the point of view in this way, students can acquire the mental concentration needed to learn the individual parts of plays and their possibilities. The approach will eventually show that each element is inseparable from the whole meaning, an understanding that is the bedrock of artistic unity. When formalist analysis is done well, it can feel almost like the play is acting, directing, and designing itself.

A list of questions about the topics covered is found at the end of each chapter. These questions are important learning tools. They are meant to stimulate creative thinking as actors, directors, and designers engage in the production process. By reviewing the topics one by one, students will be certain to cover most of the important dramatic possibilities found in a play.

Appendix A is a list of supplementary topics for script analysis, and Appendix B is an introduction to the genres and styles of drama, but in general, I have assumed that readers concerned with outside information and different methods of criticism will consult some of the excellent books already available on those subjects. The Selected Bibliography at the end of this book supports the point of view of the book and is a learning device.

Play analysis is a practical craft that is best explained by concrete examples, but since this book is likely to be used with an anthology chosen by the teacher, I have tried to keep it reasonably self-contained. The plays used in the examples were carefully selected to represent a wide range of playwrights, periods, genres, and styles. Those who wish to get the most out of the book should read all the plays to which I refer. They are:

Oedipus Rex (ca. 430 BC) by Sophocles
Hamlet (ca. 1600) by William Shakespeare
Tartuffe (1669) by Molière
The School for Scandal (1777) by Richard Brinsley Sheridan
The Wild Duck (1884) by Henrik Ibsen
The Hairy Ape (1921) by Eugene O'Neill
Mother Courage (1937) by Bertolt Brecht
Death of a Salesman (1949) by Arthur Miller
A Raisin in the Sun (1959) by Lorraine Hansberry
Happy Days (1961) by Samuel Beckett
Streamers (1976) by David Rabe

The scripts are widely available in both single editions and anthologies. In my own teaching, students select three plays for careful study: one historical, one realistic, and one modern nontraditional. For the realistic play, they may choose from the list or select a title of their own.

Besides being a system of classification and an intellectual attitude, formalist analysis may also be used as means of entry into a playscript. When analyzing plays, it's helpful to begin with a plan, and taken all together, the classifications embody such a plan. This implies that students can go through them one by one, and in the beginning, they are encouraged to do just that. Formalist analysis is an attempt to organize the study of a play, and the system of classification is the necessary basis of such organization. Of course, some people simply cannot start with a plan, and they end up staring at a jumble of disconnected classifications. Play analysis takes practice, just as any kind of logical thinking does. In these cases, it may be better just to study the play randomly, letting one thought lead to another without worrying about classifications. Later on it should become clear what has been left out or misplaced. Then it may be easier to return to a plan and study the topics left out of the unorganized first attempts.

The book can successfully accommodate different teaching strategies. Although it is purposefully organized and arranged, there is no absolute need either to cover all the topics completely or to study them in the order they are presented. Some teachers may select fewer categories to form the organizing principles for the course; others may choose to assign the readings differently. I mention only three points. First most of the book is within reach of serious beginning students, but the material in Chapter 8, Tempo, Rhythm, and Mood, and Chapter 9, The Style of the Play, is probably better suited to students with wider experience in play reading and production. Second it's a good idea to keep the course moving and not become involved in prolonged examinations of individual plays. This goal may be accomplished if, instead of teaching the plays, the teacher focuses on teaching the skills needed to analyze the plays. Third a great deal can be gained by studying as many topics as possible in their original order. I have found that with enough practice most students gradually develop a mode of quick, automatic understanding. Eventually they are able to go directly to those topics that apply to their needs and disregard the rest.

Readers should glean from my remarks what they need to know about the scope of this book, but I wish to add a few more comments. There are many ways to understand plays, and this book is concerned with only one of them. Although in the twentieth century much of the systematic writing about plays has been in this tradition, it is not hard to find objections to formalist analysis from those who favor other methods. Therefore since we are concerned in this book primarily with the closed context of the play itself, I emphasize that the attention given to this aspect does not imply that other kinds of analysis do not exist or are not important. I have simply agreed to set them aside in favor of discovering the relationships expressed within the play itself. No single method can ever be completely true, but I aim to convince readers that a large number of playable dramatic values can be discovered using this approach.

Writing a textbook on play analysis is a challenge. This is partly because there is no consensus in the profession about terms and definitions but also because those who deal with plays on a daily basis eventually develop their own favorite aims, methods, and terms. It follows logically that there are a number of hotly contested issues involved. The topics of crisis, climax, catastrophe, and resolution, for example, have proven to be extremely vexing for critics and theorists, and sometimes it seems as if there are as many definitions of dramatic action and objectives as there are actors and directors. In other words although the topics in this book have been carefully defined, it is not hard to find different, if not contradictory, meanings in the works of other writers and practitioners. Undoubtedly we could devote a lot more thought to these topics if we wished to, but in a practical book, it isn't a good idea to test the patience of readers with too much theory. Besides for working artists, the conditions in the play itself are ordinarily more important. I hope the terms and definitions as well as the comments about the plays are at least sound and practical. They are not meant to be prescriptive or to take the place of the teacher. Readers who originally learned about them somewhere else may wish to use my definitions as a basis for comparison with their own instead of thinking of them as conclusive statements of which there are very few in art anyway.

Acknowledgments

This book would not have been possible without the help of others, and the list of those to whom I am obligated is long. It begins with Fran Hodge, whose knowledge of play analysis and directing has set standards that in my opinion no one has matched. He taught me how to think seriously about plays and play production, and his approach to the analytical process (treated in *Play Directing: Analysis, Communication, and Style*) has helped to shape the general outline of this book. None of the errors found here should be attributed to him, but most of what is good and useful can be traced to his influence.

For the invaluable opportunity to attend their rehearsals, classes, and lectures and for their patience with my endless questioning, I would like to thank the eminent artist-teachers of the Moscow Art Theatre School–Studio, namely, Oleg Tabakov (Rector), Anatoly Smelyansky, Oleg Gerasimov, Ivan Moskvin-Tarkhanov, Vladimir Komratov, and Mikhail Lobanov. Diligent readers will discover that I have additional sources, probably more than I even know myself. Among these sources are the writings of George Pierce Baker, Eric Bentley, Michael Chekhov, Harold Clurman, Francis Fergusson, John Gassner, Frank McMullan, Constantin Stanislavski, F. Cowles Strickland, and Georgi Tovstonogov. A number of colleagues read parts or all of the manuscript over the last two years and made helpful comments and criticisms. Among these are Stuart Baker, Dan Carter, John Franceschina, Richard Hornby, Gil Lazier, and Jim Wise. To all, my thanks.

I also wish to acknowledge the reprinted selections:

Excerpts from *The Oedipus Rex of Sophocles*, translated by Dudley Fitts and Robert Fitzgerald, copyright 1949 by Harcourt Brace Jovanovich, Inc. and renewed 1977 by Cornelia Fitts and Robert Fitzgerald, reprinted by permission of the publisher.

Hamlet by William Shakespeare, *The School for Scandal* by Richard Brinsley Sheridan, and *The Wild Duck* by Henrik Ibsen are from *Plays for the Theatre: An Anthology of World Drama*, Oscar G. Brockett, ed. (New York: Holt, Rinehart, and Winston, 1984).

Tartuffe by Molière from *The Misanthrope and Other Plays*, translated by John Wood (Penguin Classics, 1959). Copyright © 1959 by John Wood. Excerpts by permission of Penguin Books Ltd.

The Hairy Ape by Eugene O'Neill (New York: Random House, 1921).

Mother Courage and Her Children from *Collected Plays*, Volume V, by Bertolt Brecht, translated by Ralph Manheim. Copyright © 1972 by Stefan S. Brecht. Reprinted by permission of Pantheon Books, a division of Random House, Inc.

From *Death of a Salesman* by Arthur Miller. Copyright 1949, renewed © 1977 by Arthur Miller. Used by permission of Viking Penguin Books USA Inc.

A Raisin in the Sun by Lorraine Hansberry (New York: Random House, 1959).

Happy Days by Samuel Beckett (New York: Grove Press, 1961).

Streamers by David Rabe. Copyright, as an unpublished work, 1970, 1975 by David William Rabe. Copyright © 1976, 1977 by David William Rabe. Reprinted by permission of Alfred A. Knopf, Inc.

Script Analysis
for Actors, Directors,
and Designers

Introduction

WHAT IS FORMALIST SCRIPT ANALYSIS?

Although some readers may often have heard the term *formal,* they may not have a firm idea of what it means. This is understandable because it has taken on many meanings over time. Formal may be associated with the practice of doing something for appearance's sake as in a formal wedding. Or it may convey a feeling of primness and stiffness. Maybe readers harbor an unconscious feeling that formal means fixed, authoritarian, and inflexible. All these meanings have in common the notion of an arrangement that gives something its essential character or what Aristotle described as "the inward shaping of an object." The etymology of the word substantiates this. Formal is based on the idea of form or shape. The Latin word *forma* means that which shapes or has been shaped, but especially the shape given to an artistic object. The English word *formula* is related to it as are conformity, inform, reform, transform, and uniform.

Studying the etymology leads to the present meaning of *formalist analysis:* the search for playable dramatic values that reveal a central unifying pattern that informs or shapes a play from the inside and coordinates all of its parts. Playable dramatic values are those features that energize actors, directors, and designers in their work. To accomplish its goal, formalist analysis uses a traditional system of classifications to break up a play into its parts to understand their nature and relationship.

Some writers may call the formalist approach *descriptive* because it is concerned with describing a play in terms of its own internal artistic context. Or it may be called *analytical* because it analyzes the elements in a play as parts of an artistic totality. Others might describe this approach as *Aristotelian* because it is based on the parts of a play originally described by Aristotle. All these are acceptable alternatives. At the risk of seeming to split hairs, however, I should point out that formalist analysis is very different from *formal analysis,* which means the study of a play in relation to the form or literary genre to which it belongs. In any event, the underlying assumption of formalist analysis is that the plays themselves ought to be studied instead of the abstract theories or external circumstances under which they are written. For theatre students especially, plays should not be merely a means to other kinds of studies, but rather the primary objects of attention.

Formalist analysis of drama is customarily associated with the principles and methods of Aristotle. His *Poetics* (335–322 BC) treats the six elements of drama, unity of action, probability, features of the tragic hero, plot requirements, and other subjects related to plays. Although the term *poetics* is derived from the same Greek source as is the word *poetry*, in Aristotle's sense it more correctly means creatively making, constructing, and arranging an artistic work, in this case drama. The common-sense conclusions he reached continue to influence Western literature and drama even today, and his expressions and descriptions have become part of our critical heritage.

From his survey of the writing, construction, and arrangement of the best plays of his time, Aristotle deduced principles and methods for their analysis and evaluation. His work is the basis of the formalist approach. First he summarized the basics of drama and analyzed their inner workings and possible combinations. Second he insisted on the importance of the artistic nature of plays. Third he reduced concern with outside realistic or moral issues and emphasized instead strict attention to inner structural design, placing special emphasis on the importance of plot as a unifying feature. Fourth his method was inductive rather than prescriptive. These four principles together make up the heart of the formalist tradition in criticism.

During the Roman period and later during the Renaissance and the seventeenth-century, scholars treated Aristotle's insights as rigid prescriptions. Inquiring into the historical motives behind this phenomenon is beyond the scope of this book, but we know now that the practical outcome left Aristotle with an undeserved reputation for pedantry some of which lingers on to the present. As succeeding writers interpreted Aristotle with more insight and sensitivity, his reputation as a critic was for the most part restored.

Around the turn of the nineteenth century in Russia, scholar and critic Alexander Veselovsky extended the Aristotelian tradition by developing a system of carefully defined aims and methods for the study of literature and drama. His system, like Aristotle's, was based mainly on the importance of plot. Veselovsky was a member of the literary committee of the Maly Theatre and promoted his principles directly among Moscow's working theatre artists. His ideas strongly influenced actor Mikhail Shchepkin, artistic director of the influential Maly company, and Vladimir Nemirovitch-Dantchenko, a member of the same committee and cofounder of the Moscow Art Theatre with Constantin Stanislavski. Perhaps inspired by Veselovsky's emphasis on plot and artistic unity, Nemirovitch-Dantchenko and Stanislavski promoted similar principles and methods among their own students. Their goal was practical, not scholarly: to help actors understand and perform plays as orderly arrangements of actions.

Later, around the time of the Russian Revolution, formalist ideas began to be applied on an even larger scale by a group of critics known as the Russian formalists. Headed by Victor Shklovsky and Evgeny Zamyatin, the formalists were characterized by their meticulous attention to the artistic aspects of literature as opposed to its social or moral connections.

After 1928, Russian formalism was suppressed in the Soviet Union for political reasons, but its major concepts and strategies can be found in the New

Criticism, which first appeared during the 1930s and flourished during the 1940s and 50s in the West. The New Criticism was an American movement led by John Crowe Ransom, Allen Tate, and Robert Penn Warren, all of whom were writers and poets as well as critics. In his book *The New Criticism* (1941), Ransom coined the term that identified this informal group, which also included R.P. Blackmur, Kenneth Burke, Cleanth Brooks, Robert B. Heilman, William K. Wimsatt, and Ivor Winters.

Like the Russian formalists, the New Critics advocated meticulous study of the work itself. They generally disregarded the mind and personality of the author, literary sources, historical-critical theories, and political and social implications, which they denounced as *historical criticism.* To emphasize their firm belief in the autonomy of the work itself, they referred to the literary work as the *text* and termed their analytical approach *close reading.* Their ideas were presented in four textbooks: Wimsatt and Warren's *Understanding Poetry* (1938), Brooks and Warren's *Understanding Fiction* (1943), Brooks and Heilman's *Understanding Drama* (1948), and Brooks and Warren's guide to methodology, *Modern Rhetoric* (1958). These textbooks helped to shift the focus of literary instruction away from external concerns to the work itself.

The so-called Cambridge Critics led a comparable movement in English literary criticism. Influenced by poet T.S. Eliot, this group was unofficially headed by William Empson and included F.R. Leavis, I.A. Richards, Caroline Spurgeon, and G. Wilson Knight. Knight's analyses of Shakespeare's plays, notably *The Wheel of Fire* (1930), were some of the major successes of the Cambridge Critics in the field of drama.

Many of the principles of the New Criticism were adopted by succeeding generations of American writers, including Francis Fergusson (particularly *The Idea of a Theatre,* 1949), Elder Olson, Eric Bentley, Bernard Beckerman, Richard Hornby, and Jackson G. Barry, as well as theatre educators Alexander Dean, Hardie Albright, Lawrence Carra, William Halstead, F. Cowles Strickland, Curtis Canfield, Frank McMullan, Sam Smiley, and Francis Hodge to name only a few of the most influential. Among theatre professionals, the analytical methods of the Moscow Art Theatre were self-consciously adopted by the members of the Group Theatre beginning in the 1930s. Formalist thinking supports the writing of Stella Adler, Harold Clurman, Mordecai Gorelik, Elia Kazan, Robert Lewis, Sanford Meisner, Lee Strasberg, and many of their students and followers.

Beginning in the 1960s, drama and literature were influenced by movements in politics, sociology, and religion in ways that seemed to defy traditional methods of criticism. Accordingly a new generation of literary critics emerged who became increasingly dissatisfied with the self-imposed limits of the formalist approach. Within a decade more wide-ranging critical approaches appeared based on deconstruction, poststructuralism, hermeneutics, semiotics, and theories of reception and communication. Some of them have revealed meanings previously unknown in plays, and their fresh interpretations seem promising. So far in the rehearsal hall, however, their results have not been consistently worthwhile. Perhaps this is because they have emphasized taking apart (hence *de*construction) while theatrical production by definition must be concerned with putting together.

At any rate, even though literary criticism currently seems to be committed to interests outside the play, theatre practice must continue to rely on close analysis of the play itself. Some may argue that this approach is not inherently better than any other method at its best. After all, there are selected plays and periods of history where considerations outside the script are important and should be studied. Conversely, understanding the internal nature of the play is crucial to understanding its external context. More important in the theatre, plays must eventually exist in the practical realm of live performance and not just in the intellectual realm of scholarship. On stage at least, the play itself is obliged to remain the final controlling factor. Formalist analysis corresponds with this point of view. It offers more than intellectual insights; it supplies practical suggestions that can energize actors, directors, and designers for their work.

To conclude, the principles of formalist analysis have endured in the theatre because they correspond closely with the nature of the thing to which they are applied. They are an outcome of how actors, directors, and designers naturally think about plays, and they are based on the assumption that what these artists need to know about plays is actually what is important. Although we may not always be consciously aware of it, the principles of formalist analysis help to make plays work out in production. Without them, playscripts would seem unfinished and maybe even unintelligible.

Here then in outline form are the classifications of formalist analysis and their main subdivisions as they are used in the first eight chapters of this book:

1. Foundations of the plot: given circumstances
   - Time
   - Place
   - Society
   - Economics
   - Politics and law
   - Intellect and culture
   - Spirituality
   - The world of the play
2. Foundations of the plot: background story
   - Technique
   - Identification
3. Plot: physical and psychological action
   - Physical action (the external plot)
   - Psychological action (the internal plot)
4. Plot: progressions and structure
   - Progressions
   - Structure
5. Character
   - Objectives

- Dramatic action
- Conflict
- Willpower
- Values
- Personality traits
- Complexity
- Relationships

6. Idea
   - Words
   - Characters
   - Plot
   - The main idea
7. Dialogue
   - Words
   - Sentences
   - Speeches
   - Special qualities
   - Theatricality
8. Tempo, rhythm, and mood
   - Tempo
   - Rhythm
   - Mood

This sums up what most actors, directors, and designers will need to know about the heritage of formalist analysis. The complete history, of course, is more complex than this. For example, the Freudian, Jungian, Marxian, and Existentialist critics whose ideas currently influence some of the more radical methodologies were omitted from the survey. If the contributions of Freud, Jung, Marx, and Sartre are understated, the position of the New Critics regarding the independence of the text is a little overstated. Apart from their theories, there are passages in their writing that go beyond the literary work and into the areas of politics and morals. The survey is also responsible for another necessary exaggeration. By design, it leads the reader to feel a straight chain of thinking, supporting the formalist tradition, that is unlikely for a diverse group of writers dealing with a complex subject. But having agreed about these oversimplifications, the survey is still adequate to establish the heritage of the formalist viewpoint. Those who wish to learn more can read some of the many books that have been written about the history of literary criticism. A basic listing is provided in the Selected Bibliography.

EXPRESSIVENESS OF DRAMATIC WRITING

Before we begin to study the topics in detail, it will be helpful to review some of the basic principles of reading in general. Initial learning about a play almost always begins with the written words of the script. But when we act, direct, or design a play, we not only read the play but the play reads us. If we fall short, the results are there for everyone to see. Therefore, what is done *at the table* before the rehearsals and production conferences begin is crucial. If initial perceptions are wrong, every succeeding repetition reinforces the error. If initial perceptions are confused, every succeeding repetition increases the confusion. Persistent errors and extended confusion are certain to lead down the path of artistic failure. For these reasons alone, reviewing some of the basic principles involved with reading and thinking can help theatre artists approach their work with something worthwhile to say.

When plays are treated as subdivisions of literature, they are likely to be analyzed with the same principles as those applied to fiction, poetry, and other strictly literary genres. A number of writers have pointed out, however, that there are crucial differences between literature and drama that orthodox literary analysis may not be equipped to address by itself. To begin with, the dialogue in fiction is usually supplemented with generous amounts of narration to explain plot, character, idea, and feelings not otherwise apparent. Of course, some narration is always necessary in drama. We shall discuss this subject in more detail in Chapter 2, but in general, dramatic writing depends on dialogue that conveys action, not narration. Unlike the literary author, the dramatist cannot continuously interrupt the action to offer supplementary information or to clarify complex meanings without seriously hampering the spirit of the play. Even when there is a narrator in the play, the words still must sound like normal speech within the context of the situation, and although stage directions are written in narrative form, they are not spoken by the actors and are not central to the dramatic action.

Another feature that contributes to the extra expressiveness of plays is their short length. Even in a very long play, the number of words is surprisingly small compared to those in a novel, yet although plays employ far fewer words than do novels, they must still contain at least as much dramatic potential as does a complete novel to be effective theatrically. Playwrights achieve this potency by infusing stage dialogue with a special expressiveness that is largely absent or at least less important in other literary forms. It is true that stage dialogue often looks very much like its literary cousin. Sometimes it sounds so ordinary that it seems as if it was written without any conscious effort at all on the part of the playwright. But this is a carefully crafted deception. The truth is that theatrical dialogue is an extremely concentrated and powerful form of verbal expression. Speech is more condensed on stage and each word carries far more dramatic impact than in other literary forms. Even a single utterance can pack a tremendous bang. Because of the extra measure of expressiveness put into it initially by the playwright, there is arguably more expressiveness per page in a play than in almost any other form of writing. This is confirmed by the unusually long prewriting phase required for plays during which the extra expressiveness must be prepared painstakingly. Novelist Henry James, himself an experienced dramatist and a perceptive critic, maintained that playwriting required a more masterly sense of composition than did any other kind of literary art.

Concentrated dependence on spoken dialogue plus radical compact-ness together create the need and the opportunity for extra expressiveness in dramatic writing. It follows logically that actors, directors, and designers should learn to understand this special expressiveness to energize and illustrate every last ounce of it in production. But this does not always happen. Because the first experience of a play is ordinarily a written script, the extra expressiveness is easy to overlook. There is an understandable confusion between the strictly literary activity of reading and the theatrical activity of seeing, hearing, and feeling a play on the stage. Confusion is even more likely to occur with plays that have strong literary merit like those of Shakespeare and other authors whose works are studied in dramatic literature courses. To avoid underreading, theatre students should be continuously aware of two important considerations about theatrical dialogue. First the words in a script are far, far more emotionally expressive in a live performance than they are in the solitary, concentrated act of reading, and second the words are only the starting point of what is happening in a play. Energized acting, direction, and design are always required to unleash a play's potent expressiveness completely.

ANALYTICAL READING

There are no hard and fast rules for reading plays, but certain mental powers are needed to understand the special kind of expressiveness they contain. The first important power is that of analytical reading. Unfortunately in its initial stages at least, analytical reading can be laborious work. Some people think that experienced professionals can rapidly sight-read a play the way musicians sight-read a score, but this skill is as rare in the theatre as it is in music. A professional's analysis of a play is usually a long, tedious, and painstaking process. In fact, a major characteristic of professionals is their recognition of the value of slow, methodical *table work.*

Another mental power consists of the ability to understand the many meanings of words and the dramatic force that may be expressed by them. Art students pay attention to shape and color; music students listen for pitch and timbre. Whoever wishes to make a living in the theatre should develop a sense of the expressiveness and emotion inherent in words.

Mental power also means concern for literal facts and their connections. A fact is a verifiable assertion about a thing, and literal facts are those that are frankly and openly stated in the dialogue. Literal facts in drama include identification of people, places, actions, and objects, but they may also describe wishes as well as feelings and thoughts. Learning how to deal with facts is a basic test of artistic awareness. In the earliest readings of a play, the literal, verifiable facts should be searched out conscientiously to find exactly what is being said as completely as possible. Furthermore since plays are orderly arrangements by their nature, making connections among facts is absolutely necessary for understanding the sequences and patterns invariably found in them. We call these connections *implications* and *inferences.* Implications are indications, hints, or suggestions that are deliberate though not openly stated, and inferences are deductions of unknown from known information, that is, deduced from literal facts and their implications.

Remember the short scene in the garden from Act II of Arthur Miller's play, *Death of a Salesman.* After a climactic confrontation with his son, Biff, Willy Loman decides to plant vegetables in his cherished little backyard garden late the same night. As in several earlier scenes, his absent brother Ben appears to him in his imagination, and they carry on a short dialogue. In this scene, the literal facts about planting a garden are important. We know that planting a garden requires certain physical activities and special tools. Since these can be described precisely, this part of the action is easy to understand. Some of the literal facts involved with planting a garden are present: opening packages of seeds and reading the instructions, pacing off the rows for different kinds of plants, using a hoe, and planting the seeds in the ground. But most readers will see right away that planting a garden is not all that is happening here. There are things going on that are not ordinarily associated with planting a garden. Planting is usually not done late at night with a flashlight, and a gardener does not usually carry on a conversation about life insurance with an imaginary figure the way Willy does. Willy is also possessed by a mysterious sense of urgency in his task that prevents him from paying close attention to Ben. Obviously planting a garden is no longer what we normally think it is.

Implications and inferences now become important and they do not support a literal reading of the scene. A closer examination of Willy's unusual actions relates them to his innermost feelings and thoughts, particularly his profound sense of personal failure as a father. He is no longer simply planting a garden; he is performing a ritual in preparation for his imminent death. The garden scene becomes an important clue to the meaning of the whole play, which is a conflict between Willy's love for his son Biff and his duty to him as a father. Therefore although literal facts are a helpful starting point, implications and inferences should be considered to arrive at a complete understanding. Script analysis involves piecing the known and unknown together into a consistent and meaningful pattern just as detectives do in popular crime fiction.

LOGICAL THINKING

Evidence of all kinds is important, but so is logical thinking. Unfortunately ignorance of the creative capacities of logical thinking is widespread, particularly among young artists. It usually leads to the feeling that careful study of a play is stuffy and even creatively inhibiting, but experienced professionals know that logical analysis can uncover dramatic possibilities that make plays come alive in a new way. There is another value to consider. Audiences are becoming smarter all the time because modern playwrights demand far more intelligence from them today than they did in the past. Modern plays are fashioned to pull the audience into the action and to force them to actively comprehend what is happening, not just listen inactively. A great deal of aesthetic pleasure comes from penetrating the secret thinking of the characters. Consequently modern acting, directing, and design should demand the most of audience understanding. It is essential that the artistic team should always be at least one step ahead of the audience in this regard. For unless the audience is given something exciting to think about; unless the artistic team understands and expresses the inner logic of the play, the production cannot be considered truly modern.

Bringing some of the common fallacies of logic encountered in play reading out of the subconscious, where they usually lurk, and into the open can help students avoid accidental misreading. There are only a few major pitfalls, and they are not that difficult to understand. Most of them can be classified as non sequiturs, either as conclusions that do not follow from the facts or as reasoning that does not make sense. Some readers may feel they need to restudy the principles of logical thinking before trying to deal more thoroughly with plays. The basics can be found in any good rhetoric textbook. With the help of a good tutor, this should be enough to fill in any gaps.

Affective Fallacy (Impressionism)

According to literary critic W.K. Wimsatt, this error results from confusion between the play and its results (what it *is* and what it *does*). It comes about when readers allow their favorite ideals or momentary enthusiasms or the momentary enthusiasms of the community to intrude on their judgment of the play. Maintaining enough emotional detachment is certainly necessary to analyze a play correctly, but this is not always easy to do. After all, plays are meant to be emotional experiences, and many readers respond strongly to the emotional stimuli in them. Actors, directors, and designers, for example, usually respond in overwhelmingly personal ways, as indeed they should. In the scene from *Death of a Salesman* cited above, it is possible that readers could be reminded of their own fathers. They might be tempted to confuse emotional memories of them with Willy Loman's situation in the play. Or, alternatively, readers who personally identified with Willy's economic plight might be tempted to entangle their own feelings with Willy's in the play. Intensely personal experiences like these can be interesting if readers are experienced artists or critics; but if not, they can be an excuse for loose thinking and analytical carelessness. A reader might become hopelessly bogged down in self-analysis. Nonetheless it is possible to maintain emotional distance and still respond emotionally to a play. The solution is to try continuously to separate intimate personal responses from what is objectively *there* in the play. Director Elia Kazan has stated, "The first job is to discover what the script is saying, not what it reminds you of." Absolute objectivity is impossible, but impartiality and the tracing out of both routine and unusual consequences should be maintained. Successful script analysis depends on it.

Fallacy of Faulty Generalization (Overexpansion)

Some readers are inclined to this reading error when they jump to a conclusion without having enough evidence. When a reader uses *all* or *never* in statements about the play with only a casual concern for the information in the play itself, further close reading will usually correct this mistake. But even more deadly in play reading is inattention to contrary examples. If, after reading *Hamlet,* for instance, a reader resorts to the worn-out generalities about "the melancholy prince" or "the man who could not make up his mind," he should test the conclusions with contradictory evidence. A little scrutiny will show that Hamlet is cheerful while welcoming the Players, and he's decisive while dealing with the Ghost. A few contrary illustrations like these should be enough to disprove the original sweeping assertions.

Fallacy of Illicit Process (Reductiveness)

This kind of error reduces complex issues to one thing, a frequent mistake even among experienced play readers. Reducing Hamlet to the *Oedipus Complex* is an extreme instance. So is thinking that *Mother Courage* or *Streamers* are nothing but antiwar plays, or that *A Raisin in the Sun* is a social protest play. The phrase *nothing but* is the giveaway. Related to *reductiveness* is the *genetic fallacy* or the *fallacy of origins,* which is an attempt to reduce a play to its sources in the biography or social world of the artist to explain it. There is for any play a large body of secondary writing about its circumstances, the author's life and times, and so forth. Much of this writing is pedantic in the extreme and full of banalities. For example, the question is not what does *Death of a Salesman* tell us about Arthur Miller's personal life or about American society during the 1940s but rather what does it tell us about itself? There may be some connections between a play and some external features in the life and world of the author, but they are usually not as important as people believe them to be. No point-to-point correlation exists, and although formalist analysis teaches the fundamental unity of plays, it also teaches that plays are complex independent objects deserving intellectual respect. Readers should exercise caution before attempting to trace the meaning of a play to a tendency observed in the life or times of the author.

Fallacy of the Half-Truth (Debunking)

This error in logic occurs when readers use the same explanation for everything, usually with deliberately negative implications. In this way, the author, play, or character is cunningly discredited or debunked. Henrik Ibsen's plays frequently suffer from this fallacy among readers. To say that Ibsen wrote grim social dramas carries the unspoken meaning to others that his plays are (1) gloomy and humorless, (2) the result of psychological neuroses in the author's temperament, and (3) Victorian journalism masquerading as drama. Readers holding this opinion see Ibsen's plays as boring, depressing, and outdated. Another example is the statement that: "nothing really happens in Samuel Beckett's plays—there's no plot." What is the real meaning behind this half-truth? The remedy for automatic cynicism is to study the script more than once with an open mind. This is not just a question of finding any reasonable explanation and verifying it in the script but also of testing what connects to what against many points in the script.

Intentional Fallacy

This is another of Wimsatt's formulations that is central to the principles of formalist analysis. It means trying to determine what the author's intention was and whether it was fulfilled, instead of attending to the work itself. Examples of this are easy to find because of the modern vogue for literary research and the frequency with which artists insist on writing about their own works. Take the situation of Bertolt Brecht. No one can measure the amount of misunderstanding that has resulted from misapplication of his theoretical writings to productions of his plays (that is, *alienation effect* or *epic realism*). Wimsatt in *The Verbal Icon* argues that a work of art is detached from the author the moment it is finished. After that, the author no longer has the power to intend anything about it or to control it. Wimsatt's opinion, however, should be taken as a warning more than as a strict rule. As with the other reading errors, the antidote to use against the intentional fallacy is repeated close reading of the play itself before attempting to make a definitive statement about the author's intention.

Frigidity (Insensitivity)

The next error turns in the opposite direction. *Frigidity* is author John Gardner's term for not showing enough concern—or the right kind of concern— about the characters or situations. The standard of comparison is the concern any decent human being would naturally show under the circumstances. Frigidity here means not treating the feelings in the play with importance and care they deserve. Frigidity also includes the inability to recognize the seriousness of things in general. Frigidity occurs when pulling back from genuine feeling or when only looking at the surface trivialities in a conflict. Unfortunately it is one of the chief characteristics of the current artistic scene. It leads to increasingly less concern for the characters, plot, and concrete meaning of a play, is one of the worst errors possible in play reading, and is often the root of other errors. The error is frigidity when actors, directors, or designers knowingly go into a production less than fully prepared.

Reality Testing

Related to frigidity is the fallacy that Richard Hornby terms *reality testing*. This is the error of evaluating everything in the play on the basis of its likeness to real life. When it is used as a negative judgment, a statement like "the Ghost in *Hamlet* is not believable because science tells us there's no such thing as ghosts" is a typical if crude example. This kind of thinking is a sign of a limited imagination as much as anything else. It probably stems from misapplying the idea of *reality* in acting, sometimes called *emotional honesty* by actors. But the quality of observed reality in a play has little connection with the play's potential for expressing truth. A play after all can be completely unrealistic in all its outer features and still permit emotionally honest acting. A simple door can be different from one play to another, depending on the artistic plan of the production. In one play, it can be completely realistic while in another the actor can enter simply by appearing out of the darkness in a spotlight. Emotional honesty and theatrical reality are completely separate and distinct issues and do not contradict one another. Whatever the source of the confusion, however, the lesson is that everyday reality is irrelevant to understanding a play as an artistic experience. Plays create their own realities.

Secondhand Thinking

This error is a corollary of intentional fallacy. Although it is not really a logical fallacy, it can still be troublesome for novice play readers. It stems from unconsciously relying too much on other people's opinions, especially when dealing with difficult material. The methods of the college classroom and the recent interest in radical criticism have not discouraged the habit. Unfortunately, addiction to the judgments even of experienced critics, even when they are accurate, can inhibit self-confidence and independent thinking. Artists should beware of cutting themselves off from new experiences, feelings, or words by relying on established opinion rather than on direct contact. To permit the free exercise of imagination, script analysis should initially be a solo experience. Experts can safely be consulted afterward.

Overreliance on Stage Directions

Secondhand thinking also extends to stage directions, which are notes incorporated in a script or added to it to convey information about its performance not already evident in the dialogue itself. Ordinarily they are concerned either with the actor's movements on stage or with scenery and stage effects. Plays written in the past tended to keep stage directions to a minimum, but over the years their use grew more widespread until, by the end of the nineteenth century, they were often long and very elaborate. The prefaces to George Bernard Shaw's plays, for instance, often run on for dozens of pages and contain explicit instructions for actors and producers. There is some evidence among modern playwrights, however, of a reversal of this trend.

But stage directions may not always belong to the author. According to the custom of most publishers, stage directions are as likely to be written by the stage manager from the original setting provided by the scene designer or written by the editor of the text (as in the case of Shakespeare, for example), and even when we are absolutely certain the author has written them, it is prudent to recall the advice of the late designer, Edward Gordon Craig, about the reliability of stage directions. In his treatise, *On the Art of the Theatre*, Craig contended that stage directions are an infringement on the artistic rights of actors, directors, and designers. From this he concluded that playwrights should stop incorporating them into their plays altogether. Of course Craig's prejudices are notorious, and obviously his position on this subject was extreme. He did have a point, however. Stage directions are intended to supplement the dialogue, never to replace it. They shouldn't be confused with the play itself. Many professional actors, directors, and designers as well as producers and agents will seldom read stage directions, any stage directions. They want to work directly with the play itself and allow it to tell them everything they need to know.

1

• • • • • • • •

Foundations
of the Plot: Given
Circumstances

Every play can be divided into six parts from which it derives its basic nature: plot, character, idea, dialogue, tempo-rhythm-mood (Aristotle's *music*), and production values. In this text, we are mainly concerned with the written part of a play; therefore we will deal not with production values but only with those five parts provided by the playwright. Aristotle originally arrived at this system of partitioning in his study of the functions of the parts of a play. He did not mean that all plays have these elements in the same amount or in the same way. One play may have more or fewer incidents in its plot than another, more complicated or simplified characters, or more or less attention devoted to idea. He simply meant that these six elements are present in one form or another in all those works we call plays.

The beginning of all plays is the unique combination of present and past that Stanislavski called the *given circumstances*. Other writers have used different terms— *social context, foundation of the plot, playwright's setting, texture, local detail,* or *literary landscape.* They all mean basically the same thing, the overall situation in which the action of the play occurs.

Novice play readers often think of the given circumstances as the parts they can pass over. The impulse may be naive, but it acknowledges something important. On the surface, given circumstances may not seem as exciting as are the other parts of a play. They are usually simple things—so simple that the impulse is to take them for granted. Yet assumptions that are most familiar are often hardest to recognize as important. In actuality, the given circumstances are as crucial to a play as plot and character. They put readers and audience into the *present* of the action. Without them, characters would exist in a vacuum, in some vague never-never land without any connection to real life. In effect, the given circumstances are almost like silent, invisible characters. They influence the other characters, increase tensions, create complications, and move the plot forward. As a result, they always contain important clues to other parts of the play. They may be silent or invisible, but they are likely to be the very things that make it possible to know what makes the characters tick. Bringing each given circumstance into focus will help to explain how it works. This can happen only after careful analysis forces it to stand up and be identified.

This chapter is concerned with the given circumstances that occur on stage before the audience. They spring from the time and place of the play along with the conventions, attitudes, and manners behind and around it. Under this general heading, we will be concerned with eight subtopics: time, place, society, economics, intellect and culture, politics and law, spirituality, and finally the world of the play. In the next chapter, we will turn to the past given circumstances, or *background story,* which is everything that happened before the beginning of the play.

TIME

Time in the given circumstances has three aspects: (1) the time of the play's composition, (2) the time in which the action is set, and (3) the time that passes during the course of the action.

Time of Composition

Strictly speaking, the time or date of the play's composition is not critical in the early stages of script analysis because it is not part of the written play. It will become more valuable when it is studied in connection with the biography of the author and the play's position within the body of the author's works. Although knowledge of the author's life and works is absolutely necessary for a complete understanding of any play, too much attention to them at this point is not necessary. Otherwise confusion may arise between what is learned about a play from outside sources and what is actually in it. Better to set aside external considerations for more study after script analysis is farther along.

Time of the Action

In many plays it is important we must know the exact time and season in which the action is set. This is not just for the sake of scholarly accuracy but also to help understand the whole situation better. The precision of the determination depends on the play. For instance, there are references to boxer Gene Tunney and football player "Red" Grange among Willy Loman's flash-backs in *Death of a Salesman*. These names establish the year of those scenes at about 1927 when Tunney was heavyweight champion and Grange played for the Chicago Bears. Two years later the stock market crashed, ushering in the Great Depression—important information for the play. Another incidental reference to time is the steel trust that is the target of so much bad will in *The Hairy Ape*. This citation establishes the time of that play at about 1913 when monopolies exercised an iron grip on the economic scene. The war in Vietnam, which serves as the background for *Streamers*, sets that play at between 1964–1968, the height of the volatile 1960s. Stage directions and playwright's notes sometimes offer information about the time of the action, but they are not always entirely dependable. Time should be established by searching the dialogue for direct statements or references to historical people, places, or things.

Dramatic Time

Dramatic time is the total of the time that passes during the on-stage action plus the intervals between acts and scenes. Some plays permit very precise determination. In *The Wild Duck,* it is possible without the help of stage directions to know the passage of dramatic time almost to the hour, including the time of day and day of the week for each act. Time may also be compressed or expanded to accommodate dramatic needs. Weeks pass in *The Hairy Ape,* months in *Hamlet,* and years in *Mother Courage.* Time moves forward and backward simultaneously in *Death of a Salesman,* and stands still in *Happy Days.*

There is an assortment of information about dramatic time in the opening lines of *Hamlet.*

BERNARDO: Who's there?

FRANCISCO: Nay, answer me. Stand and unfold yourself.

BERNARDO: Long live the King!

FRANCISCO: Bernardo?

BERNARDO: He.

FRANCISCO: You come most carefully upon your hour.

BERNARDO: 'Tis now struck twelve; get thee to bed, Francisco.

FRANCISCO: For this relief much thanks. 'Tis bitter cold, And I am
    sick at heart.

BERNARDO: Have you had quiet guard?

FRANCISCO: Not a mouse stirring.

BERNARDO: Well; good night.

Although Francisco is on guard duty, Bernardo makes the first remark. Why? Because he's nervous to begin with and then he becomes frightened when Francisco make a noise in the dark as he marches during his watch. Then Francisco challenges him, "Nay, answer *me.*" Francisco is the one who is on guard duty. "Stand and unfold yourself," he says, from which we understand that Bernardo is wrapped in a cloak to protect him from the cold. The clear implication is that the season is winter, a fact that is confirmed a moment later when Francisco says "'Tis bitter cold." Another comment by Bernardo openly indicates the time of day and reconfirms the darkness. The passage ends with Bernardo's expression of "good night" to further emphasize the lateness of the hour.

Ibsen uses some of the same methods for expressing dramatic time in this selection from Act II of *The Wild Duck.*

(*A knocking is heard at the entrance door.*)

GINA: (*rising*) Hush, Ekdal--I think there's someone at the door.

HJALMAR: (*laying his flute on the bookcases*) There! Again!

> (*GINA goes and opens the door.*)

GREGERS: (*in the passage*) Excuse me--

GINA: (*starting back slightly*) Oh!

GREGERS: --doesn't Mr. Ekdal, the photographer, live here?

GINA: Yes, he does.

HJALMAR: (*going toward the door*) Gregers! You here after all? Well, come in then.

GREGERS: (*coming in*) I told you I would come and look you up.

HJALMAR: But this evening--Have you left the party?

GREGERS: I have left the party and my father's house. Good evening, Mrs. Ekdal. I don't know whether you recognize me?

GINA: Oh, yes, it's not difficult to know young Mr. Werle again.

GREGERS: No, I am like my mother, and no doubt you remember her.

HJALMAR: Left your father's house, did you say?

GREGERS: Yes, I have gone to a hotel.

HJALMAR: Indeed. Well, since you're here, take off your coat and sit down.

GREGERS: Thanks. (*He takes off his overcoat.*)

Gregers' statement "I told you I would come and look you up" relates to a statement he made to Hjalmar in the previous act, which we know occurred the same evening. Its use at this point is a way of maintaining continuity of time by connecting this scene with an earlier incident in the play. Hjalmar's reply "But this evening—Have you left the party?" and Gregers' responses "I have left the party" and "Good evening, Mrs. Ekdal." reinforce the continuity of time and reconfirm the time of the current scene. We see also that Gregers is wearing an overcoat because it is winter. The season is important enough for Ibsen to remind us about it again in the accompanying stage directions.

In the opening scene of *A Raisin in the Sun*, dramatic time is openly stated in the dialogue and observed in the characters' actions; it is then reconfirmed again in the stage directions. Ruth mentions the time three times. Travis gets out of bed and exits to the bathroom, then Ruth warns Walter Lee about being late for work.

RUTH: Come on now, boy, it's seven thirty (*He sits up at last, in a stupor of sleepiness.*) I say hurry up, Travis! You ain't the only person in the world got to use a bathroom (*The child, a sturdy, handsome boy of ten or twelve, drags himself out of bed and almost blindly takes his towels and "today's clothes" from the drawers and a closet and goes out to the bathroom, which is in an outside hall and which is shared by another family or families on the same floor. RUTH crosses to the bedroom door at right and opens it and calls in to her husband*.) Walter Lee! . . . It's after seven thirty! Lemme see you do some waking up in there now (*She waits*.) You better get up from there, man! It's seven thirty I tell you. (*She waits again*.) All right, you just go ahead and lay there and next thing you know Travis be finished and Mr. Johnson'll be in there and you'll be fussing and cussing around here like a mad man! And be late too! (*She waits, at the end of her patience*.) Walter Lee--it's time to get up!

Even in nonrealistic plays, conscientious detective work searching for the passage of time will pay handsome dividends later on when dealing with more complicated topics.

PLACE

The second subdivision of the given circumstances is *place,* or physical environment. The relation of a play to its physical environment is an issue of basic concern. Some designers feel that the scenery should illustrate the physical surroundings as accurately as possible, while others believe the physical environment is only a starting point for exploring the play's inner spirit. Formalist analysis does not argue for or against either of these positions. A specific concrete picture of the environment may work for some plays and an abstract unspecified illustration for others. What is important is that the physical environment should be completely understood because it is part of the whole meaning of the play.

Geographical Locale

The first subtopic under the heading of place is *geographical locale,* meaning the country, region, or district in which the play is set. Instructions about the geography are usually available in the front notes and stage directions, but readers should always attempt to authenticate them in the dialogue if possible. This passage from *Hamlet* contains geographical references to the city of Wittenberg, where Hamlet has recently been studying, as well as to Denmark, his native country and the geographical setting for the action.

CLAUDIUS: For your intent
        In going back to school in Wittenberg,
        It is most retrograde to our desire;
        And we beseech you bend you to remain
        Here, in the cheer and comfort of our eye,
        Our chiefest courtier, cousin, and our son.

QUEEN: Let not thy mother lose her prayers, Hamlet.

HAMLET: I shall in all my best obey you, madam.

CLAUDIUS: Why, 'tis a loving and a fair reply.
        Be as ourself in Denmark.

Besides these places, the play also contains geographical references to Poland, Norway, England, and France.

The emotional associations evoked by geography can contribute strongly to the overall effect of a play. Playwrights take advantage of this fact to strengthen the emotional impact of their works. Few can read *The Hairy Ape,* for example, without sensing the emotional associations of life at sea and life in New York City. *Death of a Salesman* contains several striking examples of emotional geographical associations as in this passage when Willy Loman complains about the deterioration of the neighborhood near his home in Brooklyn.

WILLY: The street is lined with cars. There's not a breath of fresh air in the neighborhood. The grass don't grow anymore, you can't raise a carrot in the back yard. Remember those two beautiful elm trees out there? They should've had a law against apartment houses. Remember when I and Biff hung the swing between them?

In this excerpt from *A Raisin in the Sun,* Mama Younger announces that she has made a down payment on a new home. Her family has been living for many years in a crowded tenement on Chicago's South Side. They are naturally pleased about the prospect of living in a house of their own. There are negative feelings connected with the locale, however, which everyone knows is an exclusively white suburb.

RUTH: Oh, Walter . . . a home . . . a *home. (She comes back to MAMA.)* Well--where is it? How big is it? How much it going to cost?

MAMA: Well--

RUTH: When we moving?

MAMA: (*smiling at her*) First of the month.

RUTH: (*throwing her head back with jubilance*) Praise God!

MAMA: (*tentatively, still looking at her son's back turned against her and RUTH*) It's--it's a nice house too . . . (*She cannot help speaking directly to him. An imploring quality in her voice, her manner, makes her almost like a girl now.*) Three bedrooms--nice big one for you and Ruth. . . . Me and Beneatha still have to share our room, but Travis have one of his own-- and (*with difficulty*) I figure if the--new baby--is a boy, we could get one of them double-decker outfits . . . And there's a yard with a little patch of dirt where I could maybe get to grow me a few flowers . . . And a nice big basement . . .

RUTH: Walter, honey, be glad--

MAMA: (*still to his back, fingering things on the table*) 'Course I don't want to make it sound fancier than it is . . . It's just a plain little old house--but it's made good and solid--and it will be *ours*. Walter Lee--it makes a difference in a man when he can walk on floors that belong to *him* . . .

RUTH: Where is it?

MAMA: (*frightened at this telling*) Well--well--it's out there in Clybourne Park--

(*RUTH's radiance fades abruptly, and WALTER finally turns slowly to face his mother with incredulity and hostility.*)

RUTH: Where?

MAMA: (*matter-of-factly*) Four o six Clybourne Street, Clybourne Park.

RUTH: Clybourne Park? Mama, there ain't no colored people living in Clybourne Park.

MAMA: Well, I guess there's going to be some now.

Playwrights often choose geographical locales to evoke specific emotional responses as well as for realism.

Specific Locale

Closely associated with geographical locale is the *specific locale* or the scenic area of the action. A reader's first impulse is usually to rely on stage directions for information about the specific locale. Published scripts often include elaborate notes about the scenery, such as the 200-word description of the military cadre room in *Streamers* or the equally detailed transparent multilevel Loman house in *Death of a Salelsman*. Scenery notes can sometimes be interesting and useful, but normally they are only an editor's depiction of the original production, not the author's own writing. This may not be a problem for those who are reading a play only for study, but it is a serious issue for designers or directors who are preparing for a performance. Since modern theatre conventions require completely different scenery for each new production, editorial notes describing an earlier production cannot be used as a guide.

The dialogue is almost always a more productive source of information about the specific place. Statements like "So this is your quarters, Hjalmar—this is your home" in *The Wild Duck* and "Lord, ain't nothing so dreary as the view from this window on a dreary day, is there?" in *A Raisin in the Sun* are valuable references to the specific locality in those plays. Some plays may even include details about the architectural layout. Mrs. Sorby instructs the servants in Act I of *The Wild Duck*, "Tell them to serve the coffee in the music room, Pettersen."

The specific locale can also be understood through inference. In this passage from *A School for Scandal*, Charles Surface is about to auction off his family's portraits to pay some of his debts. He points out the old paintings in the portrait gallery located in his eighteenth-century house where the sale is about to take place.

(*Enter CHARLES SURFACE, SIR OLIVER SURFACE, MOSES, and CARELESS.*)

CHARLES SURFACE: Walk in, gentlemen, pray walk in--here they are, the family of the Surfaces up to the Conquest.

SIR OLIVER (*disguised as MASTER PREMIUM*): And, in my opinion, a goodly collection.

CHARLES SURFACE: Ay, ay, these are done in the true spirit of portrait-painting; no *volontière grâce* or expression. Not like

the works of your modern Raphaels, who give you the strongest
resemblance, yet contrive to make your portrait independent of
you; so that you may sink the original and not hurt the picture. No, no; the merit of these is the inveterate likeness--
all stiff and awkward as the originals, and like nothing in
human nature besides.

SIR OLIVER: Ah! We shall never see such figures of men again.

CHARLES SURFACE: I hope not. Well, you see, Master Premium, what a
domestic character I am; here I sit of an evening surrounded
by my family.

When Charles says "Walk in, gentlemen, pray walk in" we can see him
walking through a door into a picture gallery and inviting others to follow him.
When he says "here they are, the family of the Surfaces up to the Conquest." he
is pointing to the paintings hung on the walls. His humorous description of the
paintings ("the merit of these is the inveterate likeness—all stiff and awkward
as the originals, and like nothing in human nature besides.") is a clue to what
they should look like. Carefully understood, both geographical and specific
locale can be productive objects for study by actors and directors as well as
designers.

SOCIETY

Plays illustrate social groups living together under the same closed
environment. In this section we will ask "What are the social groups in the play
and what characterizes their interactions with one another?" The term *society*
covers not only the specific identity of these groups, but also the behavioral
standards shared by their members. There is usually a dominant group enforc-
ing these standards, but the possibility of secondary groups should not be
overlooked as an aid to understanding the dominant group.

Arthur Miller contends that the choice of social groups helps to
determine the dramatic form of the play. Communication among family
members, he points out, is naturally different from that with strangers, and
private behavior is different from public. Consequently interest in the family
unit might logically lead to writing realistic plays dealing with intimate family
issues, while interest in social groups other than the family might lead to
writing nonrealistic forms. Miller's observation is interesting, but it should not
be applied too rigidly. The implications that result from the choice of social
groups are numerous and complex, and there are some obvious contrary
examples. Still his ideas can sometimes help to reveal how the choice of social
groups and the meaning of a play may be related.

Families

The most common social group, and the most important, is the family.
This is logical because we are all sons, daughters, sisters, and brothers before we
are anything else. And since the family is the basic social unit, playwrights
cannot stray too far from it without losing touch with their audiences. In the
garden scene from *Death of a Salesman* that we looked at in the Introduction,

seven distinct family members are identified. They were Willy's father, Willy as a father, Willy's wife, Willy's sons Biff and Happy, Willy's brother Ben, and Ben as the uncle of Biff and Happy. Almost every member of the Loman family and their blood relationship to each other is either specified or alluded to in this short scene. Claudius' opening lines in *Hamlet* explain the family relationship to his deceased brother and his new relationship to his brother's wife, which many would interpret as dishonorable if not incestuous.

```
KING:    Though yet of Hamlet our dear brother's death
         The memory be green, and that it us befitted
         To bear our hearts in grief, and our whole kingdom
         To be contracted in one brow of woe,
         Yet so far has discretion fought with nature
         That we with wisest sorrow think on him
         Together with remembrance of ourselves.
         Therefore, our sometime sister, now our queen,
         The imperial jointress to this warlike state,
         Have we, as with a defeated joy,
         With an auspicious and a drooping eye,
         With mirth in funeral and dirge in marriage,
         In equal scale, weighing delight with dole,
         Taken to wife.
```

A study of these and other examples should convince readers how universal the attraction of family groups is for playwrights, especially in realistic drama. Families can be found at the heart of many, many other plays.

Friendships

Friendships are social groups that exist outside the family. We see important examples of friendship in David Rabe's play *Streamers*. Throughout the action the social groups are defined by the different friendships that exist among the military trainees. Similarly there is an important friendship between Hamlet and Horatio in *Hamlet,* between Gregers Werle and Hjalmar Ekdal in *The Wild Duck,* among Walter, Willy, and Bobo in *A Raisin in the Sun,* and between Willy and Charley in *Death of a Salesman.*

Love relations form another kind of social group outside the family. This involves not only heterosexual love but all love including the love of a parent for a child and the effects of obsessive love. There are many examples in the study plays—Oedipus and Jocasta, Hamlet and Ophelia, Tartuffe and Elmire, Mrs. Sorby and Mr. Werle, Mother Courage and the Chaplain, Richie and Carlyle, Winnie and Willie, to name only a few of the most obvious ones. Apart from the family unit, friendship and love are among the most interesting and potentially dramatic social groups in plays. Readers should have little difficulty finding more of them.

Occupational Groups

Still another group outside of the family is the occupational group. This group is defined by what characters do for a living and by their interactions with others having the same vocation. Merchant seamen form the central group in *The Hairy Ape,* for instance, as do professional soldiers in *Mother*

Courage and *Streamers*. Occupational groups can even occur in historical plays where we might not ordinarily expect to encounter labor issues. Professional actors, soldiers, and gravediggers are represented in *Hamlet,* process servers in *Tartuffe,* and money lenders in *The School for Scandal.* Information about occupational groups provides clues to the characters and suggests emotional values that could be emphasized in production.

Status Groups

This topic occurs when assigning characters to formal classes that determine rank in society. Formal distinctions of class usually come from inherited wealth or political position. They are based on a privileged aristocracy whose members are accustomed to giving orders and having them carried out by characters on lower rungs of the social ladder. Characters on the lower end of the scale normally show deference to those above them by means of formal titles and various kinds of conventional submissive behavior, such as bows, curtsies, and salutes. We observe that in *Hamlet* only Claudius and Gertrude address Hamlet by his given name. All the others, including Ophelia and Horatio, say "Prince Hamlet" or "my lord."

Although class distinctions can also be found in many other older plays like *Oedipus Rex, Tartuffe,* and *The School for Scandal,* they are seldom the subject of explicit attention in them. Social class was a normal part of everyday life in the past, and it's still customary in many countries today. When class distinctions are taken for granted, no special obligation exists to provide detailed explanations. There may not be much explicit information about the inner workings of the class system in *Hamlet* or *Tartuffe,* but such distinctions are nevertheless of paramount importance. Unconsciously reading modern democratic class conventions into older historical plays can be a serious mistake. Modern readers should take careful notice of social classes in older plays. Sometimes it may be necessary to supplement script analysis with outside research to understand the social context resulting from class distinctions.

Modern class distinctions may not be as overt as are their historical counterparts, but they can be just as forceful and repressive. Social status generally appears today as an outcome of education, financial position, or ethnic culture, and is easier for some of us to recognize. For example, social status based on money looms large in *The Wild Duck, Mother Courage,* and *Death of a Salesman;* status based on education is important in *The Hairy Ape;* and ethnic discrimination negatively affects the social status of the characters in *A Raisin in the Sun* and *Streamers.* Understanding overt and covert social class distinctions is essential in these and other modern plays.

Social Standards

Social standards are the shared beliefs and behaviors regarded as acceptable by the characters and to which they are expected to conform. The clearest example is "thou shalt not kill," but there are many others equally powerful though less obvious. Social standards don't need to be formally proven or even openly stated. They simply are accepted without question as true. Most characters believe in them implicitly, and conversely, their behavior and beliefs are shaped and conditioned by the social standards. These standards are often so important that violation produces shock, horror, moral revulsion, and indignation and even justifies the use of penalties to enforce conformity. Naturally those characters offended most by violations of the social standards are those who most strongly endorse them.

In former eras, social standards were largely determined by established religion, class politics, and national culture. Consequently in historical plays, the characters tend to be controlled by religious, aristocratic, or nationalistic forces. In modern Western society, the influence of older forms of social control gradually diminished. Currently it is science, belief in social equality, and the governing middle class that collectively control the standards of belief and behavior for most people. The powerful influences of social standards may be repellent to those who are independent-minded, but understanding these influences is very necessary. Now the unwritten laws of social standards are often the only laws that dramatic characters can be counted on to obey. Certainly this is true in many contemporary plays.

One useful way to understand how social standards work their effects is to look for the use of euphemisms in the dialogue. A euphemism is a socially inoffensive term that is substituted for an offensive one. Thus euphemisms are evidence of social standards at work. There are many revealing examples in *The Wild Duck*. In the first scene the servant Jensen, referring to Mr. Ekdal, says to Pettersen, "I've heard tell as he's been a lively customer in his day." They both understand that "lively customer" is a euphemism for someone who is sexually reckless, a womanizer. In the climactic scene at the end of Act I, Gregers accuses his father of having been "interested in" their former household servant Gina Hansen. In this context, *interested in* is a euphemism for sexual intercourse. Both Gregers and Mr. Werle use euphemisms when referring to the deceased Mrs. Werle. Gregers refers to her "break down" and her "unfortunate weakness." Mr. Werle says that she was "morbid" and "overstrained." He also says, "her eyes were— clouded now and then." These are euphemisms for alcoholism or possibly even drug addiction, which were almost as common in the late nineteenth century as they are today.

Social standards are disclosed in other subtle ways, too. When the servant Jensen says in his earlier line, "I've heard tell. . . ." it is a hint that there is lively gossip circulating around town about the Werle family. This is confirmed later when Mr. Werle explains to Gregers why he didn't provide more help to Old Ekdal. He says "I've had a slur cast on my reputation . . . I have done all I could without positively laying myself open to all sorts of suspicion and gossip." Then, referring to the fact that Mrs. Sorby is currently living with him, he says, "A woman so situated may easily find herself in a false position in the eyes of the world. For that matter, it does a man no good either." Clearly Mr. Werle is controlled by his fear of scandal or even rumors of scandal. More evidence of this control occurs when Hjalmar confesses that he "kept the blinds down" over the windows when his father was in prison. Euphemisms and other kinds of evidence in *The Wild Duck* show the existence of strong social standards regarding marriage, sex, alcohol, mental health, local politics, government contracts, and even relations between labor and management. The reward for conforming to these standards is economic success and social approval; the penalty for violation is malicious gossip, public scandal, social ostracism, and prison.

Social standards can create a harsh and unforgiving world for characters to live in. The old saying that sticks and stones can break our bones but words can never hurt us is not true in plays. Words are often used to criticize violations of the prevailing social standards, and they do have the power to hurt characters. They are meant to cause shame, embarrassment, and guilt for violating social standards, and they usually work very well.

ECONOMICS

Economics is concerned with the large-scale financial systems the characters collectively live under plus the daily financial activities in which the characters engage within that system. It may seem that the study of economics is far from our stated goal of concentrating on the play itself, but it is more important in script analysis than it may seem at first. A little reflection will show that from among the study plays alone *Tartuffe, The School for Scandal, The Wild Duck, The Hairy Ape, Mother Courage, Death of a Salesman,* and *A Raisin in the Sun* share an intense concern with money. A great deal of information about economics can be found in other plays, too. Sometimes money concerns appear where we are least likely to expect them, for example in the plays of Anton Chekhov. In *The Cherry Orchard*, it is necessary to know accurately detailed information about real estate development, mortgages, banking, borrowing and lending, agricultural marketing, and the daily financial operations of a large estate, not to mention the economic impact of the law passed in 1861 freeing the serfs. Clearly gaining or losing money (mainly losing it) has been, and continues to be, one of the favorite plot resources of modern dramatists.

According to economists, there are four principal financial systems. They define *mercantilism* as colonialism with state control of manufacturing and exports. In a *laissez-faire* economic system, business is permitted to follow the unwritten natural laws of economics freely. Private property, profit, and credit form the basis of *capitalism,* while *socialism* involves public ownership of manufacturing, services, and natural resources. These four systems seldom exist in isolation, but are usually present in various combinations. On a smaller scale, economics in plays concerns any private financial affairs in which the characters are involved.

Capitalism is the system with which most of us are familiar and the one we are most likely to encounter in the plays we read. Since capitalism is based on individual freedom and free enterprise, it can be rewarding for wealthy entrepreneurs, but it can be hard on characters with limited influence or financial resources. In *Death of a Salesman,* Willy Loman struggles to live within a harsh capitalistic economic system that is dominated by the selfish values of high-powered business interests. His major personal economic concerns are meeting the monthly payments for his refrigerator, automobile, life insurance, and home. Willy's personal economics are so important that they are elevated almost to symbolic status in the play. In the kitchen of Joe Meilziner's famous setting, the Hastings refrigerator is the only appliance.

Mercantilism is the system found in *The School for Scandal.* The important economic circumstances are the loans made to Charles Surface based on his credit from the family's colonial exports, the auction of his family home together with its furnishings, and the sizable financial resources controlled by Sir Oliver Surface. International trading, which plays a major role in mercantilism, influences the timing of Charles' loans and the arrival of Sir Oliver. The character of Long, the Cockney seaman in *The Hairy Ape,* incites his companions with Marxist harangues about "the damned Capitalist clarss [sic]." He also introduces Yank to New York's expensive Fifth Avenue shopping district to awaken his "clarss consciousness [sic]."

Economics can be important in script analysis, but a word of caution. Because economics is so close to each of us, special care should be taken against projecting personal convictions or experiences into a play written by someone else. As with the other analytical concepts, students should search for conditions that are objectively present in the play.

POLITICS AND LAW

The term *politics and law* refers to governmental institutions and activities including the rules of conduct that are set up by political authorities or legislation. Political and legal conditions rely on the mutual consent of the characters that in turn is revealed by the respect or disregard they show for political and legal considerations. In *Oedipus Rex,* the oath that Oedipus takes—to track down the murderer of Laius—is an example of an important political condition. For him and the population of Thebes, the oath has the absolute force of law. His complete authority is understood and accepted by everyone without question. There is no need for him to explain or justify himself.

Politics is strongly at work in the pact made between King Hamlet and King Fortinbras that Horatio discloses in Act I, Scene 1, of *Hamlet.* He tells his companions that this agreement has had serious political consequences for Denmark and Norway. First Denmark has gained political control of Norway. Second young Fortinbras of Norway has raised a military challenge against Claudius to regain his country's independence, and third Claudius has responded by placing Denmark on full military alert. Danish weapons makers are working around the clock in preparation for an impending war. The feeling of war is in the air, and everyone is frightened and tense.

INTELLECT AND CULTURE

According to the philosophers, intellect and culture are among humanity's highest activities. Every society has its intellectuals of some kind, or at least it has people who spend a large part of their time dealing with ideas. The life of the mind is protected in most societies because in an important way it helps to shape daily life. Although there may be no specialized professional roles for intellect or art, intellectual life plays a substantial role in creating high culture. Sometimes intellectuals and artists attempt to influence political action and social change.

Undoubtedly intellectual achievement is not always reserved for intellectuals or artists. It may appear in various forms. At one end of the spectrum are those characters with formal schooling and refined cultural tastes. Hamlet, for example, is most at home in Wittenberg, which is an isolated intellectual environment. He is the product of a refined university education that trained him to appreciate poetry, philosophy, and theatre. He prefers the life of the mind over the life of action advocated by Claudius, Fortinbras, and Laertes. He is clearly out of place in a warlike society such as Denmark. At the other end of the spectrum are characters who are not formally educated or who deliberately scorn the life of the mind. In *The Hairy Ape*, Yank rejects the world of learning although ironically he is the most natively intelligent character in the play. In fact, Yank's intelligence becomes his downfall. Walter Lee Younger in *A Raisin in the Sun* is similarly disdainful of the educational plans of his sister, Beneatha, as well as those of her college friend, George Murchison. In *Death of a Salesman* Willy Loman preaches against the values of formal schooling. He favors cultivating a winning personality because he believes it has made him a successful salesman.

SPIRITUALITY

In its narrowest sense, spirituality involves the formal religious elements in a play. Expression of this can be seen in the presence of religious societies, ceremonies, and traditions and in the religious values espoused by the characters. Speaking more broadly, evidence of spirituality includes any beliefs in divine, spiritual, or superstitious powers that must be obeyed or worshiped.

Spirituality does not figure prominently in modern plays. There is no direct evidence of spirituality, for example, in *The Hairy Ape, Death of a Salesman,* or *Streamers*. Spirituality plays a small but strategic role, however, in *The Wild Duck* through the character of Reverend Molvik, in *Mother Courage* through the Chaplain, and in *Happy Days* through Winnie's frequent prayers. Mama Younger's religious values are an extremely important part of *A Raisin in the Sun*. The situation is different in older plays. The action of *Oedipus Rex* contains numerous religious references, including many prayers. *Hamlet* also includes important spiritual conditions, notably the many references to religious ceremonies, traditions, and beliefs. *Tartuffe* is specifically about the hypocrisy of certain religious societies that were influential in Moliére's time.

Characters are sometimes strongly guided by spiritual considerations, many of which may remain hidden or unspoken. Readers should be on the alert for any evidence of spiritual ethics in character actions as well as in the words.

THE WORLD OF THE PLAY

The cumulative effect of all the given circumstances plus the social standards they embody creates the world of the play. The nature of that unique world the characters reveal through their behavior. They show whether the world they inhabit is a place that is good or bad, friendly or unfriendly, amusing or frightening, benign or dangerous, lovable or hateful. At the beginning of this chapter, there was a statement that without living through the given circumstances, the characters would exist in vacuums without any connection to real life. How many times has an audience experienced the feeling of looking into such a psychological vacuum while watching a play on stage? This occurs in productions that pay insufficient attention to the world of the play, and yet it's only necessary to establish which given circumstances exert the most influence over the characters and which social standards dominate their beliefs and behavior.

In *Oedipus Rex,* the characters seem to be controlled by spiritual forces. Their world is a fearful place dominated by fickle and unforgiving gods who will not hesitate to send plagues and famines to punish those who disagree with them. The world of *Hamlet* is an equally unfriendly place. As punishment for his sins, King Hamlet has been condemned to wander in agony among the living and to suffer the fires of purgatory among the dead. For his part, young Hamlet is compelled to undertake a violent and bloody revenge that he is mentally and morally unsuited to perform. There are obviously strong political forces at work, too, however. The reader will have to decide whether *Hamlet* is dominated by spiritual or political forces. The world of *Tartuffe,* on the other hand, is controlled by religion and politics working in harmony. Orgon suffers miserably at the hands of Tartuffe throughout most of the play, but in the end, the king sets everything right.

The worlds created in modern plays are more often dominated by social considerations than by gods, providence, or kings, but they can frequently be just as cruel and unforgiving. In *The Wild Duck,* a petty financial crime leads to the complete and permanent social ruin of the Ekdal family. In *Death of a Salesman,* Willy Loman becomes an unfortunate victim of a world dominated by ruthless, profit-hungry businessmen. Mindless violence and moral anarchy are the controlling circumstances in the world of *Streamers.* The world of *Happy Days* is controlled by a mysterious force that seems to enjoy maliciously ridiculing the characters as they attempt to make sense out of their lives.

Studying the world of the play also offers an opportunity to get an early feel for the characters. (Understand that any judgments about the characters at this point will necessarily be tentative and subject to many adjustments.) As already observed, the world of the play is formed by the given circumstances that control the characters. A character's point of view is the complex of factors that determines his exact relationship to the world of the play. Sometimes this concept is called the character's position or attitude.

Clearly, not all the characters will exhibit the same point of view toward the play's world. For example, each character in *Tartuffe* reveals a distinctly different point of view. The issue of morality or virtuous conduct is the controlling circumstance, and ideas about morality control the beliefs and behaviors of the characters. To Orgon morality means extravagant public devoutness. He admires Tartuffe precisely for this characteristic, which he interprets as saintliness. He looks to Tartuffe to teach him how to achieve peace of mind and how to stop worrying about what he views as his family's immoral behavior. According to Orgon, Tartuffe must take the family under control and teach them how to behave. The other characters express their own points of view toward morality. For Madame Pernelle, it means respectability; Elmire views it as a private matter of conscience; Dorine considers it a refuge for gossips; for Cleante religion is "pious flummery" or flattery; Mariane sees religion as a family duty; and for Tartuffe religion is a con game and a means to easy wealth. The King genuinely believes in morality as virtuous conduct. Once the main character's point of view is clear, it is normal to expect it to change. At the end of the play, Orgon's point of view is considerably different. He learns that public devoutness is not the same as morality. Thus each character expresses a different point of view about the forces that control the world of the play.

SUMMARY

This chapter contained a review of the given circumstances that readers should attempt to identify in the study of plays and an attempt to discover the dramatic possibilities or playable values in each one. It is not too much of an exaggeration to say that once the given circumstances are completely understood, the rest of the play will begin to fall into place more or less by itself. Of course, not all the given circumstances will be equally useful on every occasion. And when a play does not use a particular feature extensively, obviously it would not be practical to dwell on it. As in most analytical activities, readers should develop instincts for what is most useful. Because these instincts are among the unteachable skills of play analysis, this text cannot equip students with them. It can only point the way.

QUESTIONS

Time: In what year and season does the action occur? Can the passage of time during the play be determined accurately? The time between the scenes and acts? The hour of day for each scene? Each act?

Place: In what country, region, or city does the play occur? Are any geographical features described? In what specific locale does the action occur? What is the specific location for each scene including ground plan and other architectural features if possible?

Society: What are the family relationships? What are the friendships and love relationships? What occupational groups are represented? What social classes are represented? What are the social standards? How strongly are they enforced? What social group controls the standards of behavior? What are the rewards for social conformity? The penalties for violating the social standards?

Economics: What is the general economic system at work in the play? Any specific examples of business activities or transactions? Does economics exercise any control over the lives of the characters? Who controls the economic circumstances in the play? How strongly do they exert control? What are the rewards for economic success? The penalties for violating the economic standards?

Politics and law: What is the system of government that serves as the background for the play? Any specific examples of political or legal activities, actions, or ceremonies? Do politics or law exercise any control over the lives of the characters? Who controls the political and legal circumstances in the play? How strongly do they exert control? What are the rewards for political and legal conformity? The penalties for violating the political and legal standards?

Intellect and culture: What is the general level of culture and education? Any specific examples of artistic or educational activities? Any characters obviously more or less educated or intelligent than the others? Does intellect or culture exercise any control over the lives of the characters? Who controls the intellectual and cultural circumstances in the play? How strongly do they exert their control? What are the rewards for intellectual and spiritual conformity? The penalties for violating intellectual and cultural standards?

Spirituality: What is the accepted code of religious or spiritual belief? Any specific examples of religious or spiritual activities or ceremonies? Does spirituality exercise any control over the lives of the characters? Who controls the spiritual circumstances in the play? How strongly do they exert control? What are the rewards for spiritual conformity? The penalties for violating the spiritual standards?

The world of the play: Describe the world of the play, the distinctive social universe created by the total given circumstances plus all the social standards. How does the world of the play affect the conduct and mental attitude of each of the characters at the beginning of the play? What are the different points of view expressed by the characters toward that world? Does anyone's point of view to the world of the play change or develop as the action progresses?

2

Foundations of the Plot: Background Story

Now that we have finished studying the present, we can turn our attention to the past. The lives of the characters actually begin long before they first appear on stage, and understanding their pasts is necessary for understanding their lives on stage. Every dramatic story has a past, but the conventional time and space limits of the theatre usually make it impossible to present all of it on the stage. For this reason, playwrights use a special kind of narration as a literary shortcut to reveal the past at the same time the stage action is still going on. *Exposition* is the standard term for this dramatic convention, but sometimes it is also referred to as *previous action* or *antecedent action*. The word exposition comes from the Latin root *exposito*, meaning *to put forth* or *to expose*. This term has proven useful because exposition is a way of exposing the hidden parts of a play.

Exposition involves everything that happened before the beginning of the play. Often it is crucial to know precisely what went on prior to the stage action. In *Oedipus Rex*, the fate of Jocasta's infant son is an example. Did Jocasta really bind the infant's feet and turn him over to a household servant with orders to abandon him? Where did the Corinthian Messenger get the infant he gave to King Polybus and Queen Merope? He claims that he received the infant from one of Laius' herdsmen. But if so, how did the herdsman come to give the baby to him in the first place? Did the infant actually belong to the herdsman? If not, who gave it to him and why? Is the shepherd actually the herdsman who originally gave the infant to the Corinthian Messenger? If so, why is he unwilling to acknowledge it? All these questions and many more about the background story are crucial to the plot of *Oedipus Rex*.

The past becomes even more complex when it is used as Ibsen often used it in, for example, *The Wild Duck*. In the excerpt from Act I that follows, Gregers Werle has just returned home after a long absence. He has a sharp disagreement with his father about the fate of the Ekdal family, who used to be close friends of the Werles. But we should guard against making unwarranted assumptions about the past. Reliability should not depend exclusively on Gregers' recollections nor on those of any single character. Incidentally it is a good practice to get into the habit of underlining the background story in the printed script to distinguish it visually from the on-stage action.

GREGERS: <u>How has that family been allowed to go so miserably to the wall?</u>

WERLE: You mean the Ekdals, I suppose?

GREGERS: Yes, I mean the Ekdals. <u>Lieutenant Ekdal was once so closely associated with you?</u>

WERLE: <u>Much too closely; I have felt that to my cost for many a year. It is thanks to him that I--yes I--have had a kind of slur cast upon my reputation.</u>

GREGERS: (*softly*) <u>Are you sure that he alone was to blame?</u>

WERLE: Who else do you suppose?

GREGERS: <u>You and he acted together in that affair of the forests--</u>

WERLE: <u>But was it not Ekdal that drew the map of the tracts we had bought--that fraudulent map! It was he who felled all the timber illegally on government ground. In fact, the whole management was in his hands. I was quite in the dark as to what Lieutenant Ekdal was doing.</u>

GREGERS: <u>Lieutenant Ekdal himself seems to have been very much in the dark about what he was doing.</u>

WERLE: That may be. <u>But the fact is that he was found guilty and I was acquitted.</u>

GREGERS: Yes, I know that <u>nothing was proved against you.</u>

Since the interpretations of the past presented by the characters are often incompatible or at least incomplete, readers are obliged to formulate their own accounts. This involves understanding what happened and why in a very detailed way. It also means knowing whose version of the past is correct and how much of it is reliable. In the excerpt here, the characters strongly disagree about the reasons for the decline of the Ekdals. Gregers indicts his father for it, while Mr. Werle seems to lay the blame entirely on Lieutenant Ekdal, the head of the family and formerly Werle's business partner. Later in the play, Lieutenant Ekdal offers his own interpretation as do his son, Hjalmar, and his daughter-in-law, Gina. Who is right? Who benefits from each version? In such cases, readers should examine skeptically—like trial lawyers.

It is important to determine the value of the facts and their meaning apart from what the characters say about them. It's also essential to understand the past from a theatrical point of view. Unfortunately for many readers, the abstract term *exposition* is likely to call up a relatively uncritical response. According to some people, exposition tells the audience everything they need to know about the past to understand what they are going to see; it is considered a playwriting problem. It involves a certain amount of dullness, but skillful dramatists are able to handle it without holding up the action of the play. Obviously this explanation carries unpleasant overtones. Exposition seems an awkward technical requirement that obstructs the flow of the plot. The unpleasantness increases when scholars talk about protactic characters such as the Chorus in classical Greek tragedies or certain servants in modern plays, presumably introduced only for disclosing exposition.

Actors, directors, and designers can't let the matter rest here. What exposition means to theatre artists is an important element in the full-scale understanding of a play. As complicated as this subject may be, we should attempt to understand the past in a way that makes it theatrically compelling, not a clumsy obstacle to overcome. This involves several important adjustments in ways of thinking about the past in a play. First the notion that what has already happened is dull and undramatic must be set aside. For the characters themselves, it's just the opposite. After all, to them the past is not just an abstract literary concept but rather their own lives, everything good and bad that has happened to them. Second the past should be understood as an integral part of the play, not a technical encumbrance. It helps in understanding the characters who are themselves talking about the past, it creates moods, and it generates conflicts. Third to be reminded of the dramatic possibilities of the past, replace the static term *exposition* with the more lively, journalistic term *background story*. The basic lesson here for actors, directors, and designers is that background story does not interrupt the flow of the action. On the contrary, it propels the play forward in explosive surges and with an increasing sense of urgency.

TECHNIQUE

Let's first study the basic techniques playwrights employ to disclose background story and then consider some ways of identifying it. By approaching the topic in this way, it should be easier to understand the workings of the background story in the play as a whole.

Broadly speaking, background story emerges in two ways. It appears either in relatively long passages near the beginning of a play, or else in fragments distributed throughout the action. There is no advantage in craftsmanship or plausibility either way. The choice depends on the author's goals and the practical requirements of the play. Playwriting fashions also play a part. Both methods have been used successfully in a wide assortment of plays and both are capable of revealing the past without interrupting the flow of the action or harming the play's plausibility.

Historical Technique

In plays written before the nineteenth century, the background story ordinarily emerges early as extended rhetorical speeches. Note how this operates in *Hamlet*. We studied Act I, Scene 1, for its political conditions in the last chapter. Horatio's long speech consists of 29 lines explaining the reasons behind Denmark's preparations for war. In the next scene, Claudius has a speech of 34 lines expressing his gratitude to the court for their support during the recent transfer of power. He also explains his strategy for dealing with the threat posed by Fortinbras. At the end of this scene, more background story is disclosed. In a famous soliloquy of about 50 lines, Hamlet reveals his feelings about his father's recent death and his mother's hasty remarriage. Next, in Scene 3, Laertes censures Ophelia in a speech of 34 lines, warning her not to be misled by Hamlet's fondness for her. Besides being a warning to Ophelia, this is also background story. In Scene 4, the Ghost materializes, then in a discourse of 50 lines in Scene 5, he discloses the circumstances of his death. At this early point in the play, the characters have revealed nearly all the background story in five speeches totaling about 200 lines. Similarly, most of the background story in *Tartuffe* and *The School for Scandal* unfolds in a few long speeches early in those plays.

The technique of extended narration has advantages and disadvantages. On one hand, it focuses attention because it collects all the essential facts of the background story at the beginning of the play. This permits the dramatist to devote the remainder of the play to the development of on-stage action, which is a considerable writing benefit. On the other hand, extended narration can be a burden on actors and audiences. For actors, it is essential to express all the important background information clearly in lengthy speeches, while at the same time maintaining emotional honesty and logical consistency. Audiences must digest most of the background story at one time and note who the important characters are and what they did. More difficult still, they must remember all of it throughout the entire action that follows.

Early Modern Technique

For artistic reasons, another method of disclosing the background story eventually displaced the use of long speeches. Most of the background story still appeared at the beginning of the play, but now it was broken into smaller pieces and shared among several characters. Although this method seemed to provide plays with a more plausible appearance of everyday reality, its initial use was somewhat crude by modern standards. A typical instance involved an opening scene in which two servants perform routine household duties while gossiping about their employer. Use of this type of opening was so widespread in nineteenth century realistic drama that it came to be called the *below-stairs scene* because it almost always involved servants.

Ibsen used a refined variation of this method in the opening scene of *The Wild Duck*, where Pettersen, the old family servant, and Jensen, a newly hired helper, observe, explain, and otherwise account for a dinner party that's happening off stage at the same time. The concurrent off-stage scene lends plausibility to the on-stage discussion, but there is another refinement as well. Unlike other early realistic playwrights, Ibsen seldom treated his secondary characters simply as dramatic functionaries. He provided each of them with a distinct character and with an intense personal interest in the plot. Not only are Pettersen and Jensen distinctive characters in themselves, they also have plausible reasons for gossiping about the people at the party.

In his later work, Ibsen refined the method further. Instead of continuing to reveal so much of the background story in the early scenes, he began to distribute it in fragments throughout the entire play. Scholars call this the *retrospective method* because the on-stage action moves forward while the past unfolds backward, retrospectively. The key to its effective use was to keep from revealing the most significant background information until as late as possible in the action when it was most effective theatrically. As time went on, Ibsen and other early modern dramatists—chiefly Anton Chekhov, August Strindberg, and George Bernard Shaw—became very adept at this method. They learned how to distribute the background story in small bits and pieces throughout their plays, and they knew exactly where and how to place the information so that its disclosure would be as dramatic as possible. In their best works, no single piece of background story is revealed until it is of maximum service to the action. The past develops one small fact at a time with an extremely skillful sense of theatrical timing.

The retrospective method seemed new, but actually it was a rediscovery of an historical model that had remained largely unused for nearly 2400 years. Few dramatists ever handled it better than Sophocles did in *Oedipus Rex*. The plot of this play is essentially a kind of murder mystery told retrospectively. A detective (Oedipus) searching for a murderer digs step-by-step into his past and discovers to his horror that the criminal turns out to be himself. In spite of its early date of composition, *Oedipus Rex* remains an excellent example of retrospective technique. Both *Oedipus Rex* and *The Wild Duck* are models of background story craftsmanship that will reward patient analysis.

Modern Technique

Beginning in the 1940s, certain avant garde authors began to push the limits of the retrospective method. They did so by concealing the background story so deeply that audiences had a difficult time even detecting its presence. This new approach might be called *deep background story*. Audiences were initially perplexed by these unorthodox plays. After all, without understanding the past it was next to impossible for anyone to know what was going on except the actors, and they were frequently as befuddled as the audience was. The early absurdists—notably Edward Albee, Samuel Beckett, Jean Genêt, and Harold Pinter—were particularly skilled at crafting deep background stories. In their plays and in those of many like-minded dramatists, the background story is so carefully concealed that it is almost impossible to uncover without a great deal of diligent detective work.

Appearances to the contrary, most plays continue have a past of some kind. Even the absurdists and their followers could not abandon the need for it altogether. Critics were fond of attributing the unusual moods in these plays to intellectual factors like the "illogical and purposeless nature of existence." But this is obfuscation masking as erudition. What the absurdists really did was to rediscover the entertainment value of being cryptic. Curiosity and attention can be heightened if the audience is not allowed in on the secret. Mysterious undertones are created when the background story is deliberately withheld, a technique used effectively by August Strindberg in *The Ghost Sonata* in 1907 and by Edgar Allen Poe as early as 1841 in his detective fiction.

Naturally enough, absurdist plays and their stylistic relatives needed a new approach to acting and production to meet the challenge of expressing the dark psychological undertones that were their hallmark. Fortunately, talented young directors, actors, and designers developed innovative performance techniques exactly suited to these unusual works. Now that we have observed the background story technique of the absurdists in use for over a generation, we understand that there was really no magic involved in what they were doing. Deep background story is essentially a radical extension of the retrospective method employed by early realistic playwrights. The main difference lies in severely limiting the quantity of background story and then disclosing what is left of it by means of extremely intricate, complicated hints instead of by frank narration. To perform absurdist plays successfully, actors and directors need to pay close attention to two important factors. They must first employ patient and imaginative detective work during the analytical phases of rehearsal to expose every last ounce of background material. Second they should use meticulous application of tempo, rhythm, and mood in production to illuminate every veiled hint and casual allusion that these plays depend on for their effects.

The plays of Albee, Beckett, Genêt, and Pinter may have been perplexing at first, but it is instructive to remember that for similar reasons the plays of Ibsen, Chekhov, and Strindberg were also difficult for their contemporaries to understand. Ibsen felt compelled to provide detailed stage directions, and Strindberg wrote explanatory prefaces to help actors understand their then-unconventional plays. We know too that Chekhov's plays were misunderstood when they were originally produced. It required the special talent of Stanislavski with considerable assistance from Nemirovitch-Dantchenko to communicate the hidden qualities of his plays successfully.

IDENTIFICATION

Granting that plays require some kind of background story, of what does it usually consist? Normally background story takes on several forms: events, character descriptions, and feelings. Which of these is most important is determined by the nature of the play, the characters, and the situations in the play.

Events

An event is simply something that happened to a character in the past, especially something momentous. Past events are always important in a play because they provide the source material for the on-stage conflicts. Here are some background passages that contain important past events. In *Streamers,* Sergeant Cokes boasts, "I told 'em when they wanted to send me back [to Vietnam] I ain't got no leukemia; they wanna check it. They think I got it. I don't think I got it." The fateful event here is Cokes' denial to his superiors that he had leukemia so he could be allowed to return to the war. Two crucial past events are disclosed in Mama Younger's announcement to her son Walter in *A Raisin in the Sun,* "Son—do you know your wife is expecting another baby?" The surprises for Walter are that Ruth is pregnant and that he didn't know about it. Another example is Hjalmar Ekdal's confession in *The Wild Duck* that his father considered suicide when he was sent to jail. Hjalmar says to Gregers, "When the sentence of imprisonment was passed—he had the pistol in his hand." In *Oedipus Rex* when Oedipus asks who found him as an infant, the

Corinthian Messenger discloses a momentous past event, "It was another shepherd gave you to me." At this moment Oedipus learns that he is not the son of Polybus and Merope. In *Mother Courage,* the Recruiter reveals an important past event when he says to the Sergeant, "The general wants me to recruit four platoons by the twelfth." The fact that the general will probably have him shot if he doesn't enlist 90 men by the end of the week explains why the Recruiter doesn't show much sympathy when dealing with potential recruits later in the play. Background stories are mainly composed of pivotal events like these.

Again, the caution is that readers should not always take descriptions of past events at face value. It's not that characters lie necessarily; they tell their own versions of the truth. Even a lie (told as a truth), however, can reveal character if it is studied carefully. In Hjalmar Ekdal's scene discussed in the first paragraph of this section, his accidental use of the word "considered" instead of "attempted" when he speaks about his father's experience is revealing. For one thing, an attempted suicide is far different from a considered suicide, which implies a kind of double cowardice. Moreover even though the near-suicide was probably real enough, it is not as important at this moment in the play as the use Hjalmar is making of it. His purpose in confessing the event to Gregers is not so much to gain sympathy for his father but rather to express how he suffered personally from his father's social disgrace. This is also a useful example of how background story can provide important information about other dimensions of the play, like character.

Character Descriptions

Recalling the events of the past naturally leads to a consideration of the characters involved in them. In *Tartuffe,* Orgon offers this evaluation of his daughter's suitor: "I had promised you to Valere, but apart from the fact that he's said to be a bit of a gambler, I suspect him of being a free thinker." Orgon is disclosing his evaluation of a character in the past. Horatio reveals to Hamlet his recollection of King Hamlet's character: "I saw him once; he was a goodly king." Joseph Surface receives this admiring description from Sir Peter Teazle in *The School for Scandal:* "Joseph is indeed what a youth should be— everyone in the world speaks well of him." Speaking to Gregers Werle, Dr. Relling says of Lieutenant Ekdal in *The Wild Duck:* "The old lieutenant has been an ass all his days." Willy Loman recalls his brother Ben in *Death of a Salesman:* "There was the only man I ever met who knew all the answers," and Mama Younger in *A Raisin in the Sun* fondly recalls her deceased husband, "God knows there was plenty wrong with Walter Younger—hard-headed, mean, kind of wild with women—plenty wrong with him. But he sure loved his children." Such character descriptions in the background story often reveal as much about the speaker as they do about the person being remembered.

Feelings

Characters reveal their past feelings and their current feelings about the past in various ways. When in *The Wild Duck* Hjalmar Ekdal's father went to prison for fraud, it was also a terrible time for Hjalmar emotionally: "I kept the blinds drawn down over both my windows. When I peeped out I saw the sun shining as if nothing had happened. I could not understand it. I saw people going along the street, laughing and talking about indifferent things. I could not understand it. It seemed to me that the whole of existence must be at a standstill—as if under an eclipse." To which Gregers Werle adds significantly, "I felt that too, when my mother died." In *Happy Days*, Winnie expresses her happiness about three memorable events in her past: "My first ball! (*long pause*) My second ball! (*long pause, close eyes*) My first kiss!" In *Death of a Salesman*, Willy Loman tells Linda how he feels when he's traveling alone on the road: "I get so lonely—especially when business is bad and there's nobody to talk to. I get the feeling that I'll never sell anything again." Paddy, the sentimental Irish stoker in *The Hairy Ape*, remembers what it felt like to be at sea when he was young: "A warm sun on the clean decks. Sun warming the blood of you, and wind over the miles of shiny green ocean like strong drink to your lungs." The frustration of Walter Younger's past expresses itself through sense impressions in *A Raisin in the Sun*: "Sometimes it's like I can see the future stretched out in front of me—just plain as day. The future, Mama. Hanging over there at the edge of my days. Just waiting for me—a big, looming blank space—full of *nothing*." Feelings in the background story are also a valuable resource for beginning to understand character.

Combining Events, Character Descriptions, and Feelings in Extended Passages

To learn how past events, character descriptions, and feelings work together in longer passages of dialogue, we will consider two extended examples. The first passage uses traditional narration, and the second one uses the retrospective method. *Hamlet* falls into the class of play in which background story appears in large portions of narration early in the action. The death of King Hamlet is clearly the single most important fact of the background story. In Act 1, Scene 5, the Ghost reveals to Hamlet the circumstances surrounding this event in several long speeches. Background story in this scene is a seamless merging of events, feelings, and character descriptions. The Ghost begins by disclosing his experiences in purgatory since his death. Again background story is underlined.

GHOST: I am thy father's spirit,
        Doom'd for a certain term to walk the night,
        And for the day confin'd to fast in fires,
        Till the foul crimes done in my days of nature
        Are burnt and purg'd away.

In the next 11 lines he describes in sensory terms how Hamlet would probably feel if he knew what his father has had to endure.

GHOST: But that I am forbid
        To tell the secrets of my prison-house,
        I could a tale unfold whose lightest word
        Would harrow up thy soul, freeze thy young blood,
        Make thy two eyes, like stars, start from their spheres,
        Thy knotted and combined locks to part,
        And each particular hair to stand on end,

```
Like quills upon the fretful porpentine.
But this eternal blazon must not be
To ears of flesh and blood.
```

Now the Ghost discloses that he was murdered, which is the pivotal event of the background story. He adds his personal feeling that blood ties and incest made the crime even worse.

```
GHOST: List, List, O, List!
       If thou didst ever thy dear father love--

HAMLET: O God!

GHOST: Revenge his foul and most unnatural murder.

HAMLET: Murder!

GHOST: Murder most foul, as in the best it is;
       But this most foul, strange, and unnatural.
```

A few lines later, the Ghost picks up the thread of the events once again.

```
GHOST:                    Now, Hamlet, hear;
       'Tis given out that, sleeping in my orchard
       A serpent stung me; so the whole ear of Denmark
       Is by a forged process of my death
       Rankly abused; but know, thou noble youth,
       The serpent that did sting thy father's life
       Now wears his crown.

HAMLET: O my prophetic soul!
        My uncle!
```

The Ghost adds a character description of Claudius, condemning his incestuous relationship with Gertrude and the murder of his own brother.

```
GHOST:  Ay, that incestuous, that adulterate beast,
        With wicked witchcraft of his wits, with traitorous gifts--
        O wicked wit and gifts that have the power
        So to seduce--won to his shameful lust
        The will of my most seeming virtuous queen.
```

Now follows 11 lines contrasting King Hamlet's honorable love of Gertrude with Claudius's dishonorable lust.

```
        O Hamlet, what a falling off was there,
        From me, whose love was of that dignity
        That it went hand in hand even with the vow
        I made to her in marriage; and to decline
        Upon a wretch whose natural gifts were poor
        To those of mine!
```

The next 16 lines are a vivid account of the murder itself.

```
        But soft! methinks I scent the morning air.
        Brief let me be. Sleeping within my orchard,
        My custom always of the afternoon,
        Upon my secure hour thy uncle stole,
```

```
With juice of cursed hebona in a vial,
And in the porches of mine ears did pour
The leprous distillment; whose effect
Holds such an enmity with blood of man
That swift as quicksilver it courses through
The natural gates and alleys of the body;
And with a sudden vigour it doth posset
And curd, like eager droppings into milk,
The thin and wholesome blood. So did it mine;
And a most instant tetter bark'd about,
Most lazar-like, with vile and loathsome crust,
All my smooth body.
```

Seven lines of religious feelings develop from these.

```
Thus was I, sleeping, by a brother's hand
Of life, of crown, of queen, at once dispatch'd;
Cut off even in the blossom of my sin,
Unhousl'd, disappointed, unanel'd;
No reck'ning made, but sent to my account
With all my imperfections on my head.
O, Horrible! O, Horrible! most horrible!
```

The Ghost concludes the scene by challenging Hamlet to revenge his murder. The background story in this scene has been disclosed by one character during several long narrative speeches composed of a seamless blend of events, feelings, and character descriptions.

In *A Raisin in the Sun,* the background story is disclosed by a number of characters speaking about the past retrospectively and in small fragments. This scene between Walter and his wife, Ruth, occurs near the beginning of the play. It centers around Walter's scheme for buying a liquor store. Unfortunately his project will require $10,000 from his father's life insurance. Skillfully mixed within the action going on between Walter and Ruth are background story events, character descriptions, and feelings.

WALTER: You want to know what I was thinking 'bout in the bathroom this morning?

RUTH: No.

WALTER: How come you always got to be so pleasant?

RUTH: What is there to be pleasant 'bout?

WALTER: You want to know what I was thinking 'bout in the bathroom or not?

RUTH: I know what you was thinking 'bout.

WALTER: (*ignoring her*) 'Bout what me an' Willy Harris was talking about last night.

RUTH: (*immediately--a refrain*) Willy Harris is a good-for-nothing loud mouth.

WALTER: Anybody who talks to me has got to be a good-for-nothing loud mouth, ain't he? And what you know about who is just a good-for-nothing loud mouth? <u>Charlie Atkins was just a "good-for-nothing loud-mouth" too, wasn't he? When he wanted me to go into the dry-cleaning business with him. And now--he's grossing a hundred thousand dollars a year. A hundred thousand dollars a year!</u> You still call him a loud mouth?

RUTH: (*bitterly*) Oh, Walter Lee.

(*She folds her head on her arms over the table.*)

WALTER: (*rising and coming over to her and standing over her*) You tired, ain't you? Tired of everything. Me, the boy, <u>the way we live</u>--this beat up hole--everything. Ain't you? So tired--<u>moaning and groaning all the time, but you wouldn't do nothing to help, would you? You couldn't be on my side that long for nothing, could you?</u>

RUTH: Walter, please leave me alone.

WALTER: A man needs for a woman to back him up. . .

RUTH: Walter--

WALTER: Mama would listen to you. <u>You know she listen to you more than she do me and Bennie. She think more of you, too.</u> All you have to do is just sit down with her when you drinking your coffee one morning and talking 'bout things like you do--(*He sits down beside her and demonstrates graphically what he thinks her methods and tone should be.*)--you just sip your coffee, see, and say easy like that you been thinking 'bout <u>that deal Walter Lee is so interested in, 'bout the store, and all,</u> and sip some more coffee, like what you saying ain't really that important to you--and the next thing you know, she be listening good and asking you questions and when I come home--I can tell her the details. <u>This ain't no fly-by-night proposition, baby. I mean we got it figured out, me and Willy and Bobo.</u>

RUTH: (*with a frown*) Bobo?

WALTER: Yeah. <u>You see, this little liquor store we got in mind cost seventy-five thousand and we figured the initial investment on the place be 'bout thirty thousand, see. That be ten thousand each. Course, there's a couple of hundred you got to pay so's you don't spend the rest of your life just waitin' for them clowns to let your license get approved--</u>

RUTH: You mean graft?

WALTER: (*frowning impatiently*) Don't call it that. See there, that just goes to show you what women understand about the world. Baby, don't <u>nothing</u> happen in this world 'less you pay <u>somebody</u> off!

RUTH: Walter, leave me alone! (*She raises her head and stares at him vigorously--then says, more quietly.*) Eat your eggs, they gonna be cold.

WALTER: (*straightening up from her and looking off*) That's it. There you are. Man say to his woman: I got me a dream. His woman

say: eat your eggs. (*sadly, but gaining in power*) Man say: I
got to take hold of this here world, baby! And a woman will
say: Eat your eggs and go to work. (*passionately now*) Man say:
I got to change my life. I'm choking to death, baby!. And his
woman say--(*in utter anguish as he brings his fists down on
his thighs*)--Your eggs is getting cold!

RUTH: (*softly*) Walter, that ain't none of our money.

WALTER: (*not listening at all or even looking at her*) <u>This morning,
I was lookin' in the mirror and thinking about it . . .
I'm thirty-five years old; I been married eleven years and I
got a boy who sleeps in the living room</u>--(*very, very quietly*)--
<u>and all I got to give him is stories about how rich people
live. . .</u>

RUTH: Eat your eggs, Walter.

WALTER: <u>Damn my eggs . . . damn all the eggs that ever was!</u>

RUTH: Then go to work.

WALTER: (*looking at her*) See--I'm trying to talk to you 'bout myself--
(*shaking his head with the repetition*)--and all you can say is
eat them eggs and go to work.

RUTH: (*wearily*) Honey, <u>you never say anything new. I listen to you
every day, every night, and every morning, and you never say
nothing new.</u> (*shrugging*) So <u>you would rather be Mr. Arnold
than be his chauffeur.</u> So--I would *rather* be living in Buck-
ingham Palace.

WALTER: That's just what is wrong with the colored women in this
world. . . .Don't understand about building their men up and
making 'em feel like they somebody. Like they can do something.

RUTH: (*dryly, but to hurt*) There *are* colored men who do things.

WALTER: No thanks to the colored woman.

RUTH: Well, being a colored woman, I guess I can't help myself none.

Modern realistic treatment of background story is deliberately calculated to create the illusion of everyday life. This means that characters must be
able to talk about the past without obviously seeming to do so and without
interrupting the advance of the story that's occurring on stage. Disclosing
the past in this way certainly does provide a surface feeling of credibility, but
there is a trade off. Since the past is mixed with the present, it's more difficult
to distinguish between them during the rapid unfolding of the action. This is
further complicated by the fact that, in the retrospective method, unspoken
implications and inferences play a much larger role than they do in historical
narrative technique. The lesson to be learned about realistic background
story is that actors, directors, and designers need to exercise special care
during analysis and in performance and that audiences need to exercise
attentive listening.

SUMMARY

We have been reviewing the topic of background story, noting what is normally done and studying the adjustments playwrights have made to accommodate particular needs. We have seen that, since the background story is crowded with significant information, it is essential to know as much about it as possible and in detail. Another important part of learning about background story is understanding that for theatre workers it involves much more than the theoretical term exposition. Most readers who have followed the discussion so far should see that background story is as dramatic as on-stage action. Frequently it is more so.

QUESTIONS

Technique: Is the background story disclosed in long speeches? In short statements? In subtle hints and veiled allusions? How reliable are the characters who disclose the background story? Is the background story disclosed near the beginning of the play? Throughout the entire play? Any disclosed near the end of the play? How much background story is there compared to on-stage action? Where does the action of the play begin in relation to the background story? In relation to the end of the action?

Identification: What specific events are disclosed in the background story? How long ago did they occur? What is the original chronology of events? In what order are the events disclosed in the play? Besides events, are there any character descriptions in the background story? Any feelings or sense impressions?

Summary: Provide a complete report of the background story as told by all the characters. Write a complete report of each character's background story.

3

• • • • • • • •

Plot: Physical and Psychological Action

Etymologically, the word *plot* is influenced by the Old French word *complot*, meaning "a secret scheme." It has an added sense of its parts being closely packed together. Plot also has parallel meanings related to secret intrigues or conspiracies and to suspense. Aristotle believed that plot was the first principle and the soul of drama. He described it as the imitation of the action and the arrangement of the incidents. He also said that a plot should have a beginning, a middle, and an end and that it should present a single complete action.

Writers from Voltaire to Bertolt Brecht have debated Aristotle's expectations about plot, but that is not of concern here. Most audiences—and that includes actors, directors, and designers—expect some kind of plot, even if it's wrong to expect it. Plot means the story line, the sense that things are moving, that the play is getting somewhere, and that the action is moving forward. In this basic sense, plot serves to sustain interest in wanting to learn how everything does or doesn't come together in the end. It causes the questions: "What happened?" "What is happening?" and "What is going to happen?"

It is not necessary to define plot more than this, but someone who tried would be obliged to deal with at least four basic principles: (1) physical action, (2) psychological action, (3) progressions, and (4) structure. A plot could conceivably be deficient in one of these, but if that happened there would be a sense that something was missing. A play with such an unfinished feeling rarely succeeds. Physical and psychological action will be the organizing principles of this chapter. Chapter 4 will deal with the plot's progress and arrangement.

PHYSICAL ACTION (THE EXTERNAL PLOT)

The first responsibility of plot is to provide the physical action needed to carry out the story practically. Try to understand the plot on its most basic level—that of what the characters are actually doing on stage. When such physical activity is specified in the dialogue, it is considered an elementary mechanical part of the plot. In *Creating a Role,* Stanislavski used the term *physical action* to describe these kinds of external activities. He was interested in their role in stimulating the actor's imagination. He believed the life of a play begins with physical actions then moves forward to include psychological actions.

Once again when reading only for private study, there is probably no harm in supplementing the dialogue with the stage directions to discover information about physical action. In most cases, stage directions are a reasonably accurate record of the original production. If analysis is intended for a production, however, extreme caution should be exercised in using the stage directions as authority for anything. This text advocates relying on the dialogue as much as possible. Even when there is no obvious physical action disclosed in the dialogue, it can usually be supplied by deduction without consulting other people's suggestions. Most of the interpretive physical action created by professionals does not come from the stage directions anyway but rather from information found in the dialogue.

Entrances and Exits

Entrances and exits in drama are roughly equivalent to attack and release in music; they start and stop the action. In a play, the action normally, though not always, starts with an entrance and concludes with an exit (or a curtain or blackout, which are essentially the same thing). Entrances and exits differ from one another in terms of characters and physical conditions, but they all share the same components. Reading the dialogue in the literal sense is helpful to illustrate this lesson, but there is no obligation always to be so strict in production.

The following simple example from early in *Oedipus Rex* shows Sophocles presenting an important entrance. Notice his use of repetition for dramatic reinforcement.

CHORUS: He is coming. Creon is coming.

Shakespeare infuses a little more emotion into the following two examples from *Hamlet*. The first is Horatio's warning to Hamlet of the appearance of the Ghost; the second is the Ghost's departure.

HORATIO: Look, my lord, it comes!

. . .

GHOST: Adieu, adieu, adieu! Remember me.

Molière includes both strong emotion and information about specific locale in this exit from *Tartuffe*.

ORGON: I'm so incensed . . . I shall have to go outside to recover myself.

Ibsen's talent for innuendo may be seen in the following entrance. Here Gina Ekdal gently scolds her father-in-law about his tardiness while hinting that she knows he has been drinking again. In the second example, Ibsen has concluded a family dispute with an exit that also involves important information about character motivation. The third passage shows Ibsen using an exit to provoke a sense of "What's going to happen next?"

GINA: How *late* you are today, Grandfather!

                        . . .

GREGERS: When I look back upon your past I seem to see a battlefield
         with shattered lives on every hand.

WERLE: I begin to think that the chasm that divides us is too wide.

GREGERS: (*bowing with self-command*) So I have observed, and therefore
         I take my hat and go.

WERLE: You are going? Out of the house?

GREGERS: Yes. For at last I see my mission in life.

WERLE: What mission?

GREGERS: You would only laugh if I told you.

                        . . .

GREGERS: Put on your hat and coat, Hjalmar; I want you to come for a
         long walk with me.

Mama Younger expresses her feelings about Beneatha's new boyfriend in this exit from *A Raisin in the Sun.*

MAMA: Lord, that's a pretty thing just went out of here!

Of course not all entrances and exits are openly stated in the dialogue as these are. Nonetheless, they always merit careful study. Who is coming and going are basic parts of the plot. Arrivals and departures will often effect the action of a scene significantly. Moreover the surrounding dialogue can reveal information about character.

Blocking

Blocking is the movement and location of the characters. The ability to visualize blocking while reading is a difficult skill, yet the spatial relationships among the characters serve to clarify the story and express emotion. Characters physically adjust to each other corresponding to their mental attitudes. They alternately attract and repel each other like polarized magnets. They are close in climactic or affectionate moments and apart at other times. This blocking may be recognized in the dialogue.

Here are some examples of *indigenous blocking,* or physical action required for the practical execution of the plot. Such instances as these are needed to explain the basic logic of the events. In the first line, Oedipus provides a picture of the stage positions of the Chorus members as well as some of their costume accessories. The words *strewn* and *before* (in this translation, at least) indicate that the characters are probably located around the thymele, the central altar, which was a standard architectural feature of Greek theatres.

OEDIPUS: My children . . .
         Why have you strewn yourselves before these altars
         In supplication, with your boughs and garlands?

Hamlet's following line in the *mousetrap scene* is both a stage direction and a sexual pun. Ophelia is seated on the floor before the Players' makeshift stage. Hamlet jokingly asks permission to lay his head on her lap while watching the play.

HAMLET: Lady, shall I lie in your lap?

In this line from *Tartuffe*, Elmire provides detailed directions to Orgon for hiding under the table. He must position himself carefully to avoid being seen by Tartuffe during the following scene. Her persistence shows that Orgon is a reluctant participant.

ELMIRE: Help me to bring the table up. Now get under it . . . You
        shall see in due course. Get under there and, mind now, take
        care that he doesn't see or hear you.

A moment before the next line, from *Death of a Salesman*, Biff has accidentally discovered his father in a hotel room with another woman. Willy hides her in the bathroom because he doesn't want Biff to see her.

WILLY: All right, stay in the bathroom here, and don't come out. I
       think there's a law in Massachusetts, so don't come out.

In *A Raisin in the Sun*, Nigerian student Joseph Asagai visits Beneatha's apartment. Her family is packing for their move to Clybourne Park. It's not necessarily an important entrance in itself, but his line still contains hints about the stage picture and blocking as well as a little of the personal charm that makes him attractive to Beneatha.

ASAGAI: I came over . . . I had some free time. I thought I might
        help with the packing. Ah, I like the look of packing crates!
        A household in preparation for a journey!

Use of Properties

A third type of physical action is the use of stage or hand properties. What makes their use special is their physical actuality on stage. Since properties are among the few things that are objectively real in a performance, they provide a link with the real world and offer opportunities for stage business. Like blocking, the use of properties has both a logical and an emotional aspect. Logic is served when characters use properties to explain the story; emotion is released when properties are used for the expression of personal feelings.

After Hamlet has spoken with the Ghost, he makes his friends promise not to reveal what they have seen. His line shows that he is using his sword as a cross on which his friends are expected to place their hands ritualistically.

HAMLET: Swear by my sword
        Never to speak of this that you have heard.

This line from *The School for Scandal* requires close attention to the context of the makeshift auction that is about to take place. There are three references to properties: (1) a chair used as the auctioneer's pulpit, (2) a parchment with a listing of the family tree, and (3) the same parchment used as the auctioneer's gavel.

CHARLES: But come, get to your pulpit, Mr. Auctioneer; here's a gouty
      old chair of my grandfather's will answer the purpose. . . .
      What parchment have we here? Oh, our genealogy in full. Here,
      Careless, you shall have no common bit of mahogany, here's the
      family tree for you, you rogue! This shall be your hammer. . . .

Hjalmar's warning to Hedvig about the fatal pistol in *The Wild Duck* is a physical action that also prepares crucial plot information. Playwrights technically call this practice *funding* or *foreshadowing,* terms that refer to the accumulation or disclosure of important information prior to an action.

HJALMAR: Don't touch that pistol, Hedvig! One of the barrels is
      loaded, remember that.

In this line from *Mother Courage,* Anna Fierling shows her identity papers to the Sergeant. It's characteristic of Brecht to provide opportunities for character illustration through the use of ordinary, everyday objects like these.

MOTHER COURAGE: Here are my papers, Sergeant. There's a whole missal,
      picked it up in Alt-Otting to wrap cucumbers in, and a map of
      Moravia. . . .

Readers should be aware that properties are meant to be expressively important when they are described frankly in the dialogue as these are. Playwrights plan their properties to express dramatic effects.

Special Physical Activities

This group of physical actions comprises all the unusual kinds of activities that are not covered under the previous topics. Examples include stage combat, playing musical instruments, dancing, acrobatics, and any other movements that require special knowledge or skill on the part of the actors. The distinctive attention warranted by all lines describing physical action is particularly true here. When playwrights make an effort to describe unusual physical activities in their plays, it is because they have endowed those activities with playable dramatic possibilities.

Hamlet's accidental stabbing of Polonius with a sword is a major turning point in *Hamlet* and must be played as such. Polonius, of course, has been hiding behind the arras to eavesdrop on Hamlet.

POLONIUS: (*behind*) What ho! help, help, help!

HAMLET: (*draws*) How now! a rat?
      Dead for a ducat, dead!

      (*kills POLONIUS with a pass through the arras*)

POLONIUS: (*behind*) O, I am slain!

In *The Wild Duck,* Mrs. Sorby's piano playing is the subject of this line. When she returns to the other room, she begins to play cheerful tunes on the piano. The cheery music continues in the background during the next scene in which it serves as an ironic commentary on the confrontation between Gregers and his father.

GUEST: Shall we play a duet, Mrs. Sorby?

MRS. SORBY: Yes, suppose we do.

GUESTS: Bravo, bravo!

These three short lines from *The Hairy Ape* contain stage combat. Yank is on a rampage in jail. It takes several guards plus a water hose and a straight jacket to restrain him. There are only a few lines, but they describe a moment that is very complicated to stage successfully.

GUARD: Hey, look at dat bar bended! On'y a bug is strong enough for dat!

YANK: Or a hairy ape, yuh big yellow bum! Look out! Here I come!

GUARD: Toin on de hose, Ben!--full pressure. And call de others--and a straitjacket!

A specific Nigerian folk dance is the subject of these lines in *A Raisin in the Sun.*

RUTH: What kind of dance is that?

BENEATHA: A folk dance.

RUTH: What kind of folks do that, honey?

BENEATHA: It's from Nigeria. It's a dance of welcome.

Cleaning the floors of the barracks is one of the many special activities called for in *Streamers*. The physical action may not seem important, but a closer study shows that the act of cleaning relates to the main idea of the play. Cleaning is a ritualized experience in the military. The characters are trained in how to work according to standard procedures, using government issue equipment. It's a small example of the types of dehumanizing activities the characters are forced to undergo in the play.

BILLY: I'll go get some buckets and stuff so we can clean up, okay? This area's a mess. This area ain't standin' tall.

A knowledge of these and other special physical activities will help readers to appreciate their practical importance as well as their dramatic potential. The benefit is that when readers understand these activities, they will be able to see how they may be used to increase the emotional expressiveness of plays.

PSYCHOLOGICAL ACTION (THE INTERNAL PLOT)

Plot is often understood exclusively as outer physical action. According to this argument, plays with strong plots contain plenty of entrances and exits, hazards and rescues, and similar types of clever and interesting activities, but this is a misunderstanding. Plot is more than a collection of inventive physical activities; for besides its external features, it also occurs inside the characters, changing their inner states as well as their outer conditions. This internal dimension of the plot is usually referred to as *psychological*, or *inner action* to distinguish it from physical action or activity.

Psychological action concerns the mental, spiritual, or emotional lives of the characters rather than their physical lives. When psychological action is expressed openly in the dialogue, it normally appears in three forms: assertions, plans, and commands. There is nothing unusual or mysterious about these forms. They simply describe the attitude of the character toward what is being said. They are similar to the grammatical principle of mood, whether making a statement (indicative), posing a future situation (subjunctive), or giving a command (imperative). In the following section, the way psychological action is expressed directly in the words of the characters will be examined. Psychological action also has non-verbal aspects that will be discussed in Chapter 4.

Assertions

Assertions are the simplest forms of psychological action spoken in the dialogue. In one way or another, they appear on almost every page of a script. The principle behind an assertion is so obvious that it hardly needs explaining. An assertion is simply a statement of fact, a positive declaration that something is true. Saying, for example, "The book is Jill's" or "John has arrived" is openly asserting the simple fact of the book's ownership or of John's current whereabouts. As a rule, assertions identify people, places, things, or events like these. Several examples follow with the dialogue treated literally for instructional reasons, but there are times when psychological actions should not be read this way. Sometimes characters deceive themselves or even lie. Even these occasions, however, are instructive because dialogue must be read literally before it can be read in other ways.

In these lines from *The School for Scandal*, Rowley announces to Sir Peter Teazle the surprise arrival in London of Sir Oliver Surface. When working on a script, it's helpful to highlight the psychological action so that it stands out visually from the rest of the dialogue. Therefore here, and in the rest of this chapter, the plot information is in bold.

ROWLEY: **Sir Oliver is arrived, and at this moment is in town.**

Rowley's announcement involves three clear assertions—first a person ("Sir Oliver"), then an event and time ("is arrived . . . at this moment"), and finally a place ("in town").

The following climactic moment from *The Wild Duck* consists of an assertion of an important event: that Hedvig Ekdal has shot herself. Note how repetition increases the impact.

RELLING: What's the matter here?

GINA: **They say Hedvig shot herself.**

HJALMAR: Come and help us!

RELLING: Shot herself!

When assertions involve serious offenses, they grow in importance and become *accusations*. In this selection from *Oedipus Rex*, Oedipus accuses Teiresias of conspiring with Creon to murder King Laius. Angered at this triple accusation of treason, conspiracy, and murder, Teiresias responds by accusing Oedipus himself of the murder. These two accusations are essentially assertions about an offense involving three persons and one event.

OEDIPUS: I'll tell you what I think:
    You planned it, you had it done, you all but
    Killed him with your own hands: if you had eyes,
    I'd say the crime was yours, and yours alone.

TEIRESIAS: So? I charge you, then,
    Abide by the proclamation you have made:
    From this day forth
    Never speak again to these men or to me;
    You yourself are the pollution of this country.

Accusations also appear when Damis condemns Tartuffe for attempting to seduce Elmire: accusations involving a person (Tartuffe) and an event (the seduction). Note that the number of words in this speech devoted solely to plot is actually quite small. Most of the words describe Damis' feelings.

DAMIS: **We have interesting news for you, father. Something has just occurred which will astonish you.** You are well repaid for your kindness! The gentleman sets a very high value on the consideration you have shown for him! He has just been demonstrating his passionate concern for you and he stops at nothing less than dishonouring your bed. **I have just overheard him making a disgraceful declaration of his guilty passion for your wife.** She in kind-heartedness and overanxiety to be discreet was all for keeping it secret but I can't condone such shameless behavior. I consider it would be a gross injustice to you to keep it from you.

Three characters and five assertions appear in this passage from *Mother Courage*. First Swiss Cheese asserts that he did not steal the payroll. Second the Sergeant asserts that Mother Courage was an accomplice in the theft. Third Swiss Cheese asserts that she had nothing to do with it. Fourth Swiss Cheese asserts that he is innocent. Fifth Mother Courage asserts that she does not know Swiss Cheese. The moment moves quickly, but it is important because it shows Mother Courage denying her own son, even if for seemingly justifiable reasons.

(Voices are heard from the rear. The two men bring in SWISS CHEESE.)

SWISS CHEESE: Let me go. **I haven't got anything.** Stop twisting my shoulder, **I'm innocent.**

THE SERGEANT: **He belongs here. You know each other.**

MOTHER COURAGE: **What makes you think that?**

SWISS CHEESE: I don't know them. I don't even know who they are. I
    had a meal here, it cost me ten hellers. Maybe you saw me
    sitting here, it was too salty.

THE SERGEANT: Who are you anyway?

MOTHER COURAGE: We're respectable people. And it's true. He had a
    meal here. He said it was too salty.

THE SERGEANT: Are you trying to tell me you don't know each other?

MOTHER COURAGE: Why should I know him? I don't know everybody. I
    don't ask people what their name is or if they're heartless;
    if they pay, they're not heathens.

Assertions can be composed of announcements, identifications,
accusations, and rhetorical questions. In any form, they are intimately connected with the plot of the play. Actors and directors should see to it that such
elementary information is not overlooked.

Plans

A *plan* is any detailed method, formulated beforehand, for doing
something. Some plans may be very simple as in "First we'll meet at Mike's
house, then we'll go to the movies," or they may be elaborate, involving
complex sets of dependent actions leading to a final goal like the plans for
landing an astronaut on the moon. Because plans are a practical, economical
method for advancing the plot, their use in plays is widespread. As the following examples show, playwrights with diverse personal styles have made use of
plans under a wide assortment of dramatic conditions.

An illustration of a simple and direct plan occurs in *Mother Courage*
when Anna Fierling hides the platoon's cash box. She is afraid her son will be
charged with the theft.

MOTHER COURAGE: I'd better get the cash box out of here, I've found a
    hiding place. All right, get me a drink. (*KATTRIN goes behind
    the wagon.*) I'll hide it in the rabbit hole down by the river
    until I can take it away. Maybe late tonight. I'll go get it
    and take it to the regiment.

Hamlet's well-known lines also describe a plan, in this case one that has
profound results. An event in the background story sets up the plan.

HAMLET: I have heard
    That guilty creatures, sitting at a play,
    Have by the very cunning of the scene
    Been struck so to the soul that presently
    They have proclaim'd their malefactions;
                · · ·
                   I'll have these players
    Play something like the murder of my father
    Before mine uncle. I'll observe his looks;
    I'll tent him to the quick. If 'a do blench,
    I know my course.
             · · ·

```
The play's the thing
Wherein I'll catch the conscience of the King.
```

Later in the same play Claudius arranges a complicated plan with
Laertes to use an unbated foil (that is, without a protective button on the point)
tipped with poison to murder Hamlet. Shakespeare is justly praised for being
able to maintain the rhythm of his verse even when he is describing ordinary
actions like the ones in these lines.

```
CLAUDIUS:                    But good Laertes,
    Will you do this? Keep close within your chamber.
    Hamlet return'd shall know you are come home.
    We'll put on those shall praise your excellence,
    And set a double varnish on the fame
    The Frenchman gave you; bring you, in fine, together,
    And wager on your heads. He, being remiss,
    Most generous, and free from all contriving,
    Will not peruse the foils; so that with ease
    Or with a little shuffling, you may choose
    A sword unbated, and, in a pass of practice,
    Requite him for your father.
```

In *Tartuffe,* Dorine prepares an elaborate plan to frustrate Orgon's
earlier plan to marry his daughter Mariane to Tartuffe. Mariane's boyfriend
Valere helps her.

```
DORINE: We'll try everything we can. Your father can't be serious and
    it's all sheer rubbish, but you had better pretend to fall in
    with his nonsense and give the appearance of consenting so
    that if it comes to the point you'll more easily be able to
    delay the marriage. If we can only gain time we may easily set
    everything right. You can complain of sudden illness that will
    necessitate delay; another time you can have recourse to bad
    omens--such as having met a corpse or broken a mirror or
    dreamt of muddy water. Finally, the great thing is that they
    can't make you his wife unless you answer 'I will'. But I
    think, as a precaution, you had better not be found talking
    together. (to VALERE) Off you go and get all your friends to
    use their influence with her father to stand by his promise.
    We must ask his brother to try once again, and see if we can
    get the stepmother on our side.
```

In *The Wild Duck,* Gregers' misguided advice to innocent Hedvig proves
to be an insidious plan because it results in her death.

```
GREGERS: (coming a little nearer) But suppose you were to sacrifice
    the wild duck of your own free will for his sake?

HEDVIG: (rising) The wild duck!

GREGERS: Suppose you were to make a free-will offering, for his sake,
    of the dearest treasure you have in the world?

HEDVIG: Do you think that would do any good?

GREGERS: Try it, Hedvig.
```

HEDVIG: (*softly, with flashing eyes*) Yes, I will try it.

GREGERS: Have you really the courage for it, so you think?

HEDVIG: I'll ask grandfather to shoot the wild duck for me.

GREGERS: Yes, do. But not a word to your mother about it.

HEDVIG: Why not?

GREGERS: She doesn't understand us.

HEDVIG: The wild duck! I'll try it tomorrow morning.

Plans can be productive psychological actions to study because normally they appear quite openly in the dialogue as plans. Their treatment seldom varies. First the characters discuss the tactical details, then they put them into effect. Plans provide conspicuous demonstrations of how psychological action advances the plot.

Commands

A *command* is a statement with a built-in feeling of urgent necessity as in, "This must be done!" The following excerpts demonstrate different kinds of commands.

When Claudius formally commands Hamlet to leave for England, he is expressing his absolute authority as king.

CLAUDIUS: Hamlet, this deed, for thine especial safety--
Which we do tender, as we dearly grieve
For that which thou hast done--must send thee hence
With fiery quickness. Therefore prepare thyself;
The bark is ready, and the wind at help,
Th' associates tend, and everything is bent
For England.

HAMLET: For England!

Orgon takes advantage of the inherent authority of his paternal role when he commands his daughter, Mariane, to marry Tartuffe.

ORGON: What have you to say about our guest Tartuffe?

MARIANE: What have I to say?

ORGON: Yes, you! Mind how you answer.

MARIANE: Oh dear! I'll say anything you like about him.

ORGON: That's very sensible. Then let me hear you say, my dear, that he is a wonderful man, that you love him, and you'd be glad to have me choose him for your husband. Eh?

Mama Younger expresses another kind of parental authority in this stern command from *A Raisin in the Sun*. In the preceding moment, her daughter Beneatha has repudiated the need for God in her life.

(*MAMA absorbs [BENEATHA's] speech, studies her daughter and rises slowly and crosses to BENEATHA and slaps her powerfully across the face. After, there is only silence and the daughter drops her eyes from her mother's face, and MAMA is very tall before her.*)

MAMA: **Now--you say after me, in my mother's house there is still God.** (*There is a long pause and BENEATHA stares at the floor wordlessly. MAMA repeats the phrase with precision and cool emotion.*) **In my mother's house there is still God.**

BENEATHA: In my mother's house there is still God. (*a long pause*)

MAMA: (*walking away from BENEATHA, too disturbed for triumphant posture. Stopping and turning back to her daughter.*) **There are some ideas we ain't going to have in this house. Not as long as I am the head of this family.**

BENEATHA: Yes, ma'am.

The following passage contains examples of military commands as expressed in David Rabe's *Streamers*. The military police have arrived in the cadre room to find that two soldiers have been brutally murdered.

(*As a MILITARY POLICE LIEUTENANT comes running in the door, his .45 automatic drawn, and he levels it at ROGER.*)

LIEUTENANT: **Freeze, soldier! Not a quick move out of you. Just real slow, straighten your ass up.**

(*ROGER has gone rigid; the LIEUTENANT is advancing on him. Tentatively, ROGER turns, looks.*)

ROGER: Huh? No.

LIEUTENANT: **Get your ass against the lockers.**

ROGER: Sir, no. I--

LIEUTENANT: (*hurling ROGER away toward the wall lockers*) **MOVE!** (*As another M.P., Pfc HINSON, comes in, followed by RICHIE, flushed and breathless*) **Hinson, cover this bastard.**

HINSON: (*drawing his .45 automatic, moving on ROGER*) Yes, sir.

(*The LIEUTENANT frisks ROGER, who is spread-eagled at the lockers.*)

RICHIE: What? Oh, sir, no, no. Roger, what's going on?

LIEUTENANT: I'll straighten this shit out.

ROGER: Tell him to get the gun off me, Richie.

LIEUTENANT: **SHUT UP!**

RICHIE: But, sir, sir, he didn't do it. Not him.

LIEUTENANT: (*Fiercely he shoves RICHIE out of the way.*) **I told you, all of you, to shut up.**

These commands given by Winnie to her husband, Willie, reveal an important dimension of their relationship in Beckett's play *Happy Days*. Readers will recall that in this off-beat fantasy, Winnie is continuously buried up to her waist in an earthen hill and Willie is buried out of sight behind her.

WINNIE: (*She cranes [her neck] back and down.*) **Go back into your hole now, Willie, you've exposed yourself enough.** (*Pause.*) **Do as I say, Willie, don't lie sprawling there in this hellish sun, go back into your hole.** (*Pause.*) **Go on now, Willie.** (*WILLIE invisible [to the audience] starts crawling left towards hole.*) **That's the man.** (*She follows his progress with her eyes.*) **Not head first, stupid, how are you going to turn?** (*Pause.*) **That's it . . . right round . . . now . . . back in.** (*Pause.*) **Oh I know it's not easy, dear, crawling backwards, but it is re warding in the end.** (*Pause.*) **You have left your Vaseline behind.** (*She watches as he crawls back for Vaseline.*) **The lid!** (*She watches as he crawls back towards the hole. Irritated.*) **Not head first, I tell you!** (*Pause.*) **More to the right.** (*Pause.*) **The *right*, I said.** (*Pause. Irritated.*) **Keep your tail down, can't you!** (*Pause.*) **Now.** (*Pause.*) **There!** (*All these directions loud. Now in her normal voice, still turned towards him.*) **Can you hear me?** (*Pause.*) **I beseech you, Willie, just say yes or no, can you hear me, just yes or nothing.**

Commands push the play ahead by causing events that the characters must carry out. Close reading will also disclose the presence of *driving characters*, strong-willed characters who produce the plans that are needed to drive the plot forward.

SUMMARY

Physical and psychological action is important in the understanding of plot. Physical action includes entrances and exits, blocking, use of properties, and special physical activities that contribute to carrying out the basic external plot. Psychological action consists of assertions, plans, and commands that comprise the inner plot. The reason for evaluating these features is not that the act of classification is at all important but to give the broadest possible scope to our understanding of plot.

By analyzing the different categories, it should be possible for actors, directors, and designers to make whatever adjustments are needed in their techniques for a wider theatrical application of plot. For example, every assertion, plan, and command contributes to the forward motion of the plot. Accordingly actors and directors will wish to *point* these moments (embellish them theatrically) to make sure that the plot information is clearly and unambiguously expressed. Designers who are sensitized to the function of entrances and exits in the plot may find it less difficult to determine their most expressive form and placement within the scenic space. In other words, once the physical and psychological actions are known, there is an obligation to express them as fully as possible on stage, whether through performance or design. Fortunately, we are aided in this by the emotional dynamics and arrangement of the plot, which will be discussed in the next chapter.

QUESTIONS

Physical action: Identify the entrances and exits explicitly described in the dialogue. How do they contribute to the advancement of the plot? Are there any movements or positions of the characters described in the dialogue? What function do they play in progressing the plot? Are any practical uses of properties described in the dialogue? Are any special physical actions described in the dialogue, like dancing, fighting, cooking, or anything else besides routine blocking? Do they advance the plot or do they have some other purpose?

Psychological action: Locate and highlight all the important assertions (including identifications and accusations) about people, places, things, or events that take place in the present action. Any detailed plans for doing something? How do they advance the plot? Any commands issued by an authority figure? Any official orders given by someone exercising political or military power? Any directions or instructions in the form supervision? Describe how each of these psychological actions moves the story ahead.

4

· · · · · · · · ·

Plot: Progressions and Structure

There is a progressive growth in the events of a play, and that growth is purposefully arranged to achieve the maximum dramatic effect. Actors, directors, and designers, if they are seriously concerned with craftsmanship, should learn to understand the process of growth and pattern in a plot. If they do not, if they consider one event as important as another or overlook their relationship to each other or to the whole play, the result will be misreading and artistic disorder. This may be high-sounding and trite, but it has to be repeated because so few understand its obvious implications. A production which is "flat," that is, lacking in emotional dynamics, is a sure sign that too little attention has been given to this important principle.

PROGRESSIONS

Plays are written to create the impression that things are constantly moving, that they are getting somewhere. By this we don't always mean a chronological movement but sometimes a psychological one. Even in a play without much physical action, one like *Happy Days,* the plot is advancing emotionally constantly. The feeling of forward motion comes from the dramatists' method of always making the next event more interesting than the last. We're uncomfortable when our interest in the play declines or if there is a feeling of going backwards. We're not even satisfied to maintain the same level of interest. Forward motion is a fundamental necessity of plot.

But a plot does not progress at the same continuous rate throughout the entire play. That would be almost as uninteresting as no forward motion at all. What really happens is this. A question is introduced and developed to an emotional peak, then a new question is introduced that immediately begins to grow toward another peak. Emotional intensity may drop a little after the first peak, but interest will never fade completely because a new question will emerge and begin moving toward another peak almost immediately. This is how a play moves forward in progressions, which rise, crest, and fall away like waves on the seashore.

Progressions are arranged in groups according to size, technically called beats, units, scenes, and acts. Literature employs progressions, too, called *paragraphs, chapters,* and *books.* In drama as in literature, progressions help to create interest, maintain suspense, develop the story logically, and bring everything to a satisfactory conclusion. The study of progressions begins by subdividing the play into a chain of storytelling pieces. After this has been done, it becomes possible to determine the inner logic or through-line that connects them. From this process, the story of the play emerges.

Since progressions are also related to character, some readers may be concerned that we do not discuss character objectives and actions at this point in the book. The principal reason is organizational convenience. In this chapter, we are interested in the basic storytelling function of progressions, and the main task is to identify them by studying the outward features of the story. Admittedly, some of the descriptions to be referred to are not *actions* or *objectives* in the narrow sense employed by Stanislavski and his followers. Plot may be adequately discussed without using Stanislavski's vocabulary rules for analyzing characters. A reasonable explanation of the activities of the characters is satisfactory and saves time. Chapter 5 will consider how progressions are also affected by character. There is no urgent need of course to stick with this organizational strategy. Readers who wish to study character objectives and actions before learning about beats and units can jump ahead to Chapter 5 for that information then return to this chapter.

Beats

The smallest dramatic progressions are called *beats.* In a play, these work like paragraphs in prose, but without their visible identification marks. Their purpose is identical—namely, to introduce, develop, and conclude a single small topic that adds to the progress of the whole story. Any collection of consecutive lines can compose a beat as long as it expresses a single, complete topic (or action, objective, or conflict as we will see in Chapter 5). A beat normally consists of about six lines of dialogue, but many are longer or shorter, and some contain only physical or psychological action with little or no dialogue. The requirements are flexible. The length, internal arrangement, and purpose may vary according to the playwright's intentions and personal style.

Beats are basic features of playwriting technique and therefore may be identified objectively in the script. Ideally different readers analyzing the same play should arrive at the same pattern of beats. Unfortunately we are so accustomed to seeing dialogue flow uninterrupted on the page that we may not realize how much the practice of grouping by beats helps our understanding. But the effect of dialogue without beats is like a passage of prose without paragraphing. It is almost impossible to make sense of a continuous river of dialogue undivided into beats. Disregarding beats means always having to deal with countless unrelated lines. Script analysis identifies beats and forces them into the open where they can be used productively by actors and directors.

At this point, consider two pieces of advice about beats. First even though beats are present objectively in the script, it's easy to become confused trying to identify them. Beats are obviously about something, but playwrights are crafty and inventive about revealing the real subjects of their writing. Even though playwrights should insure that their subject is always clear, in practice many of them disguise what's really happening. Readers should make allowances for beats aiming at artistic effects—where the playwright's objective is to deliberately keep the audience guessing—for the sake of a delayed surprise, for example. Even when authors do not try to conceal their subjects, learning about beats can still be frustrating. It's perfectly natural to experience confusion at first because learning to recognize beats takes practice. Do not become trapped in endless mental gymnastics, but make an educated guess then test the results in rehearsals. Practically speaking, early rehearsals are often used to identify and explain the beats in the play.

Second in a book on script analysis we are naturally talking about beats in the written part of the play, or *textual beats*. In the vocabulary of some actors and directors, the term *beat* sometimes also refers to an independent physical acting task—for example, eating a meal or packing a suitcase within the context of a scene. Understanding textual beats can help in the performance of so-called acting beats, but there is not necessarily a point-to-point correlation.

To understand textual beats, we will look at the opening moments of David Rabe's play, *Streamers*. The setting is the cadre room in an army training camp a few years before the Vietnam conflict became a major war. It is early evening. The play begins just as Richie has fortunately interrupted Martin's latest suicide attempt. Beats are not formally identified in a play, of course, so we have illustrated them here with a solid line marked through the script. This is a useful practice for actors and directors to get into the habit of doing. In addition, studying the words of one character at a time can make the topics of conversation and their associated beats easier to comprehend.

Beat 1 ───

RICHIE: Honest to God, Martin, I don't know what to say anymore. I
      don't know what to tell you.

MARTIN: (*beginning to pace again*) I mean it. I just can't stand it.
      Look at me.

RICHIE: I know.

MARTIN: I hate it.

RICHIE: We've got to make up a story. They'll ask you a hundred
      questions.

MARTIN: Do you know how I hate it?

RICHIE: Everybody does. Don't you think I hate it, too?

MARTIN: I enlisted, though. I enlisted and I hate it.

RICHIE: I enlisted, too.

MARTIN: I vomit every morning. I get the dry heaves. In the middle of
      every night.

> *(He flops down on the corner of BILLY's bed and sits there, slumped forward, shaking his head.)*

Beat 2 ————————————————————————————

RICHIE: You can stop that. You can.

MARTIN: No.

RICHIE: You're just scared. It's just fear.

MARTIN: They're all so mean, they're all so awful. I've got two years to go. Just thinking about it is going to make me sick. I thought it would be different from the way it is.

RICHIE: But you could have died, for God's sake.

> *(RICHIE has turned now; he is facing MARTIN.)*

MARTIN: I just wanted out.

RICHIE: I might not have found you, though. I might not have come up here.

MARTIN: I don't care. I'd be out.

> *(The door opens, and a black man in filthy fatigues--they are grease-stained and dark with sweat--stands there. He is CAR-LYLE, looking about, RICHIE, seeing him, rises and moves toward him.)*

This conversation consists of two beats. We said before that an important story-telling function of beats is to disclose a new topic. In the first beat, the topic is Martin's hatred of military life and his related appeal for sympathy. This appears in his line, "Do you know how I hate it?" Richie protects Martin from further harm as can be seen in his line, "We've got to make up a story." The beat rises to a small crescendo at the moment Martin flops on Billy's bed, and it ends there. It contains ten lines and concludes with a decisive physical action.

The second beat begins with Richie's line "You can stop that. You can." He warns Martin about the seriousness of his actions. Martin, on the other hand, wishes to show Richie why he wants to get out of the military so badly. He specifies this in his line beginning, "They're all so mean." The beat lasts for eight lines and ends with Carlyle's entrance. A physical action also punctuates this beat. To summarize the topics that constitute these two beats:

Beat 1. Martin appeals for sympathy; Richie protects him.
Beat 2. Martin wants out at any cost; Richie warns him against it.

There may be other ways to describe these two beats, but at least the reasons for these descriptions should be clear. Notice also this important feature, almost a law of dramatic writing. In each beat, the characters are restricted to one small topic, and once that topic is finished, there is no longer any need to talk about it. The characters may discuss additional issues related to the original topic, but they will never repeat the topic in the same way. Without this economy, the dialogue we just studied would have a negligent, unfinished feeling about it. Again readers should remember that there are other ways to describe beats, and Chapter 5 will present some of them for study. In this chapter, the only concern under discussion is their most obvious role in the advancement of the plot.

Units

Beats follow each other without a break but are not lined up mechanically without connections. They are tightly connected and interact with one another in the development of a larger progression called a *unit* or sometimes *event* or *episode*. In other words, while a beat is a group of related lines, a unit is a group of related beats. Compare beats with *measures* in music—a group of related notes—and units with *phrases*—a group of related measures. The key distinction is the relative importance of the progression. A unit is structurally more influential in the play because it contains several beats.

Some writers maintain that units are different from beats in terms of their larger size and all-around importance, while others use the two terms interchangeably. Can these two points of view be reconciled? To clarify the situation, it might be helpful to look at the historical picture. Following the practice of contemporary Russian critics, Stanislavski employed the procedure of objectively subdividing a play into its component pieces. He explained the process in *An Actor Prepares* where he spoke of the subdivisions simply as *kouski*, meaning literally pieces. He didn't make any further size distinctions except to speak of larger pieces (*bolshe kouski*), medium pieces (*sredni kouski*), and smaller pieces (*menshe kouski*). In her English translation of *An Actor Prepares*, Elizabeth Hapgood designated the larger pieces as *units* and the smaller ones as *bits*. According to Hapgood, the term *beat* first appeared when early Russian teachers of Stanislavski's system in America used the same English terms, only mispronouncing the word *bit*, so initially at least it seems there was a size distinction. Bits (beats) were finer subdivisions of pieces (units).

Stanislavski was interested mainly in the larger progressions, and Hapgood's English terms were chosen to represent his viewpoint. He maintained that detailed development of beats is sometimes needed to disclose the subtleties in a unit, but he did not believe in dealing with more subdivisions than necessary. Of course, these are only historical distinctions, and they should always be adapted to suit our own needs. The lessons are that beats are subdivisions of units and that the larger and fewer the progressions, the easier it will be to understand the whole play.

To explain units, we will study the remaining beats that collectively form the first unit of *Streamers*.

Beat 3 ——————————————————————————

(*The door opens and a black man in filthy fatigues--they are grease-stained and dark with sweat--stands there. He is CAR-LYLE, looking about. RICHIE, seeing him, rises and moves toward him.*)

RICHIE: No, Roger isn't here right now.

CARLYLE: Who isn't?

RICHIE: He isn't here.

CARLYLE: They told me a black boy livin' in here. I don't see him.

>   *(He looks suspiciously about the room.)*

RICHIE: That's what I'm saying. He isn't here. He'll be back later. You can come back later. His name is Roger.

Beat 4 ————————————————————————————————

MARTIN: I slit my wrist.

>   *(Thrusting out the bloody, towel-wrapped wrist toward CAR-LYLE.)*

RICHIE: Martin! Jesus!

MARTIN: I did.

RICHIE: He's kidding. He's kidding.

CARLYLE: What's was his name? Martin?

>   *(CARLYLE is confused and the confusion has made him angry. He moves toward MARTIN.)*

>   You Martin?

MARTIN: Yes.

Beat 5 ————————————————————————————————

>   *(As BILLY, a white in his mid-twenties, blond and trim, appears in the door, whistling, carrying a slice of pie on a paper napkin. Sensing something, he falters, looks at CARLYLE, then RICHIE.)*

BILLY: Hey, what's goin' on?

CARLYLE: *(turning, leaving)* Nothin', man. Not a thing.

Beat 6 ————————————————————————————————

>   *(BILLY looks questioningly at RICHIE. Then, after placing the piece of pie on the chair beside the door, he crosses to his footlocker.)*

RICHIE: He came here looking for Roger, but he didn't even know his name.

BILLY: *(Sitting on his footlocker, he starts taking off his shoes.)* How come you weren't at dinner, Rich? I brought you a piece of pie. Hey, Martin.

Beat 7 ————————————————————————————————

>   *(MARTIN thrusts out his towel-wrapped wrist.)*

RICHIE: Oh, for God's sake, Martin!

(He whirls away.)

BILLY: Huh?

MARTIN: I did.

RICHIE: You are disgusting, Martin.

MARTIN: No. It's the truth. I did. I am not disgusting.

RICHIE: Well, maybe it isn't disgusting, but it certainly is disappointing.

BILLY: What are you guys talking about?

(Sitting there, he really doesn't know what is going on.)

MARTIN: I cut my wrists. I slashed them, and Richie is pretending I didn't.

RICHIE: I am not. And you only cut one wrist and you didn't slash it.

Beat 8 ────────────────────────────────────

MARTIN: I can't stand the army anymore, Billy.

(He is moving now to petition BILLY, and RICHIE steps between them.)

RICHIE: Billy, listen to me. This is between Martin and me.

MARTIN: It's between me and the army, Richie.

RICHIE: *(Taking MARTIN by the shoulders as BILLY is now trying to get near MARTIN.)* Let's just go outside and talk, Martin. You don't know what you're saying.

BILLY: Can I see? I mean, did he really do it?

RICHIE: No!

MARTIN: I did.

BILLY: That's awful. Jesus. Maybe you should go to the infirmary.

RICHIE: I washed it with peroxide. It's not deep. Just let us be. Please. He just needs to straighten out his thinking a little, that's all.

BILLY: Well, maybe I could help him?

MARTIN: Maybe he could.

Beat 9 ────────────────────────────────────

RICHIE: *(Suddenly pushing at MARTIN, RICHIE is angry and exasperated. He wants MARTIN out of the room.)* Get out of here, Martin. Billy, you do some push-ups or something.

(Having been pushed towards the door, MARTIN wanders out.)

BILLY: No.

```
RICHIE: I know what Martin needs.

        (RICHIE whirls and rushes into the hall after MARTIN, leaving
        BILLY scrambling to get his shoes on.)

BILLY:  You're no doctor, are you? I just want to make sure he doesn't
        have to go to the infirmary, then I'll leave you alone.

        (One shoe on, he grabs up the second and runs out the door
        into the hall after them.)

        Martin! Martin, wait up!

        (Silence. The door has been left open. Fifteen or twenty sec-
        onds pass. Then someone is heard coming down the hall. . . .)
```

From what we know so far, the locus of dramatic interest in the unit seems to be Martin's attempted suicide. We count nine beats in all. In the third beat, Carlyle enters and demands to know where Roger is. The fourth beat is Martin's attempt to gain sympathy from Carlyle by showing him his injured wrist. Billy enters and Carlyle exits in the fifth beat. In the sixth beat, Martin attempts to gain Billy's sympathy. Richie scolds Martin in the seventh beat. In the eighth beat, Billy attempts to help Martin, and in the ninth beat, Richie leaves with Martin. This represents one unit or one complete step in the story's progress. The general topic of conversation is obviously Martin's attempted suicide. The next unit begins with the tenth beat when someone is heard coming down the hall.

In outline form, the composition of the first unit is roughly:

> Unit 1. Martin's attempted suicide.
>   Beat 1. Martin appeals to Richie for sympathy.
>   Beat 2. Martin wants to escape.
>   Beat 3. Carlyle enters.
>   Beat 4. Martin appeals to Carlyle for sympathy.
>   Beat 5. Billy enters; Carlyle exits.
>   Beat 6. Martin appeals to Billy for sympathy.
>   Beat 7. Richie scolds Martin.
>   Beat 8. Billy offers to help Martin.
>   Beat 9. Richie departs with Martin.

There may be disagreement about the exact wording of this outline. Some of the items, for example, cannot be considered actions or objectives in the strict sense, only loose descriptions of general kinds of activities. It should make the basic principle at stake understandable. Each beat has a distinct identity, but it also interacts with other beats in the development of its parent unit, itself distinct from other units.

Like most ordinary garden-variety units in modern realistic plays, this one consists of little more than one page of printed dialogue in the sort of acting script published by Samuel French or Dramatists Play Service. The playing time is probably be about three minutes. Such a coldly premeditated way of describing units may seem too clinical at first, but there is no need to be concerned about it. There are undoubtedly exceptions. The length is based simply on the practical requirements of storytelling in front of an audience. Readers can draw a further lesson from that fact that the unit begins and ends with decisive physical actions although once again this may not occur in all cases. Because units have no clear identification marks or fixed length and seldom have a clear indication of physical action, they are not always easy to identify. Understanding them at this point may be a challenge, but effort will be rewarded in production.

Scenes

A *scene* is a progression of related units that is shaped dynamically like a play. This is one reason why scenes are popular choices for acting or directing classes: they're miniature plays. The function of a scene in the plot is roughly equivalent to that of a chapter in a book—to introduce, develop, and conclude a single, large event. Some plays are subdivided into formal scenes for explicit reasons such as a change in locale or the entrance or exit of a major character. In other plays, scenes may be more difficult to perceive because they are not divided formally ahead of time. For this reason, occasional confusion about the outermost limits of units or informal scenes should be expected. A scene is similar to a unit because its action is continuous and its locale is constant, but the important difference is that a scene is longer and more substantial than a unit is because it is composed of several units. Moreover the ending of a scene is far stronger and more decisive than is that of a unit because the consequences of the action are greater. In fact, the strength of the ending is what gives a scene its characteristic identity.

In many older plays like *Tartuffe* or *The School for Scandal,* it was common practice to include many formal scenes. Greek tragedies do not contain such divisions, but scenes are identified by alternating choral odes with episodes. Modern plays, however, hold the situation longer to take more advantage of a scene's dramatic potential. The result is fewer formal scene divisions and longer scenes.

In any one of the French neoclassical plays, like those by Pierre Corneille or Jean Racine, there seem to be dozens of scenes in each act. This of course is not completely accurate. It was the convention of that period to consider a scene finished when any character entered or left the stage. This so-called *French scene* is not always a scene in the standard sense used here. By this rule, the first unit of *Streamers,* for example, contains three French scenes. They are identified by character groups: (1) Martin and Richie; (2) Martin, Richie, and Carlyle; and (3) Martin, Richie, and Billy. Practically speaking, French scenes usually denote beats or units, not always scenes. Even though in *Streamers* the stage is left empty at the end of the first unit, however, the emptiness does not mark the ending of a complete scene. We know that the scene continues because Billy returns after a few moments and resumes the action with Roger. Despite its obsolescence, the French scene remains a useful device for delimiting beats and units if not traditional scenes. Some directors also find French scenes useful as subdivisions for rehearsal schedules.

To understand how scenes work together to advance the plot, we might look again at the opening pages of *Streamers.* No scenes are formally defined in Act I, but based on the logic of the action, the act can be subdivided into five informal scenes. We'll look at the first one, composed of the first four units of the play. After the first unit, the scene continues as Billy reappears. The general subject of the unit is Billy's frustration with other people. In the third unit, Richie returns and ridicules his own playfully effeminate behavior. The fourth unit begins after Richie leaves. It involves Billy's expression to Roger of concern about Richie's behavior. The first scene ends there. The general topic of conversation is Billy's distrust of people who are different from himself. The next unit begins where the previous one ends, and the process is repeated this way until all the units in the play have been collected into their parent scenes.

The four units of this scene complement one another even though they may not appear to do so at first. To understand this, we must reexamine our initial perception of Unit 1 by focusing on Billy instead of on Martin or Richie. Seen from Billy's viewpoint, the first unit deals largely with his shocked response to Martin's attempted suicide. In outline form, Scene 1 looks like this:

> Scene 1. Billy distrusts people who are *different*.
> Unit 1. Billy is shocked by Martin's behavior.
> Unit 2. Billy confides in Roger.
> Unit 3. Billy is suspicious of Richie.

We should be able to understand the logical economy of the scene as it develops in these three units. There is no dramatic need to repeat a topic after it is finished, and therefore each succeeding unit is free to introduce a topic of its own.

In play analysis, it is frequently necessary to reconsider first impressions as more is learned about a play. After reading the remainder of Scene 1, for example, we learned that our initial attention to Richie was probably incorrect or at least not completely accurate. Rethinking first impressions is perfectly all right. After all, it is easy to overreact to Martin's attempted suicide, but it is really Billy, not Richie, who occupies the dramatic focus in the scene, and the main interest is his suspicion of people with values different than his (although at this point in the play he is only dimly aware of his feelings.) Our example shows that the virtues of flexibility and willingness to discard favorite impressions are crucial for successful script analysis. The initial reading may have been reasonable, but this is a healthy reminder that almost all readings must be considered temporary guesses based on available evidence. There should never be embarrassment about rethinking, particularly in rehearsals. As new evidence emerges, the artistic courage to change course if necessary must be present.

Acts

The largest dramatic progression within a play is an *act*, which may either be scenically continuous or divided into formal or informal scenes. An act is characterized further by the dramatic quality of its ending. The ending of opening and interior acts will usually leave a clear expectation of something important to come in the next act. The ending of the final act will normally use all the dramatic potentials of the theatre to create a decisive impression.

The Roman author Horace was the first to define the act as divisions of a play. His dictum was based on an understanding of the five divisions traditionally found in classical Greek tragedy. Largely because of Horace's influence, the five-act arrangement became the official standard for many centuries. Shakespeare didn't arrange his plays into acts, that was done for him afterwards by editors; but a number of his plays seem to fall naturally into five parts. The practice of writing in four or three acts developed during the nineteenth century, and in the twentieth century, full-length plays with two or even only one long act have become popular. Today in New York and other theatre centers, long one-act plays are produced regularly. There are many reasons for this historical tendency. This is the end of a stylistic era. We have seen it all, have no time, have more important things to do, and require more detailed understanding, new techniques, or a deeper penetration of character psychology. Whatever the reason and despite the obvious historical trend, the need to subdivide a play into large, semi-independent masses of action has not altogether disappeared. Most playwrights continue to collect scenic progressions into acts or their equivalents.

The next logical step with *Streamers* is to assemble the related scenes into acts. Since the analytical routine is essentially the same as has been described before, let's pass over the intermediate explanations and just collect the scenes into their parent acts. At this advanced point in analyzing progressions, individual details can be repressed temporarily and situations described in very broad terms to see the big picture. Once again, there is no need to be too concerned with verbal nuances, only with describing the advancement of the plot.

Act I. Billy encounters the real world ("I'm not like *"them!"*)
1. Martin's despair
2. Richie's homosexuality
3. Carlyle's threats
4. Billy's warning
5. Cokes' and Rooney's war stories
6. The story of Billy's friend
7. Carlyle's fear

Act II. Billy revolts ("I must put a stop to *"them!"*)
Scene I. Carlyle's threat
1. Billy's conscience
2. Carlyle's proposal
3. Going to town
Scene II. Billy's defense
1. Carlyle's warning
2. Billy's defiance

3. Carlyle's attack on Billy
4. Carlyle's attack on Rooney
5. The military police
6. Cokes' lament

After studying the entire play, it becomes clear that the center of attention is indeed Billy. The play may be seen as the story of a naive idealist who encounters the inhumanity in his society, in effect declares, "I am nothing like you," and in doing so he is never more like it. As the break-down shows, the dramatist has selected and arranged the material to emphasize Billy's importance. Readers should be able to understand the thinking behind these descriptions even though they may not completely agree with them in every case. Acts are coherent groups of related scenes. To understand their role in storytelling completely, it's necessary to understand how each scene contributes to its parent act just as each unit contributes to its parent scene, each beat to its unit, and each line to its beat.

STRUCTURE

The relationship of the parts of the plot to each other and to the whole play is called the *structure*. Just as literary critics sometimes speak of the *gestalt*, the unified pattern, of the whole work, we can speak of the beats, units, scenes, and acts comprising the harmonious structure of a play. Regardless of the individual arrangement of these parts, each continues to perform its assigned function in the whole play. The main structural difference from one play to the next lies in the amount of emphasis devoted to each of its constituent parts.

Textbooks about drama usually suggest that the structure of the plot consists of *rising action* (complications or obstacles), *climax,* and *falling action* (resolution, dénouement, or closure). German critic Gustav Freytag originally described this arrangement as a pyramid, the so-called *Freytag pyramid.* In his explanation, the tension of the plot rises through complications to a climax (the apex of the pyramid) after which it gradually subsides until the end. The rising and falling may consist of several parts or of a single scene, but the climax, according to Freytag's arrangement (today we say the major climax) is usually a single big scene somewhere in the middle of the play.

Freytag points out that Shakespeare often used a regular pyramidal structure like this. In *Hamlet,* for example, he placed what Freytag argues is the most intensely emotional scene squarely in the middle of a five-part structure. The first half of the play shows Hamlet searching for conclusive proof of Claudius' guilt. Then, after the mousetrap scene, Hamlet sets in motion the second half of the play, which leads to the deaths of Ophelia, Polonius, Rosencrantz and Guildenstern, Gertrude, Laertes, Claudius, and Hamlet himself.

Despite the widespread appeal of Freytag's theory in classrooms, there is no law that requires such a symmetrical structure. Those who are determined to search for it at all costs may overlook all the climaxes except the one that might be in the middle of the play. A more practical approach would be to consider the typical dramatic structure not as a symmetrical pyramid but rather as a line ascending upward at an angle, interrupted by one or more minor climaxes in each act, and terminating with a major climax. *Oedipus Rex, Tartuffe, Death of a Salesman,* and *A Raisin in the Sun* are all examples of plays with such uneven rising structures. Their climaxes appear at or near the end of the final act. A few modern plays, like *Happy Days,* employ an unusual structure that is deliberately flat and free of any traditional climaxes whatsoever, but more about this later. The structure of most dramatic works normally involves several obvious moments of high tension whose placement varies from one play to another.

Now that we have considered the general nature of structure, we will explore the individual parts of the rising and falling action. Their nature and organization help determine the relative amount of restriction or freedom in the development of the story.

Point of Attack
The first part of the rising action to consider is the *point of attack,* the moment when the play begins in relation to the background story at one end and the climax at the other. When the on-stage action begins relatively late in the background story and closer to the climax, the play is said to have a late point of attack. *The Wild Duck* has such an arrangement. The on-stage action reveals only the last two days of a story that actually began more than 19 years earlier. A play with a late point of attack, like *The Wild Duck,* compresses a great deal of background story and on-stage action into a comparatively brief performance time frame. Because of this compression, the plot is technically considered fairly restricted because it is densely packed with action. *The Wild Duck* is a modern realistic play, but the use of a late point of attack isn't restricted to the modern period or to the style of realism. *Oedipus Rex* and *Tartuffe* also employ late points of attack.

Conversely a play has an early point of attack when there is relatively little background story and a long stretch of on-stage dramatic time between the opening curtain and the climax. The background story for *Hamlet* begins only a few weeks before the start of the play, while the on-stage action covers a period of several months. Once again, the treatment of the point of attack is independent of the play's historical period or style. *The Hairy Ape* and *Mother Courage* also have early points of attack. Because of the longer on-stage dramatic time involved, the plot is technically freer. There is less moment-to-moment tension and a comparatively looser plot organization than is found normally in plays with a late point of attack. The manner of treatment of the point of attack is characteristic of the temperaments of individual playwrights and of the writing fashion in vogue when they wrote.

Inciting Action
The *inciting action* is the single event that sparks the main action of the entire play. It occurs at the point when the leading character is actually set in motion or where a feeling arises in the character that sets the action in motion.

It becomes the chief driving force for all the succeeding action of the play. In *Hamlet,* the inciting action occurs in the fifth scene when the Ghost informs Hamlet about the murder and challenges him to revenge. The inciting action in *Oedipus Rex* occurs in the Prologue when Creon informs Oedipus of the Oracle's warning. In *The School for Scandal,* it happens in Scene 2 when Sir Oliver Surface returns unexpectedly to London. In *The Hairy Ape,* the inciting action occurs in Scene 3 when Yank comes face to face with Mildred for the first time. The inciting action may appear in a variety of different positions early in the play and may take on many different forms. It may be short or long; it may be an incident, an idea, a wish, or a plan in the mind of the leading character. One writer asserts that sometimes the inciting action may even occur while the protagonist is offstage. If that is so, it is surely a missed opportunity for the dramatist because the inciting action is potentially one of the most exciting events in the play. The main action can begin only after the inciting action takes place. It forms the transition between the introductory material and the body of the play, and its location in the overall structure helps to shape the emotional dynamics of the entire play.

Complications or Obstacles

On the stage as in life, all planned behavior encounters difficulties as it tries to reach its goal. Invariably characters meet others who have opposing wishes, or they run into opposing events. Complications, sometimes called obstacles by actors, are the countermovements in the plot created by these conflicting wishes and events. Note that, according to this definition, complications must be about common points of disagreement shared by at least two characters. Without a shared disagreement, there is no opportunity for a complication. It is the complications that produce the increasing levels of tension in the play. The plot thickens and becomes more complex, and the internal tensions begin to show. Previously diverse parts of the play begin to connect, and it feels as if the play has movement. Complications appear in a variety of different forms and illustrations, and they tend to become progressively more interesting and exciting as the play progresses.

To explain we will review the complications found in Act I, Scene 1 of *A Raisin in the Sun.* The play occurs in the living room of the Younger family's apartment somewhere on Chicago's South Side, a predominantly African-American neighborhood. It is early Friday morning. On stage are Walter Younger, his wife and son, and his mother and sister. The complications in the scene proceed in seven steps. As Ruth is awakening the family, the first complication begins when she objects to Walter's question about the impending arrival of the insurance check. Her criticism of Walter for staying up late with his friends the night before forms the second complication. Complication number three occurs when Ruth refuses to give Travis an extra 50¢ for school, and Walter disagrees with her. Next, there is a moderately longer complication involving Ruth's objection to Walter's incessant talk about becoming a big success. Beneatha's appearance provides the pretext for the fifth complication when Walter objects to her dream of becoming a doctor. The sixth complication is a short discussion between Ruth and Mama about her own plans for the money. Mama's objection to Beneatha's disavowal of God is the seventh and final complication, or obstacle, of Scene 1.

This opening scene furnishes virtually all the information needed to understand the characters, situation, and background story for what is to follow. It also introduces the main action—Walter's dream for the future as represented by his wish to buy a liquor store with the insurance money. Each of the seven complications adds to the total level of tension in the scene. This scene is a model of realistic playwriting craftsmanship and will reward patient analysis.

Obligatory Scene

This is the English term for the French *scène à faire* originally described by critic Francisque Sarcey. The obligatory scene denotes an intensely emotional scene that the author is obliged to include because the audience has been led to anticipate it. Technically speaking, the obligatory scene is an open confrontation about the main conflict that takes place between the two major opposing characters. For instance, in *Hamlet* the orthodox obligatory scene occurs in Act IV, Scene 3, when Claudius confronts Hamlet about Polonius' murder. Similarly, the final scene between Biff and Willy in *Death of a Salesman* is considered an obligatory scene. In *The Wild Duck*, the scene in which Hjalmar Ekdal condemns his wife Gina for her secret affair with Mr. Werle may be considered an obligatory scene. Obligatory scenes are not found in all plays, but when they are, they are obviously important because the dramatic interest and emotional intensity is certain to be strong.

Crises

Crises are points in the action when the tension reaches a peak and some kind of change in the course of events becomes necessary. They reveal characters making major decisions about the important things in their lives. There are two crises in the formal scene we examined from *A Raisin in the Sun*. In the first one, Beneatha reminds Walter that the insurance money belongs to their mother and that nothing he can say or do will tempt her to invest it in a liquor store. At this sharp reminder, Walter angrily storms out of the apartment. If Walter had remained, he would have been obliged to confront his mother about the money immediately, and the remainder of the play would have been radically different. As it is, he departs and the critical issue of who will control the insurance money remains unresolved for the time being.

The second crisis occurs when Beneatha's liberal views about God present a serious challenge to Mama's firm religious convictions. Mama triumphs in this particular crisis by slapping her daughter hard across the face and demanding an apology. This physical action shows vividly that Mama is capable of defending her values. If she had walked away from Beneatha instead of challenging her, Walter's later confrontations with her about the insurance money would have been significantly weaker by comparison. These two crises illustrate the opposing values of the two major characters in the play: Walter's stubborn selfishness versus his mother's stern traditional morality. Note that each of these crises is punctuated by a decisive physical action: slamming a door, slapping a face.

Climax

A climax is a prominent peak of emotional intensity in the play. It is the point when the complications appear strongest and most decisive. Although climaxes are usually found at the culmination of a great accentuated scene, like crises, they may be major or minor. The major climax is the highest peak of emotional intensity. It is surrounded on either side by connecting scenes that form the rising and falling action, and it logically dominates any other climax. The major climax can appear at an assortment of distances from the end of the play. In *A Raisin in the Sun*, it appears in the final scene with Walter, Mr. Lindner, and the family. The end of the play after that occupies only two and a half pages of dialogue. In *Oedipus Rex*, it occurs near the end of Episode 4, and the last two scenes are devoted to the *catastrophe* (scene of physical violence) and the resolution. *The Wild Duck* has its major climax very near the end of the play just after Hedvig kills herself. In *Streamers*, the major climax occurs midway through Act II, Scene 2, when Billy publicly condemns Carlyle. In these examples and many others readers can point to, playwrights use all their writing skills to insure that the major climaxes are the most dramatic and memorable moments in the play.

Though major climax is ordinarily preceded by a minor climax in each act, some plays contain only one minor and one major climax in spite of running several acts. In *Hamlet*, the minor climax occurs during the mousetrap scene that is located in middle of the play. With its tense, complicated interplay among Hamlet and Claudius, the Players, and the members of the court, it is one of the most effective scenes in the theatre. The second and major climax of this play occurs in the final scene when Hamlet kills Claudius. *The School for Scandal* contains five acts, but it also has only one minor climax besides the major one. It is the famous screen scene in Act V, Scene 2, traditionally a model scene for comedies. The major climax occurs in the last scene of the play when Joseph Surface is finally exposed as a scoundrel.

Simple and Complex Plots (Recognition and Reversal)

Before we move on to the remaining elements of structure, it might be helpful to pause and examine the characteristics of climaxes in a little more detail. The word *climax* is really a composite term used to describe two distinct psychological activities that usually unfold simultaneously in a performance: recognition and reversal. Recognition, according to Aristotle, is a change from ignorance to knowledge, usually on the part of the leading character. At the climax of *A Raisin in the Sun*, for example, Walter Younger at last recognizes that he has earned not respect but rather contemptible humiliation. He has failed utterly as husband, father, and human being. The most effective kind of recognition is accompanied by a reversal (radical change in fortune). In Walter Younger's case, the reversal is from bad to good fortune. After a considerable amount of inner turmoil, he eventually achieves self-respect by sacrificing his personal dream of success for his family. In view of Walter's personal enlightenment, the lost insurance money is no longer an important issue for him.

In *Death of a Salesman*, Willy Loman's recognition is somewhat the same, but the reversal is in the opposite direction. Like Walter Younger, Willy also discovers that he has been a failure as a father, but then, instead of changing his point of view the way Walter does, he decides to sacrifice his life for his son for the sake of the life insurance money. Reversals from good to bad fortune like Willy Loman's are frequently accompanied by a catastrophe. Willy's suicide is a catastrophe in the technical sense as are Oedipus' self-mutilation and Hamlet's death. Although Walter does lose the money, there is no technical catastrophe in *A Raisin in the Sun* because there is no violence. In any event, the intense emotions that characterize a climax are the direct result of sympathies and antagonisms generated by recognition and reversal. (Incidentally with both plays, we are again reminded of the omnipresence of getting or losing money as a major given circumstance.)

Aristotle described plots with traditional climaxes (those containing recognitions and reversals) as technically complex. He believed that complex plots were inherently dramatic and therefore the most effective types to use in the theatre. He described plots without climaxes (that is, those without recognitions and reversals) as technically simple. Although Aristotle believed that simple plots were relatively undramatic, nevertheless many playwrights, even classical Greek playwrights, have made effective use of them. The plots of *Mother Courage* and *Happy Days,* for example, are technically simple because they contain no recognitions or reversals in their leading characters, yet no one would accuse them of being undramatic.

Among modern playwrights, Bertolt Brecht, Samuel Beckett, and Anton Chekhov routinely used simple plots. In their plays, they chose to substitute other dramatic values for the emotional excitement ordinarily provided by traditional climaxes. Brecht employed narration, poetry, music, and emphatic social commentary. Beckett used pantomime, detailed character drawing, unusual moods, and vivid intellectual meaning. Chekhov used detailed character description, intensely lyrical moods, and contrasting actions. Plays with complex plots have no built-in advantage over those with simple plots. In the hands of a skilled playwright, either kind can be effective. The main difference lies in the presence or absence of recognition and reversal.

Resolution

The *resolution* (falling action) includes all events following the major climax. Sometimes this is also called the *dénouement* (unraveling) of the complications. The resolution is characterized normally by a gradual quieting of the tension and a return of the original opposing forces to a state of near equilibrium or adjustment. The resolution in *Oedipus Rex* begins after the Messenger recounts the double catastrophe of Jocasta's suicide and Oedipus' self-mutilation. It consists of the final lament of Oedipus and his banishment by Creon. The resolution in *Hamlet* is quickly accomplished with the arrival of Fortinbras and the removal of Hamlet's body from the stage. Still shorter is the resolution in *Tartuffe.* It consists of the Officer's announcement of Tartuffe's arrest and the return of the estate to Orgon. The final scene, or requiem, is the resolution in *Death of a Salesman.* It also acts as a kind of epilogue (formal concluding scene) to the play. The resolution in *Streamers* consists of Sergeant Cokes' drunken tale of violence and his singing of "Beautiful Dreamer." It can also be considered an epilogue. By definition, plays with simple plots have no climax and therefore no formal period of resolution. At the peak of a continuously rising structure, they just end like *Mother Courage* and *Happy Days*.

SUMMARY

In the study of plot, readers are likely to devote most of their attention to understanding the basic physical and psychological actions, but, as we have shown, this is not all of what goes into crafting a successful plot. Besides identifying the actions, readers will also need to explore their progress and arrangement. Initially it may be difficult to catch the flow of dramatic progressions and to develop a sense of how they relate within the whole play. The temptation is to read plays merely as sequential arrangements of scenes without much regard for their internal or external arrangements, but analyzing the progressions and structure is essential and should not be undervalued. Regardless of the kind of play or what it means, dramatic interest depends not only on the story but also on how it is told.

QUESTIONS

Progressions: Take time to subdivide the action of the play (or scene) into units (or beats if necessary) and ask: . What is the story logic and how does each beat and unit contribute to it? How is the action divided into scenes (informal, formal, and French) and acts? Describe how each of these larger progressions contributes to the logical development of the story.

Structure: What is the motivating force that sparks the story (inciting action)? What are the obstacles (complications)? Is there an open confrontation between the two major opposing characters in which the major conflict is frankly discussed (obligatory scene)? What are the peaks of emotional intensity in each act? Rank them in their order of importance. What is the highest peak of emotional intensity (minor climax) in the act? In the play (major climax)? What is the overall pattern of emotional intensity (formed by the collective crises and climaxes)? Does the leading character or any character undergo a psychological recognition (complex plot)? If so, describe it. If not, why not (simple plot)? Is there an important change of fortune (reversal) for the leading character? If so, what is it? Does the reversal lead to better or worse fortune? What important actions, if any, occur after the highest peak of emotional intensity (resolution)? How would the decline in tension be described at this point in the play?

5

• • • • • • • • •

Character

The term *character* has taken on many meanings over time. Originally it was from a middle English root associated with something fixed and permanent, like a distinguishing mark or a sign on a building. During Shakespeare's time, character was still considered a permanent feature. It was said to stem from certain bodily fluids (called *humours*) that historically were thought to shape a person's disposition. In the nineteenth century, character continued to mean a fixed state of development though with added moral implications as in, "She had character." This meaning was associated with moral strength, self-discipline and, most important to the Victorians, a sound reputation. The modern meaning of character is more comprehensive. Today we consider character the entire pattern of behaviors that identify a person. This is the definition we will examine in this chapter. In drama, character is not a static object fixed forever in time but rather a dynamic pattern of features that gradually develops over the course of the play. Some writers think this suggests that characters can actually change during a play, while others claim they only reveal formerly hidden traits. It's an interesting puzzle, but it needn't detain us here. To recognize that character is composed of a shifting pattern of mixed elements is satisfactory for most practical purposes.

Although sometimes stage characters are studied as if they were real people, they truly are artificial because they are objects created by playwrights. It's risky to depend too heavily on psychoanalytical methods to understand them. Psychoanalysis is a method of examining mental disorders, and its main purpose is medical treatment of those disorders. Occasionally its methods can be useful in artistic circumstances, but character analysis is essentially an artistic enterprise, not a medical one. Dramatic characters may be performed by real people and their emotional lives may be similar to those of real people, but the resemblance stops there. Compared to real people, stage characters are highly predictable. In life, few people are as relentlessly absorbed with a single overpowering goal as are characters in plays. The expressiveness of drama implies sacrifice and reduction to essentials. To portray character, the whole array of ordinary human behavior is purposely sacrificed to concentrate on a few carefully selected features.

This chapter will study character under eight headings: (1) *Objectives* equip the characters with goals to aim for. (2) *Dramatic actions* are the behavioral tactics they use to pursue those goals. (3) *Conflict* describes the tensions in situations between characters, and (4) *willpower* is the amount of force they use in the pursuit of their objectives. (5) *Values* are the intangible things the characters consider good and bad. (6) *Personality traits* are those minor strokes of individuality that show how characters look, feel, and think. The topic of (7) *complexity* is about how aware of their situations characters are. Finally under (8) *relationships* fall the primary and secondary associations characters have with one another. These topics provide the general lines of inquiry that can be used to understand dramatic character. Some actors think of them as individual *layers* that collectively form the complete character. Rehearsing layer by layer is a useful way to come to terms with a character without having to deal with everything at one time.

OBJECTIVES

Character desires Stanislavski and his followers called *objectives,* or, more simply, *goals.* Boleslavsky, the members of the Group Theatre (formed by Harold Clurman, Lee Strasberg, and Cheryl Crawford in 1929), and their students and followers have used the term *spine* or *intention. Want* is another variation. The terms may vary, but they all mean essentially the same thing: the character's basic desire or plan of action. Objectives are part of the soul, the inner self of the character. They stem from strong religious, social, political, or artistic feelings, from dreams of personal glory or empire, or from whatever controls the inner nature of the character.

A single objective for an entire play can be a very extensive undertaking, however. It may be so large that it is impossible to complete all at once. For this reason, it is necessary to subdivide it into minor objectives that are easier to understand and accomplish. This turns out to be entirely practical because minor objectives are closely tied to the progressions that already exist objectively in the plot. The largest objective, ordinarily called the *main objective,* is the one that arises from the whole play and governs its limits. Secondary objectives are tied to beats, units, scenes, and acts and define their limits. The *through-line* of the character is Stanislavski's term for the controlled process that ties all the character's secondary objectives together under the control of the main objective.

Objectives should not be complex abstract statements. On the contrary, they should be described in the form of basic human drives understandable by everyone, professionals and nonprofessionals alike. In *An Actor Prepares,* Stanislavski suggested a number of guidelines for discovering, if not actually explaining, objectives. As usual, his guidelines are practical and easy to understand. Five of the most important are: (1) Objectives should come from the characters' goals, (2) be directed at the other characters (as opposed to oneself or the audience), (3) describe the inner life of the character (as opposed to the outward physical life), (4) relate to the main idea of the play, and (5) be framed in the form of an infinitive phrase from an active (transitive), concrete verb.

It is important that the last guideline be very clear. From Stanislavski's point of view it was absolutely necessary for the actor to know the character's objectives ahead of time. He asserted that objectives must lure the character into physical action while simultaneously challenging the actor's imagination. Burnet Hobgood has correctly reminded us that Stanislavski was helped in this understanding of objectives by a grammatical feature in the Russian language called *verbal aspect,* that doesn't appear in English. When he described objectives, Stanislavski always used verbs in the *perfective aspect,* which in Russian invariably signifies future action. Stanislavski's model objective goes, "I want to [verb] in order to [statement of purpose]," and the verb and its corresponding purpose are carefully selected to explain the character under study. In English, the use of the infinitive indicates a similar sense of the future. Stanislavski's grammatical practice supports his assertion that objectives should express something the character believes will happen or is about to happen in the future. It helps to explain why he insisted that characters be understood as eagerly desiring to reach objectives that always lie ahead of them.

Objectives are best understood in relation to a specific play, and so study *A Raisin in the Sun.* In order to learn Walter Younger's major objective for the play, first find out what he wants to do with his life. In a scene early in Act I, he tells his wife Ruth that he has been planning to use the life insurance money to invest in a liquor store. "I got me a dream," he says, "I got to take hold of this here world . . . I got to change my life." When Ruth expresses doubts about his determination, he responds, "This morning, I was lookin' in the mirror and thinking about it . . . I'm thirty-five years old; I been married eleven years and I got a boy who sleeps in the living room—and all I got to give him is stories about how rich white people live." From these lines and other evidence in the play we might agree that Walter's main objective is to buy a liquor store in order to achieve success. This would be essentially correct, but most readers would agree that it leaves out a large part of Walter's character, notably his love for his family. A more completely accurate objective would be to buy a liquor store in order to gain the respect of his family. Several other equally workable alternatives are possible, but in any case, this is an acceptable choice because it clearly conditions everything Walter does in the play.

Under the circumstances, Walter's dream is an ambitious one. To accomplish it, he must subdivide it into more manageable pieces (secondary objectives) that are tied to the individual progressions in the play. For example in Walter's first unit, he gives Travis extra spending money despite Ruth's protests. His objective for this unit might be to appear generous with money in order to obtain Travis' admiration. In his next unit, Walter turns to Ruth to disclose his personal frustrations in order to obtain Ruth's sympathy. When his sister Beneatha enters, Walter wishes to belittle her in order to destroy her expensive dream of becoming a doctor. In the important scene with his mother later in the act, Walter reveals how desperate his dream has made him. She's a very moral person, and strongly objects to the prospect of anyone in her family owning a liquor store. He forces a confrontation with her over the issue. His objective is to ridicule his mother's objections as old fashioned in order to obtain the insurance money from her. Each secondary objective defines its own unique progression while also adhering to Stanislavski's basic guidelines. Walter's secondary objectives clearly follow from his main objective; they are directed at specific characters and not at the world in general; and they obviously relate to his inner life. Walter's through-line successfully combines his secondary objectives together under the command of his main objective.

As mentioned earlier, successful main objectives should also relate to the main idea of the play. Chapter 6 will explain the concept of the *main idea*, sometimes called the *superobjective* or *spine* of the play. For this discussion a convenient example will serve for demonstration. The main idea of *A Raisin in the Sun* is to struggle for a dream. It is easy to understand how Walter's objectives relate to this statement. For the description to be completely convincing, however, the major objectives of all the other characters should relate to it just as favorably. And they do successfully relate to it because everyone in the play is struggling for a dream. Ruth's main objective is to support Walter in order save their marriage; Mama's is to invest the money in the best way to help her children fulfill their dreams; and Beneatha's is to become a doctor in order to achieve personal fulfillment. Although each of these main objectives contains its own separate feelings and thoughts, each also clearly relates to the main idea of the play: to struggle for a dream. The through-line of the play successfully ties all the characters' main objectives together under the command of the play's main idea.

Director-critic Harold Clurman was always one of the strongest advocates of the use of objectives by actors and directors. In his writing, he warned actors against always looking for minor personality traits. He believed the actor's most important analytical task should be to find the character's main objective, the basic drive that determines the character's behavior in the whole play and throughout the acts, scenes, units, and beats of which the play is composed. He pointed out that, even though many of the characters will experience similar feelings of anger, joy, or sadness, it is their main objective that explains these changing feelings and thoughts by showing that they are all related to a single permanent goal.

DRAMATIC ACTION

Dramatic action is one of the most basic and important concepts in script analysis, but the variety of conflicting definitions has made it seem more complicated than it need be. Some of this confusion is understandable. Dramatic action is connected with behavior, and it is always hard to explain the subtleties of human action. It's also true that readers who haven't been introduced to dramatic action in acting or directing classes can hardly be expected to pay much attention to it in a script, much less understand it. There is also the added confusion that comes from loose thinking. In any case, just because dramatic action is a challenging subject, however, does not mean it should be avoided. Whatever theoretical differences might exist about it, there is no denying that it is an extremely important concept for actors, directors, and designers.

To begin with, dramatic action should be distinguished from objectives, at least as we understand the terms here. Objectives are the characters' goals. Although they are described with verbs, objectives are not actually done; they are something the characters aim at doing in the future. Dramatic action is described with verbs as well, but it's actually done by the characters. The key is time. Objectives occur in the future while dramatic actions happen in the present. What connects them is their joint purpose. Dramatic action is the behavioral tactics characters use to achieve their objectives. We might think of how a sailboat changes its course to adjust to an opposing wind. To make headway, the captain deliberately employs a zigzag pattern in which each course of the boat is different from other ones or from the preceding one; so also a character selects different dramatic actions to adjust to opposition from other characters when that character is working toward an objective. Characters employ not just one dramatic action but rather a whole series of different actions, changing from one tactic to another to achieve their objectives. This explanation shows that dramatic action is a crucial part of a character's outer self. It controls how that character relates to others from one progression to the next throughout the play.

Dramatic action can be illustrated in the units studied in *A Raisin in the Sun*. Recall that Walter's main objective is to buy a liquor store in order to gain the respect of his family. It follows logically that he also has a main dramatic action or a dominant way of behaving, that stems from his main objective. He believes that he deserves the insurance money because his dreams are honorable, his frustrations are real, and his scheme can't miss. It's clear that his explanations are not enough to convince his family, however, so he adopts the behavior of a bully to badger them into submission. Therefore his main dramatic action for the play is *intimidate*. Naturally within this large action, Walter adopts a variety of secondary behaviors to deal with the many different complications in which he finds himself. He *shows off* for his son Travis, then he *scolds* his wife Ruth, next he *belittles* his sister Beneatha, and then he *challenges* his mother. Walter's zigzag behaviors are the secondary dramatic actions he adopts to achieve his secondary objectives.

There are two more lessons to be learned here. First it is just as impossible to insert unrelated dramatic actions into a play as it is to insert dramatic progressions that are not related to it. Dramatic actions are inherent in the progressions that the author has already written. Second dramatic action is back and forth behavior, something the characters do to each other, not solo action. To emphasize this important condition, dramatic action is normally expressed as a transitive verb that requires a target character. Some actors even refer to dramatic action itself as *the verb*. Notice the transitive verbs and their targets in Walter's dramatic actions. He intimidates → his family; he impresses → Travis; he scolds → Ruth; he belittles → Beneatha; and he challenges → Mama. There will be many dramatic actions for every character. To remember them all, it's a good idea to write them down in the margin of the script at the point they occur (for example, John ridicules Jack, Mary threatens John). The original choices made at the table will almost certainly be refined as more is learned about the given circumstances, but after all, that is what rehearsals are for.

CONFLICT

Since the subject of conflict comes up so often in discussions about plays, it is wise to examine it closely. The word *conflict* stems from a Latin root meaning to strike together, from which comes its current meaning of a battle, quarrel, or struggle for supremacy between opposing forces. Does conflict appear in every play? If it is defined as open quarrels between characters, the answer clearly is no. There are no major quarrels, for example, in *The Wild Duck, Happy Days,* or *Mother Courage.* Moreover in these plays and in many others, the characters do not even seem to struggle conspicuously to escape from their surroundings. Looking for traditional big conflict in situations like these is a mistake.

Instead of being a single narrow concept, conflict actually appears in many different forms. There may be conflict between one character and another, between character and environment, between character and destiny or the forces of nature, between character and ideas, or even among forces inside a character. All these are legitimate types of conflicts, but not all of them produce the same kinds of tensions. Conflict from intellectual abstractions such as environment, society, or destiny, for example, produces intellectual tensions. These conflicts are useful for critics and academicians because they provide the intellectual material needed for scholarly work. They can also be useful for directors and designers in artistic work as will be seen in Chapter 6.

To achieve the kind of appeal necessary for acting, however, conflict must be more than an intellectual abstraction. It must be concrete and have a human face. In other words, it must involve the characters themselves. This kind of conflict stems from concrete conditions in the given circumstances and is firmly grounded in the world of the play. It is normally the most productive kind of conflict in the rehearsal hall because it provides the psychological tensions that stir actors' creative imaginations. Conflicts in this concrete sense may be divided into two classes: (1) role conflicts stemming from characters' opposing views of each other and (2) conflicts of objectives stemming from their opposing goals. Role conflicts and conflicts of objectives are parts of the characters' outer selves; they help to shape the way characters relate to each other. That is why the subject of conflict occurs both in this chapter and in Chapter 6.

Role Conflicts

Role conflicts arise specifically from characters' opposing views of each other. Sometimes they are called conflicts of attitude or rite-role conflicts. They come from conditions in the given circumstances that cause one character to start a disagreement and that form the opposing character's adjustments. The task is to search the given circumstances for the right conditions and to think about them exactly as the characters would. There may be a number of different role conflicts among the characters, each defined by its own conditions in the given circumstances.

For an explanation of how role conflict comes from the given circumstances, return to the scene between Walter and Ruth in *A Raisin in the Sun.* The relevant given circumstances for the scene are: The year is 1959. The Youngers are an African-American family. They live in a crowded apartment building on the strictly segregated South Side of Chicago. Thanks to the strong moral character of Walter, Sr., and Mama Younger, the family has managed to endure most of the hardships African-Americans unfortunately encountered in the

United States during the 1950s. To make ends meet, everyone in the family has to work hard at servile, low-paying jobs without any future.

About 11 years ago, Walter Younger, Jr., married Ruth, and now they have a son Travis. They have lived in the same small apartment with Walter's father, mother, and sister Beneatha since they were married. Walter's father died about a month ago, and Mama is about to receive his life insurance, amounting to $10,000, a very large sum for the financially deprived Younger family. Walter feels humiliated at the prospect of becoming the head of the family without any future ahead of him. The most important given circumstance for him is the scheme he concocted with his friends to buy a liquor store with his father's insurance money. He feels that this project will give him a real chance to become a successful husband and provider for the family. (Note once again the importance of economic given circumstances in the scheme.)

Ruth is growing increasingly disappointed with her life with Walter. When she married him, she was excited about their hopes and dreams for the future. Now she's become disillusioned with his endless scheming and disappointed with his lack of ambition. She has reluctantly concluded that Walter no longer cares for her or the family. The crucial facts are that Ruth is pregnant with their second child and has not told Walter about it. Moreover she feels that under the circumstances she must have an abortion, a prospect that disturbs her profoundly.

This summarizes the relevant given circumstances. Next it's necessary to identify the character who controls the situation. The dialogue shows that Walter is the controlling character. He insists on aggravating Ruth with his plans for the liquor store while she is trying to get the family ready for work and school. Ruth doesn't want to listen to Walter. Therefore she is the one who actually starts the conflict and continues it. Without her resistance to Walter's plan, there would be no conflict of any kind.

Now that the positions of the two characters are also clear, the heart of the role conflict becomes clear. Walter's given circumstances show why he is seeking help from Ruth in spite of her resistance. No one in the family is closer to Mama than Ruth is. She is not only Mama's daughter-in-law but also her close friend and confidante. Walter wants Ruth to intercede with his mother on his behalf for the life insurance money. This is his side of the situation. But his request immediately antagonizes Ruth. Because of the frustrations she has endured, she no longer shares her husband's hopes and dreams as she once did. In fact, she does not even consider him as her husband any more. All she's concerned about now is the baby and the disturbing possibility of an abortion.

The role conflict is clear. Walter sees himself as a good husband and father, and he expects Ruth to be a loyal, supporting wife. Ruth feels, however, that she no longer has anything in common with Walter because she considers him a failure. What sparks the conflict is the insurance money. It constitutes the shared point of dispute that brings their opposing views of each other into the open. Without the disagreement over the insurance money, the role conflict would stay hidden inside the characters.

Conflicts of Objectives

A second category of conflict comes from the ideas of the nineteenth-century French critic Ferdinand Brunetière. His so-called *law of conflict* states that drama is defined by the obstacles encountered as a character is attempting to fulfill his objectives. The key issue in this understanding of conflict is obstacles, or barriers. Characters have objectives, direct everything toward fulfilling those objectives, and try to bring everything in their lives into harmony with them. Obstacles in Brunetière's sense are the opposing objectives of other characters who stand in the way of this process. In Stanislavski's terms, opposing objectives form a counter-through-line. Crises and climaxes occur at those points where one character's through-line crosses the counter-through-line formed by the opposing objectives of another character. These clashes in turn produce the emotionally-charged scenes that make plays exciting. Aside from the emphasis on obstacles, conflicts of objectives share the same basic requirements as role conflicts do.

To prove this fact, examine *A Raisin in the Sun* one more time. Walter wants to buy a liquor store in order to gain respect, and the question is how he will succeed. He is prevented from fulfilling his objective by Mama's objective which is to invest the insurance money in the best way so that her children can fulfill their dreams. This encounter fulfills the same requirements treated under role conflict. It arises from the given circumstances and is concrete rather than abstract; Walter controls the conflict and Mama resists it; the objectives inherently clash; and the money constitutes a shared point of dispute. Walter eventually overcomes his mother's opposition, but he is defeated then by his friend Willy, whose objective is to get hold of the insurance money by deception in order to steal it. Does this encounter also fulfill the requirements? It arises logically from the circumstances; it involves a concrete dispute between Walter and Willy; Willy begins the conflict and Walter resists it; their objectives inherently clash; and finally the shared point of dispute is again the money. It's not hard to find examples of opposing objectives in other plays. The real effort is stating them so that their built-in opposition is clear.

Of the two classes, conflicts of objectives are used more often because they are more easily grasped and explained. Role conflicts may impose a more severe analytical test, but the reward is a larger assortment of acting choices. In any event, searching systematically for either type of conflict will supply many useful and exciting options. Assuming the conflicts have been correctly perceived, the final choice depends on the creative imagination of the artistic team and on what they decide to emphasize in production.

WILLPOWER

The concept of *will* has been described variously as a strong wish, a firm intention, a power of choosing, a determination to do, and an inner force used to undertake conscious, purposeful action. The key words here are *strong, firm, power, determination,* and *force*. Will is associated with strength because it is the driving force of drama. Strong-willed characters make things happen. Plays depend on them to keep things moving. Some characters may not have strong wills, but if the leading character is also devoid of will, the results may be disastrous unless other compensations are provided. Characters without strong wills are unable to create traditional types of dramatic conflicts. They may participate in events, but they seldom seem to cause them. They can't struggle against their situations, and they are often the victims of the more willful characters who control them.

Modern artistic sensibilities prefer victims instead of heroes, but it's not always easy to come to terms with passive characters. Before sympathizing with them, it's necessary to try to understand the reasons for their apparent inactivity. Instructive examples of such characters appear in *Mother Courage* and *Hamlet*. In *Mother Courage* there is Anna Fierling, the canteen woman who earns a living by following warring armies and selling basic necessities to them at high prices. The quality of her will appears early in the first scene of the play when she inadvertently loses her son Eilif to the recruiting officer. She has been distracted by the chance to make a quick profit selling a belt buckle. We know that Anna is a shrewd and determined businesswoman; yet she does nothing when her son is taken from her, a fact that Brecht emphasizes in stage directions that state, *"she stands motionless."*

Anna is equally unable to prevent her second son, Swiss Cheese, from being sacrificed for the war. She compromises with the same recruiting officer by permitting her son to enlist as a paymaster. She claims that at least he won't have to fight, but she knows he's simple-minded and will almost certainly get himself into trouble because he can't count. She's troubled by these concerns, but she justifies her decision on the grounds that the war has been good for business. Soon she finds that Swiss Cheese has panicked during an attack and fled with the cash box. When he's arrested, Anna haggles over the bribe to save his life. Meanwhile Swiss Cheese is taken before a firing squad and shot. She observes, "Maybe I bargained too long," and the stage directions indicate once again that she *"remains seated."* Afterward Anna refuses to acknowledge the body of her son rather than risk arrest. She attempts to file an official complaint about it, but after thinking it over, she changes her mind.

In another scene, Anna's son, Eilif, arrives to say goodbye before being taken away to be executed for a petty crime. Just then the cease-fire is cut short by the renewed outbreak of war. Anna is so excited by the chance to make money that she misses the chance to save Eilif's life. Further on in the play, Anna finds herself in town on business when her remaining child, the mute Kattrin, is shot sounding an alarm to warn the town of an attack. "Maybe it wouldn't have happened if you hadn't gone to town to swindle people," a peasant says to her. "I've got to get back in business," she replies. Then she hails a passing regiment and shouts "Hey, take me with you!" and the play ends.

Someone in Anna's predicament should invoke sympathy, but Brecht deliberately attempts to dispel this natural inclination. He shows Anna Fierling as a cowardly character who apparently lacks even a mother's most basic instinct for protecting her children. This would be a formula for almost certain failure in the theatre, but there are deliberate compensations that stimulate interest and sympathy. Brecht tries to show that Anna's behavior is not her fault. The play argues that her natural goodness has been exhausted by the brutal economics of war. Compelled to choose between peaceful poverty and wartime affluence, she chooses the latter. She mistakenly believes she can keep her family together despite the war by employing her shrewd business instincts. We are meant to feel that this choice hurts her deeply even though she doesn't say so. Anna Fierling never learns that she is profoundly mistaken. For many readers, Anna's story is a vivid illustration of social and economic injustice.

Besides these economic considerations, Anna Fierling's inactivity is further counterbalanced by other dimensions of the play. The changes in the course of the war, for example, unsettle everyone. Also Anna's daughter Kattrin and the prostitute Yvette show remarkable strength of will and even heroism. Other compensating features are the earthy humor and homespun intelligence of the characters, and the play's unusual production style, which employs signs, banners, musical interludes, poetry, and direct address to the audience. All these features give the play compelling social relevance, variety of feeling, and a special kind of excitement that compensate for the absence of traditional willpower in the leading character.

Another apparently weak-willed character who is attractive to modern audiences is Hamlet. A deeply sensitive person, he is burdened with the responsibility of revenging his warrior-father's murder. Hamlet has already neglected one of his major princely responsibilities by standing idly by as his uncle usurped the throne that is rightfully Hamlet's. Nor did he do anything to prevent his mother's overhasty and incestuous marriage to his uncle. By these examples of inaction, Hamlet seems to show weak will and possibly even cowardice. At his first appearance in the play, Hamlet is refusing to take part in the coronation ceremonies for the new king. His display of temperament in the scene is logically interpreted by the court as spitefulness stemming from emotional instability. Fortunately, however, his strong conscience soon regains control over his grief, and he scolds himself for his inertia. He gets a chance to make up for his initial inaction when the Ghost appears and challenges him to take revenge, but here too Hamlet throws away one chance after another to carry out his responsibility. Instead of concentrating on revenge, he is trying to comprehend the underlying meaning of the events in which he is reluctantly participating. It is Claudius who provides the force behind the play's conflict when he becomes increasingly worried about Hamlet's moodiness, interpreting it as suspicion of his own guilt.

Hamlet is sensitive, introspective, and relatively inactive, at least as compared to Claudius, Laertes, and Fortinbras. Despite appearances, however, he is not weak-willed, nor is he a coward. He's the strongest character in the play. His intensely reflective nature seems to make him incapable of fear. It drives him to undertake reckless and sometimes malicious schemes to test his uncle's guilt or to satisfy his own spiritual quest. This is what makes him so attractive to us. We feel somehow that he will eventually do something extraordinary. Eventually to test himself, he disregards Horatio's warnings and accepts Claudius' challenge to duel with Laertes. In effect, Hamlet challenges Claudius to kill him.

Hamlet has enjoyed success on the modern stage in spite of, perhaps because of, its superficially weak-willed leading character. It is the compensating features in the play which provide the attractions. For one thing, Hamlet is an extremely likable character. He loves his mother and honors his father. He has a wonderfully dry sense of humor. He is a gentleman, a poet, a scholar, and ironically a supremely well-trained swordsman and soldier. He is not cowardly but actually recklessly brave, and of course, he's intensely driven to comprehend the meaning of his life. Many of the other characters in the play are also interesting in themselves. There are the traditionally strong-willed characters of Claudius, Laertes, and Fortinbras, whose crusades for power offset Hamlet's philosophical inactivity. It is the combination of all these features plus the comic interludes and the language that make the play dramatic.

Strong wills are ordinarily required to create conflicts and make the play interesting. The leading characters in *Oedipus Rex, Tartuffe,* and *The School for Scandal* are examples of such strong wills. They are characterized by their determination to impose their wills on everyone else, regardless of the outcome. They drive the action in their plays forward and force things to happen. The leading characters in *The Wild Duck, Death of a Salesman,* and *Streamers* are technically weak in comparison. In these plays, as in *Hamlet* and *Mother Courage,* compensating features furnish the dramatic interest.

VALUES

Values are what characters are for or against in the world of the play and their ideas of good and bad and right and wrong. To achieve their objectives, characters embrace the values that gratify them and reject, or at least struggle against, those that do not do so. Values tell characters how they can best get where they want to go. They affect their personal, family, and social lives; their work; and their leisure. They define their reasons for choosing to be who they are. Values arise chiefly from personal beliefs about such things as conscience, public- and family-mindedness, ambition, success, and physical pleasure. In some characters, these beliefs will form a pattern of virtues while in others they may form an opposite set of vices. The deciding question is whether the values are deeply held convictions or merely tactics adopted for selfish ends.

Madame Pernelle, Orgon's mother in *Tartuffe,* is an example of a character whose values are designed more for social utility than they are for true morality. On the surface her values appear virtuous. She advocates decorous behavior, religious observance, modesty in dress, and respect for authority. She reveals her values in the opening scene when she reproaches the family for what she interprets as their immoral behavior. This is another way of saying that she disagrees with their values. She even criticizes Elmire's clothes, which she believes are too expensive for her position in society. Madame Pernelle also criticizes Cleante, Elmire's brother and Orgon's brother-in-law, whose religious skepticism offends her. In spite of her protests, however, the most important value for Madame Pernelle is not virtue but the appearance of virtue—otherwise known as respectability. Her values are merely a public strategy she has adopted to enable her to appear virtuous to other people, a fact that she tries unsuccessfully to conceal.

Values also play an important role in *Death of a Salesman.* As a traveling salesman, Willy deeply believes in the traditional values held by many Americans during the period following World War II. He believes in material prosperity, that the world is basically a just place, and that good friends and hard work will eventually lead to success. Early in Act I Willy discloses to Linda that he expects the same values in his son, Biff. He wants Biff to accomplish something. He fears that Biff has been on his own in the world for nearly ten years and "has yet to make thirty-five dollars a week!" Willy believes that, in "the greatest country in the world," someone with Biff's "personal attractiveness" and who is such a "hard worker" should be successful. Driven by his implicit faith in the necessity of success, Willy is determined to help Biff get a job selling. In the first flashback scene, when Biff and Happy are boys, Willy reminds them of the values he believes are important in life, "the man who makes an appearance in the business world, the man who creates personal interest, is the man who gets ahead. Be liked and you will never want."

But if money and friends were Willy's only values, he would not be a very sympathetic character. He values other things, too. First he loves nature. Besides his garden, one of the things he enjoys most is the New England scenery he sees on his travels. Respecting people as individuals is also important to him, but he senses that this value is disappearing in America and being displaced by self-interest. He complains that selling is not as attractive as it once was for someone like him, "The competition is maddening!" Willy also values loyalty, hard work, and friendship, but perhaps most important of all, he values his family. He reveals to Linda that his deepest concern is the possibility of not being able to support them the way he feels that he should.

Willy's sensitivity, kindness, sense of duty, and love for his family compensate for his selfishness. That he does not value material success in itself but rather what it can do for his family is clear. Unfortunately his single-minded faith in success conflicts with his more praiseworthy values. In the end, the narrowly materialistic values he advocates are openly discredited. Willy dies for his son, yet Biff has only contempt for his father. Ironically it is the neglected son Happy who rededicates himself to his father's discredited values. The central issue in *Death of a Salesman* is in large measure the conflict of values between a father and son.

PERSONALITY TRAITS

The word *personality* comes from the Latin *persona,* meaning mask or appearance, ergo the meaning of personality as the manner in which a character is socially perceived, the way he relates to others. Personality has certain definable properties called *traits* that include outward appearance. Traits may change in a character depending on the situation, but ordinarily there is a pattern that shows up in a variety of situations. This pattern allows the assembly a personality profile. For some actors, personality traits are the physical choices that control how the character looks, sits, stands, walks, gestures, speaks, and behaves with other characters.

Personality traits, like other aspects of play analysis, should be described as simply and clearly as possible. The process is not complicated. First list all the traits the character shows in the play. Next reduce the list to manageable proportions by combining related traits and identifying those of central importance. The result will be a concise personality profile. The most challenging part of the task is learning how to grasp personality traits mentally. Close observation of human nature is required to distinguish platitudes about personality from real behavior.

Willy Loman is a useful character on whom to apply this process. He predictably reveals several of his most important traits in the opening scene. Willy's impatience with Linda's worries shows sudden changeability, a quick temper, and a tendency to cruelty; "I said nothing happened. Didn't you hear me?" When he explains why he returned home unexpectedly, he reveals physical weakness; "I'm tired to death . . . I couldn't make it. I just couldn't make it." The explanation is also evidence of absent-mindedness, "I suddenly couldn't drive anymore. . . . Suddenly I realize I'm goin' sixty miles an hours and I don't remember the last five minutes. I'm—I can't seem to—keep my mind to it." The mental turmoil that underscores his line, "I have such thoughts, I have such strange thoughts," shows lingering anxiety. His rejection of Linda's appeal to him to ask for a desk job reveals his self-esteem; "They don't need me in New York. I'm the New England man. I'm vital in New England." Another important trait is self-reflection, which appears when Linda reminds him that Biff and Happy haven't been home for some time, "Figure it out. Work a lifetime to pay off a house. You finally own it, and there's nobody to live in it." There's also evidence of loyalty and dedication, traits already reflected in his values. So far, the list of Willy's personality traits includes sudden changeability, quick temper, occasional cruelty, physical weakness, absent-mindedness, anxiety, high self-esteem, self-reflection, family loyalty, and dedication. A few new ones appear as the action unfolds, but these traits already provide the raw material for Willy's personality profile.

For an example of personality traits in a historical play, consider *Hamlet* again. His objectives, dramatic actions, will power, and values have already been discussed. What else can be learned about him? In the first court scene, Act I, scene 2, he shows sensitivity as well as loyalty and devotion to his father. He displays a sharp wit and a lethal sense of irony. In his soliloquies, he shows his habit of intense self-reflection, his penetrating intuition, a mercurial nature, and a profound curiosity about the meaning of life. His frequent classical references and love of aphorisms indicate that he is intelligent and interested in classical learning. When meeting old friends or being introduced to new ones, Hamlet shows courtesy and sometimes a surprisingly sunny disposition. He also has a reputation for being a skilled swordsman. Ophelia sums up the general view of at least the public dimensions of Hamlet's personality;

> The courtier's, soldier's, scholar's, eye, tongue, sword;
> Th' expectancy and rose of the fair state,
> Th' observ'd of all observers.

The variety of traits in Hamlet's personality explains why he remains one of the modern theatre's most appealing characters.

COMPLEXITY

Characters are interesting to us in relation to how much they perceive about their situations. Their awareness or lack of it is what connects them with the play and determines their importance in the overall scheme. This capacity for awareness is *character complexity*. It is governed by what the characters respond to and by how they respond—from ignorant, apathetic, and compliant to perceptive, intense, and fully aware. The most complex character, the one who shows the most power to be aware and responsible, is called the main character. The others are arranged around this character in different degrees of complexity depending on their capacity for awareness. This is not a defect in the writing but rather a technical necessity resulting from the need for economy in dramatic composition.

The least complex characters are *types*. They display a single state of mind and are quickly recognized as particular kinds of people found in everyday life. In this group are domineering spouses, slow-witted or quick-witted servants, absent-minded professors, and so forth. A few examples in the study plays are sergeants Cokes and Rooney, the bragging soldiers in *Streamers;* Howard Wagner, the miserly businessman in *Death of a Salesman;* and Osric, the foppish dandy in *Hamlet*. Character types show a minimum capacity for awareness and reveal very little about themselves apart from the narrow limitations of their group. They may be inherently interesting, but their importance usually stems from their influence on other characters.

The degree of intermediate complexity includes characters who are more aware than types but who are still not as aware of the whole situation as they might be. Intermediate characters such as Linda and Happy Loman, Mama and Ruth Younger, and Gertrude and Ophelia are some of the most attractive roles in dramatic literature. By searching the given circumstances for playable details, talented actors playing these roles often create the impression that their characters are more complex than they actually are in the script.

The most complex characters are those who are capable of being fully aware of what happens to them and who allow us to be aware of it too. Normally there is only one person with this degree of complexity, the main character. He forms the organizing principle for the play, and most of the action is devoted to him. There are exceptions to this unitary principle but not as many as people may think. Walter Younger is the single main character in *A Raisin in the Sun* as are Anna Fierling in *Mother Courage* and Yank in *The Hairy Ape*. Their capacity for awareness is what makes them so appealing and identifies them immediately as main characters. Most plays may be considered biographies of single persons like these are, but sometimes a play may contain more than one complex character. Identifying the main character in these situations is not always easy as it might seem. Is *Death of a Salesman* about Willy or Biff? Is *The Wild Duck* about Gregers or Hjalmar? Is *Tartuffe* about Tartuffe or Orgon? Some of the issues involved in identifying the main character are discussed below. In addition, although there is normally only a single main character, there may be more than one character capable of being fully aware.

RELATIONSHIPS

The main dramatic interest of a play is the conflict between the leading character and the chief adversary. Citing Aristotle, writers call these the *protagonist* and the *antagonist*. The association formed by them comprises the *main relationship* in the play. Traditionally Oedipus and Teiresias provide the main relationship in *Oedipus Rex*, Hamlet and Claudius in *Hamlet*, Walter and Mama in *A Raisin in the Sun*, and Willy and Biff in *Death of a Salesman*. The relationships between these pairs of characters is meant to be the focus of attention throughout the play. Incidentally the fact that some plays contain only one character does not dispose of the necessity for a main relationship. In such cases, the antagonist may simply be offstage (that is, the wife in Anton Chekhov's play *On the Harmfulness of Tobacco*) or may be a different part of the protagonist himself (that is, young Krapp in Samuel Beckett's play *Krapp's Last Tape*).

The protagonist's and antagonist's affiliations with other characters can be considered *secondary relationships*. Although these can be frequently as interesting as is the main relationship, they are nonetheless subsidiary to it. They exist primarily to enhance the main relationship, and only enough of them is furnished to complete this function. For example, Oedipus has secondary relationships with Creon and Jocasta; these relationships, however, are a direct outcome of his main relationship with Teiresias. Walter Younger and his mother have secondary relationships with Ruth, Beneatha, and Bobo. Walter and Mama are not continuously on stage together, but their relationship is maintained by implication through the secondary relationships.

There are occasionally differences of opinion about main relationships. Modern artistic conventions presume that our understanding of plays is not absolutely fixed. Moreover within certain objective limits, the inherent meanings of plays may change from one generation to the next as society changes. This is particularly true in the choice of a main relationship, which should always be a central issue in any new interpretation of a classic. In Tyrone Guthrie's and Laurence Olivier's famous Old Vic production of *Hamlet* in 1937, the main relationship was between Hamlet and his mother. It professed to demonstrate the *Oedipus complex* that was supposed to exist between them. Sigmund Freud's theories about sex were still novel enough in 1937 for the interpretation to cause considerable controversy. Some said that the production was *revisionist*, meaning in this context that it was done simply for the sake of shock value.

It is probably true that some of the unconventional main relationships in recent revivals of older plays are revisionist in intent. But theatre is not an exact science. There is no law against a fresh understanding of the main relationship if it is based on an honest appraisal of the script and consistent with the intent of the production. A fair understanding of *Hamlet*, for example, might suggest other combinations for the main relationship—Hamlet and his deceased father, Hamlet and Horatio, Hamlet and Laertes, Hamlet and Fortinbras, or even Rosencrantz and Guildenstern. What about the relationship between Walter and his deceased father in *A Raisin in the Sun*? All of these are unconventional choices and yet all are based on a fair assessment of the information provided in the plays themselves. The key to identifying the main relationship is honest understanding based on a thorough analysis of the script.

SUMMARY

Objectives are the specific goals that characters aim to achieve. They help make sense of a character's various feelings and thoughts by relating them to a single commanding desire. Dramatic actions are the behavior tactics characters employ to achieve their objectives. Role conflicts consist of the tensions that arise from characters' opposing views of each other. Conflicts of objectives result from their opposing goals.

The degree of determination with which characters pursue their goals is their willpower. Although historical drama depends chiefly on strong-willed characters to make things happen, in modern plays many weak-willed characters and those with vacillating wills can often be found. When the leading character is weak-willed, there will usually be compensating factors to sustain the play's interest. The characters' choices of the good and bad things in life define their values. Characters' positions in relation to the other characters and their points of view to the world of their plays may be determined largely by their values. Personality traits are characters' physical and vocal identification marks together with the impulses and inhibitions that collectively reveal their individuality. To focus attention, playwrights compose their characters in progressive levels of complexity. Ordinarily, the more complex a character is, the more important that character is in the play. The main character is usually the only one who is fully aware although there are exceptions. Playwrights also arrange character relationships to further concentrate attention. The conflict between the leading character and the major adversary is traditionally the main relationship. Other relationships are secondary but contribute to the main relationship in some measurable way. All these features are meticulously predetermined by the playwright and form the collective pattern that we call *character*. Strictly speaking, dramatists create characters that exist only in the script. Actors create living characterizations from written characters.

QUESTIONS

Objectives: What is the character's main objective in the play? What are the secondary objectives for each scene, unit, and beat? (Objectives should be expressed using infinitive forms of active, concrete verbs.) How do the secondary objectives for each character form the through-line for that character's main objective? How do the main objectives for each character form the through-line for the superobjective of the play?

Dramatic action: What is the character's main dramatic action in the play? (Remember that dramatic action is always back-and-forth behavior). What are the secondary dramatic actions for the beats, units, or scenes under study? For all the beats, units, and scenes in the play? Can a dramatic action be discovered for each line of dialogue as well?

Conflicts: For the unit or scene under study, what are the characters' opposing views of one another (role conflicts)? For the play as a whole? Do the characters' main and secondary objectives clash with those of other characters? Where do those oppositions express themselves?

Willpower: How much determination does the character possess to carry out objectives? Why? Is the character's willpower steady, or does it vacillate? If it vacillates, where in the play does it do so? Why?

Values: What is the character for and against? What does the character consider to be right and wrong? Good and bad? How do the character's values relate to those of the other characters? To the world of the play?

Personality traits: What is the character's energy level? Is it consistent or does it vary from one scene to another? How old is the character? What occupation? How does the character look? How does the character move? How does the character sound? What is the character's mental and emotional outlook? What are the character's psychological impulses and inhibitions?

Complexity: How aware is the character? Is the character a type or an intermediate or a fully complex individual? Why? Who is the most complex (main) character? Why? Who are the secondary characters? Why?

Relationships: What is the main character relationship? Why? Could any other relationship be recognized as the main relationship? Why? What are the secondary character relationships? Why? How do they relate to the main relationship?

6
. . . .
Idea

The word *idea* comes from Greek meaning the inner form of a thing as opposed to its physical reality. From this root comes the current English meaning of a thought or a mental image. Idea is also closely related to the word *ideal*, meaning a model or an original pattern. To some extent, idea has been discussed already in connection with given circumstances, background story, plot, and character. Earlier chapters, however, treated each feature's contribution to idea, not the element itself. This chapter will concentrate on idea as a basic element of drama.

Many people think of idea in connection with *idea plays*, sometimes called problem plays, thesis plays, propaganda plays, or social dramas. Idea plays began in France during the early nineteenth century with the works of Alexandre Dumas the younger, Henry Becque, and Eugène Brieux. The tradition was expanded by Ibsen and Shaw and by later dramatists. They are a part of today's theatre tradition. Idea plays treat specific issues from a didactic, or instructional, point of view and frequently offer, or at least imply, a solution. Sometimes idea plays simply call attention to perceived shortcomings in society; at other times, their intention is more radical. Shaw originated the *discussion play*, a kind of idea play in which current social, political, or economic issues are openly debated as part of the action.

Although idea and discussion plays usually aim at social reform, the concept of idea under discussion now is broader than simply these two types of plays. It is the thought pattern expressed by the whole play. Some writers refer to this as the superobjective, spine, meaning, outlook, or world view of the play. Idea is present in all plays in one form or another, but we should stress that dramatic ideas are not always as significant as those found in *Oedipus Rex*, *Hamlet*, or *Happy Days*. Idea is usually most important in serious plays and satires. Idea appears in light comedies, too, but in such plays, character and plot are ordinarily more important. It is usually least important in farce and old-fashioned melodrama; the absurdists, however, have even managed to invest farce with intellectual significance.

According to critic Francis Fergusson in *The Idea of a Theatre,* the idea "points to the object which the dramatist is trying to show us, and we must in some sense grasp that if we are to understand his complex art." In other words, the dramatic idea controls the direction analysis and subsequent artistic work should take. Learning to deal with idea is also a good exercise because it tests the quality of our thinking about the play. Idea lays the foundation for intelligible discussions about plays and is essential for communication among the members of the artistic team.

Differences of opinion about idea illuminate one of the major distinctions between studying plays for purposes of rehearsal and for other purposes. Despite idea's centrality in script analysis, it cannot be everything in a production. Even though idea is important, the intellectual issue a play expresses usually does not provide the total entertainment element. In *Mother Courage, Happy Days,* or *The Hairy Ape* the idea intrigues but the play's characters and unusual styles are what entertains. In other words, idea may hold a play together, but normally it is not its chief interest. Idea is mainly used to shed more light on the characters and plot. That is why actors, directors, and designers need to guard against the notion that playwrights are philosophers and that plays are meant to demonstrate intellectual issues. Idea is not imposed on a play but rather formed from within it. Idea determines what a play is about on its deepest level, forming the organizing plan of the entire work.

Plays express idea in many ways, but there are two general methods, *direct* and *indirect.* The idea in *Death of a Salesman* is expressed directly because it is stated frankly in the words of the characters. On the other hand, the idea in *Streamers* is expressed indirectly through the implications of the plot and characters. The use of one method does not exclude the use of the other at the same time or in the same play.

WORDS

The standard verbal devices for conveying literary meaning include the titles, discussions, epigrams, allusions, set speeches, and imagery and symbolism. In some plays the urge to talk about idea is so strong that the plot seems only a pretext for a discussion about intellectual issues, for example, in the plays of George Bernard Shaw. Characters talk about ideas in such a way that their words can almost be removed intact from the dialogue and used for a composition on the intellectual issues in the play. Most of the time, playwrights are more subtle than this. Discussion or comments about ideas are embedded in personal conversations so that a feeling of continuous everyday speech is maintained. Dramatists may occasionally turn their attention to intellectual issues, but they seldom overlook the basic need for dialogue to advance the plot *and* reveal character.

Title

Playwrights will frequently slip messages to audiences in titles. The title of *A Raisin in the Sun* is a line from a poem by Langston Hughes about frustrated idealism. The titles of *The Wild Duck, Happy Days,* and *Streamers* indicate the dramatic idea by implication. The important task with implications of course is interpreting them accurately within their contexts. More often the title simply points to the subject of the play as in *Oedipus Rex* and *Hamlet.* A title that refers to both the subject and the idea is *Death of a Salesman.* Willy Loman, the salesman, is the main subject of the play, but the title also points by implication to the dramatic idea. Ordinarily we would expect a title like "The Death of . . ." to refer to an important person such as a member of royalty or a famous artist. In the United States, however, a salesman is considered an average person. Thus Miller's decision to use the word *salesman* instead of someone traditionally more important is a clue to the idea of the play. The titles of *The Hairy Ape* and *The School for Scandal* were probably chosen for their surprise value as well as their ability to express dramatic idea.

Discussions

Characters will sometimes step back from the plot and engage frankly in discussions about an assortment of ideas. When this happens, the principle of artistic unity assures that the discussion topics will relate in some way to the main idea of the play. As was mentioned earlier, lengthy debates are a characteristic of discussion plays but shorter examples may occur in any kind of play. In *Oedipus Rex*, Sophocles included discussions about the capriciousness of the gods, the nature of political power, the role of chance in human affairs, and the credibility of oracles. Shakespeare is decidedly not an intellectual dramatist, but he included discussions about a wide assortment of ideas in *Hamlet*. Some of them are grief, love, duty, afterlife, revenge, divine providence, indecision, *ennui*, ambition, suicide, the art of acting, the responsibilities of public office, divine forgiveness, honor, and guilt. The uneducated working-class characters in *Mother Courage* openly discuss their opinions about the social impact of war, economics, means and ends, military strategy, religion, and politics.

Discussions exist not only in serious plays but also in comedies. Discussions about religious principles and tolerance in *Tartuffe* have already been pointed out. In *The School for Scandal*, there are discussions about personal reputation, literary fashions, and relations among social classes. Discussions may not always point directly to the central idea, but usually they can lead to it when carefully considering the context in which they occur.

Epigrams

The term *epigram* comes from a Greek word meaning a written inscription. We use the word in script analysis to cover proverbs, precepts, maxims, rejoinders, famous sayings, self-evident truths, sententious generalizations, and inversions—in other words, all the brief, quotable sayings that compress human experience into a verbal generality. For example, architect Miës van der Rohe's observation, "God is in the details." is considered an epigram, as is Thoreau's statement, "It is never too late to give up your prejudices." Unlike discussions, epigrams are not lengthy dialogues or statements about particular matters. They are short statements about universal principles.

Sophocles introduced a large number of epigrams into *Oedipus Rex*. Some of the most notable are:

> There is no fairer duty than that of helping others in distress.
> No man can judge the rough unknown or trust in second sight, for wisdom changes hands among the wise.
> Time, and time alone, will show the just man, though scoundrels are discovered in a day.

Hamlet's enjoyment of epigrams is one of his most memorable personality traits.

> Frailty, thy name is woman.
> Foul deeds will rise, though all the earth o'erwhelm them, to men's eyes.

Hamlet enjoys epigrams so much that he often writes them down in his *table book*, a personal accessory Elizabethan gentlemen kept handy specifically for this purpose: "My tables—meet it is I set it down / That one may smile, and smile, and be a villain."

The value of epigrams in revealing idea depends on the intellectual acuteness and credibility of the character who is speaking. When epigrams are spoken by untrustworthy or unscrupulous characters, they can express an opposite meaning from what is intended. For instance, in *Hamlet* Polonius is also fond of epigrams. His famous farewell advice to Laertes is often cited out of context as a model for moral behavior. Knowing what a hypocrite Polonius is, however, it is hard to take him seriously when he says things like "To thine own self be true, and it must follow, as the night the day, thou canst not then be false to any man."

Irony also characterizes the use of epigrams in some modern plays. In *Mother Courage*, Brecht uses epigrams that sound like simple folk sayings.

> If you want the war to work for you, you've got to give the war its due.
> On the whole, you can say that victory and defeat cost us plain people plenty.
> The best thing for us is when politics gets bogged down.

Dramatists employ epigrams to emphasize certain key ideas that in turn help to create a pattern of meaning throughout the play.

Allusions

An *allusion* is an implied reference, sometimes to another work of literature or to a person or an event outside the play. It is a way of sending a message about the idea to the culturally literate members of the audience. Even though not everyone may recognize an allusion, nothing crucial is lost if it is missed. On the other hand, those who do catch it are provided with additional insights. The most popular sources for allusions have traditionally been the Bible and classical literature, history, and mythology. Today, however, there may be a variety of hidden references in a play, including many that refer to current affairs and popular culture.

One dramatist who is widely known for his skillful use of allusions is Samuel Beckett. His play *Happy Days* contains many examples. Sometimes they are frankly set off from the dialogue like epigrams, and at other times, they are well integrated into the dialogue and require very close reading to uncover. Scholars have discovered over two dozen different sources for the allusions in *Happy Days*, ranging from the works of classical Greek playwright Menander to songs by Viennese composer Franz Lehar. Even the physical action of the play is an allusion. The reference is to Dante's *Inferno*, where characters in one level of hell lie half-buried in the earth as punishment for their sins. All the allusions relate in some way to the nearness of death and the transitory nature of earthly things, issues that are directly connected to the idea of the play.

Allusions may be frustrating for some readers, but they are meant to be more than scholarly exercises. In the hands of a skilled playwright, allusions can enrich plays by association. Like the other conventions described in this chapter, they can form a coherent pattern of meaning that points to the central dramatic idea if not directly illuminating it. Moreover allusions are a practical test of artistic awareness because their understanding depends on our cultural literacy, or knowledge of our common cultural heritage.

Set Speeches

Set speeches are long uninterrupted speeches in which important issues in the play are emphasized. They generally stand out from the surrounding dialogue not only because they are longer but also because they are more carefully written and orchestrated. There may be one or several set speeches in a play on a variety of subjects or viewpoints. In all cases, however, they embody at that moment the essence of the scene or the entire play. Because of their self-conscious craftsmanship, set speeches appear more frequently in older, nonrealistic dramas. Laertes' admonition to Ophelia in Act I, Scene 3 of *Hamlet* in which he warns her against expecting too much from Hamlet's affection for her is an example of a set speech. In the context of saying goodbye to his sister, he explains the responsibilities of kingship for Hamlet. Laertes' speech lifts the story out of the realm of individual personalities and reinforces the social and political significance of the play. There are three obvious set speeches in *Tartuffe*. The first two appear together in Act I when Cleante describes the ideal qualities of a genuinely religious person and the third takes place at the end of the play when the Officer pays tribute to the wisdom and generosity of the king.

Set speeches present plausibility problems in realistic plays, but Arthur Miller managed to include one by Charley in the Requiem of *Death of a Salesman*, and David Rabe included several in *Streamers*. Because set speeches are deliberately intended to call attention to important issues in the play, they are reliable sources of information about idea. Moreover they are like windows into the heart of the play and normally provide excellent acting opportunities. They're usually longer than adjacent speeches, are carefully orchestrated to achieve particular emotional effects, and emphasize issues that are crucial in the play.

Imagery

About imagery (and the next topic, symbolism) what has already been written in literature textbooks doesn't need to be repeated here. It is enough to point out that imagery may refer to any words used to represent people, places, or things; feelings or ideas; or sensory experiences. By expressing ideas in sensory form, imagery increases the resources for understanding plays. Critics have found that the image of light, for example, is important throughout *Oedipus Rex*. G. Wilson Knight (*The Wheel of Fire*) and Caroline Spurgeon (*Shakespeare's Imagery and What It Tells Us*) have found that imagery plays a crucial role in Shakespeare's plays. For example, *Hamlet* contains a large number of intentional images of decay. Numerous post-apocalyptic images can be found in *Happy Days,* and imagery about bodily functions appears in *Mother Courage.* Imagery creates patterns of meaning that illuminate the play as a whole. Studying the imagery may not be as immediately productive as analyzing other features, but it can clarify thinking and help resolve confusions that might exist. Perhaps the main practical value lies in the ability of imagery to influence designers' imagination in harmony with the main intellectual issues of a play.

Intentional Symbolism

A symbol is something that represents something other than itself. The word *symbol* comes from a Greek verb meaning to throw together, its noun form means a mark or sign. Symbols may vary in complexity and purpose, but here consider only *intentional symbols,* those in which there is a direct equation (that is, scales equals justice, owl equals wisdom) either because of a commonly accepted meaning or because of being purposely designated as a symbol in the play. In contrast, *incidental symbols* are imposed on the play by the reader. They are of minor or casual interest and have little practical value in script analysis.

Normally the author who uses intentional symbols slips them in cunningly. If they stand out too obviously from the context, they may distract from the play and make it too much like a sermon. In the hands of a skilled playwright, intentional symbols can enrich by association—like allusions or imagery only more obvious and therefore more potent. By constantly evoking abstract ideas and feelings in concrete form, intentional symbols function as connections between the play and the outside world. They can often reveal more about the main idea, and reveal more emphatically, than any other single literary element.

The wild duck in the play of the same name is an example of an intentional symbol. Gregers, the radical idealist, enjoys the use of symbols. He designates the wild duck as an intentional one when he says to Hjalmar in Act II "I almost think you have something of the wild duck in you." Other characters in the play reveal that when a Scandinavian wild duck is even slightly wounded, it doesn't try to escape but instead dives into the water and clings to the weeds on the bottom. Readers also learn that a wild duck is easily tamed and despite its name thrives in captivity. The symbol of the wild duck reinforces behavior patterns that Gregers thinks he sees in Hjalmar. According to Gregers, the wild duck represents Hjalmar's failure to cope with the catastrophes in his life. He also believes that Hjalmar has forsaken his youthful ideals for a comfortable existence. The meaning of the wild duck is clear because the playwright has made it part of the story.

Other intentional symbols are the ape in *The Hairy Ape,* Mama's potted plant in *A Raisin in the Sun,* the pregnant ant in *Happy Days,* Anna Fierling's canteen wagon in *Mother Courage,* and perhaps the name *Oedipus* (wounded foot) in *Oedipus Rex.* As was said before, symbolism as a device for expressing idea should be treated carefully. It may be an appealing exercise to impose incidental symbols on a play, but there is a risk that the result may only express the reader's ideas. By definition, intentional symbols are objectively present in the play, therefore they are normally more helpful in script analysis than are symbols the reader imposes.

Prologue or Epilogue

The prologue and epilogue are other literary devices playwrights use for presenting the idea directly. The *prologue* (literally, the speech before) provides necessary background story and introduces what the play is about. The *epilogue* (the speech after) summarizes the idea by restating it at the end of the play within a larger context. In a classical Greek tragedy such as *Oedipus Rex*, the prologue and epilogue intentionally frame the action according to accepted tragic form. They highlight the dramatic idea directly not only by their characteristics as formal parts of the play but also through the words of the Chorus. The Requiem at the end of *Death of a Salesman* is a formal epilogue that has similar functions. The nature of the funeral scene leads us to expect a summing up, which we find frankly in the words of Linda, Biff, Happy, and especially Charley.

CHARACTERS

Another way idea may be expressed directly is through conventional kinds of characters. Expressing idea in this way involves definite technical restrictions, however, because characters cannot speak openly for the playwright without seriously harming the play. They can say only what is permitted within the limits of their own identities and while addressing other imaginary characters. With these restrictions in mind, playwrights have developed conventional characters who can embody idea directly but without straining plausibility. These characters do not appear in every play. Moreover when they do appear, there is no rule against a single character fulfilling several conventional duties at the same time.

Be careful not to depend too much on conventional characters to learn about idea for that comes dangerously close to one of the reading fallacies discussed in the Introduction. Interest in the ideas that characters express and the technical functions they perform should not lead to misunderstanding the characters themselves. Some characters may technically embody part of the idea, but in the best plays, they are never merely mouthpieces for the playwrights. Characters behave primarily as characters because they are governed chiefly by artistic considerations and only secondarily by technical requirements.

Narrator or Chorus

The narrator or chorus tell a story to the audience and actively participate in it with the other characters. Because they always know more than do the other characters, usually they can be consulted reliably for information about the idea. In *Mother Courage*, Anna Fierling, Eilif, Yvette, and the Chaplain step out of the action several times and speak or sing directly to the audience as narrators. They explain the play in musical numbers like "The Song of the Old Wife and the Soldier," "The Song of Fraternization," and "The Song of the Great Capitulation." Choruses in Greek tragedies also play the dual roles of narrators during the choral odes and normal characters during the episodes. When the narrator or chorus frankly interrupts the action to talk about the idea the objective is to explain the meaning to the audience.

Raisonneur

Another character who knows more than the other characters is the *raisonneur*, a type of narrator who always remains within the action. Although participating continuously in the action, the *raisonneur* ordinarily has little direct effect on it, thus traditionally furnishing this character with objectivity and credibility. The *raisonneur* is often a skeptic, wishing to offer sound advice or to convince through reason. A classic example of a *raisonneur* is Cleante in *Tartuffe*. He always remains within the action, yet his skeptical personality permits him to comment on it without obviously appearing to do so. Although he has no major effect on the plot, he freely expresses his opinions about intellectual issues in the play. Dr. Relling in *The Wild Duck* is another example of a *raisonneur*. After his introduction during the lunch scene in Act III, he takes an active part in the plot only four more times. He objects to Mrs. Sorby's marriage plans, admonishes Gregers' misplaced idealism, locates the missing Hjalmar, and provides medical help for Hedvig. Relling says that he is "cultivating the life illusion" in others. Despite an inclination to preach, *raisonneurs* like Relling are most effective in performance when they are understood as part of the world of the play and not as sermonizers.

Confidant

A *confidant* (or female *confidante*) is a character with the technical function of listening sympathetically to the private feelings and thoughts of the leading character. Like a *raisonneur*, this character has little direct effect on the action even though remaining within it continuously. Since others willingly confide in this character, however, the confidant is more often a trusted friend than a skeptical observer—generally a well adjusted character without serious personal conflicts. A typical objective might be to help the leading character contend with a difficult situation. In this capacity, a confidant provides an opportunity for talking about matters that are deeply important to the leading character.

Charley, Willy Loman's next-door neighbor in *Death of a Salesman*, is a typical confidant. Aside from Willy's brother Ben, he is the only person in whom Willy confides his private feelings. In Act I, Charley listens compassionately and helps Willy to take his mind off his troubles. In Act II, he gives Willy practical help with offers of money and a job. Other examples of confidants are Horatio in *Hamlet*, Ruth in *A Raisin in the Sun*, and Roger in *Streamers*. By definition, confidants are outside the main action most of the time. This inherent weakness is easily compensated for by their strong desire to help. By offering the chance to talk safely about private matters, confidants provide the leading character with support and encouragement unobtainable from anyone else in the play.

Norm Character

Literary critics borrowed the term *norm character* from the social sciences. It describes someone who has successfully adjusted to the dominant social standards in the world of the play. The norm character is another example of a character who knows more about the situation than do the other characters, except in this case superior awareness results more from personal insight than from direct information. Norm characters do not appear in every play. They appear chiefly in comedy that needs a technical reference point against which to compare the eccentric behavior of other characters. Comic writers know that eccentricity is more clearly illuminated if it is displayed against a background of common sense.

In *Tartuffe,* the norm character is Orgon's wife, Elmire. Despite Madame Pernelle's harsh opinion of her, Elmire is well adjusted to the social standards of her society. She is independent-minded, good-natured, tolerant, and wise in the ways of the world. For her, religion is a private matter of the individual not a commodity for public discussion. Although Elmire strongly disapproves of Tartuffe, she does not overreact by publicly condemning him, an act she knows would almost certainly backfire. Instead, her objective is to dispose of Tartuffe behind the scenes without embarrassing Orgon. This is part of her main objective, which might be to rescue Orgon from the fanatical influence of his mother.

In *The School for Scandal,* Rowley performs the dual functions of norm character and confidant, as does Charley in *Death of a Salesman.* Mrs. Sorby is the norm character in *The Wild Duck* as is Joseph Asagai in *A Raisin in the Sun.* For sound dramatic reasons, norm characters are of central importance in a play. An essential point is that they are too intelligent to be pressured by social conventions. And since they don't take themselves too seriously, they frequently display well-developed senses of humor. They should be understood as appealing characters or else the comedy may misfire.

Having reviewed the ways playwrights present idea directly through the words, we should be careful of assuming that the words spoken by a character invariably reveal the main idea. This does not mean that characters never say anything trustworthy. It's only that they have their own personalities, and what they say is ordinarily shaped by their situation from moment to moment. Although their words may be appropriate in one instance, they may not explain the entire play.

PLOT

Thornton Wilder said that playwriting springs from an instinctive linkage between idea and action. Although dramatists may occasionally present the idea directly in the words of the characters, a successful play works principally through action, not verbal statements. Plays are not philosophical treatises. There is seldom much obvious talk in them about ideas. No matter how intellectual a play may seem on the surface, its essential idea is always presented most forcefully through the plot, the pattern revealed by the actions. Plot is part of the expressive system of drama. Just as dialogue and character conventions can express idea, so too can conventions in the plot. This section will study plot conventions in an effort to understand how dramatists express dramatic idea through them.

Parallelism

Playwrights who feel the need to express a series of equivalent or similar ideas sometimes use a plot device called *parallelism*. When characters are intentionally linked with other characters, the issues connecting them will be reinforced by means of repetition and contrast. Shakespeare frequently used parallelism to point up the ideas in his plays. An analysis of *Hamlet*, for example, reveals a number of intentional parallelisms linking the characters of Hamlet, Fortinbras, and Laertes. Hamlet's and Fortinbras' fathers were both recently deceased and warrior-kings. Both Hamlet and Fortinbras are princes as well as being rightful heirs to their respective thrones, yet neither holds the throne in his respective country. Hamlet's and Fortinbras' uncles are both usurpers who have gained their thrones through questionable means. Moreover there are or were extremely close personal relationships between the three parallel sets of fathers and sons: Hamlet and King Hamlet, Fortinbras and King Fortinbras, and Laertes and Polonius. Certain actions of Hamlet, Fortinbras, and Laertes are also intentionally parallel. Hamlet has embarked on a course of revenge for his father's murder. For equivalent reasons, Fortinbras threatens to retake lands his father lost in Denmark and Poland, and Laertes threatens to revenge the murder of Polonius. From these and other similarities, it seems clear that Laertes, Fortinbras, and Hamlet are foils for each other—that is, they intentionally enhance one another by contrast.

When there are enough similarities to insure that parallelisms exist objectively in the play and are not simply projected into it by the reader, clues about idea can be found. Although all three characters aim to revenge the deaths of their fathers, only Fortinbras and Laertes seem genuinely committed to their tasks. Hamlet's reluctance seems to indicate that he's more like a poet or philosopher than a soldier. The contrasts between the personality traits and willpower of these three characters provide clues to the main idea of the play. The parallelisms also emphasize the variety of different traits Hamlet displays compared to those displayed by Fortinbras and Laertes.

Parallelism in modern plays appears in more subtle forms. In *The Wild Duck*, the activities of the Werle and Ekdal families constitute parallelisms. The main idea expresses itself through Gregers' and Hjalmar's contrasting ideals and through their relationships with their parents, particularly with their fathers. The parallelisms in *Death of a Salesman* also reiterate the relations between fathers and sons. The secondary plots in this play are only briefly developed, but Miller has provided enough of them to reinforce certain key issues connected with the main idea. Obviously readers shouldn't look for parallelisms in every play, but whenever their presence can be objectively identified, readers are justified in studying them for clues about idea.

Conflict

Chapter 5 explained that some kinds of conflict produce intellectual tensions that may be useful for directors and designers in their artistic work. In this context, artistic work means work on the play as a whole. The conflict being studied here stems from the opposition of the customs or beliefs of a society against a different order or perhaps against no order at all. The intellectual tensions between different social systems, between character and environment, character and destiny, or character and the forces of nature are inherently interesting. When intellectual conflict of this kind appears in the plot, the tensions illuminate ideas.

Consider the ideas that can be drawn from the intellectual conflicts in the plot of *Streamers*. At first sight the sordid violence appears to be the only striking thing about the play, but after deeper analysis, the violence begins to illuminate one of modern society's most pressing intellectual dilemmas: the decline of moral values. Billy believes in the orthodox values he grew up with in the Midwest, but society has changed radically since he was a boy and so have its values. The play offers no glimpse of what the new order might be, but it does show the moral disorder that characterizes modern society and the fate that awaits a naive idealist who clings to an extinct set of beliefs. Gregers in *The Wild Duck* is an impractical dreamer just as Billy is. His idealism causes serious harm to others, but Gregers lives on and his impact on society is negligible. In contrast, Billy destroys not only the lives of others but also his own life. Moreover by his stubborn refusal to deal with reality, he actually contributes to the kind of moral anarchy that so horrified him.

The opposition between Billy's old-fashioned morality and modern society's amorality is the source of the intellectual conflict in the play. Combined with the supporting issues of racial relations, sexuality, and militarism, *Streamers* offers a rich supply of intellectual tensions. Abstract conflicts like these are normally too generalized to be of more than secondary interest for actors, but they can be immediately useful for directors and designers. By setting the play in a context larger than itself, intellectual conflicts contribute to those aspects of staging and design that depend on seeing the play in its entirety.

Climax

Director Elia Kazan observed that the climax of the play is the most concrete illustration of its main idea. All the parts of the play converge at this point, and everything appears in its most vivid theatrical form. The quality of a play's climax is judged by how successfully it fulfills these functions. All the essential forces of the play at work can be seen most clearly in the climax.

This may be explained by studying an effective climax in detail. In *The Wild Duck,* the climax begins almost at the end of the play when the characters learn that Hedvig has shot herself. The various responses to her death are illuminating. Old Ekdal attributes her death to mythological forest demons. He flees into the garret to comfort himself with his pets and with liquor. Reverend Molvik is always drunk anyway. He mumbles a few prayers over Hedvig's body, but his gesture is embarrassing rather than consoling. Hjalmar Ekdal, Hedvig's father, reacts in typical fashion by thinking only of himself. When Dr.

Relling tries to comfort Hjalmar by assuring him that Hedvig's death was painless, Hjalmar cries "And I! I hunted her from me like an animal! . . . She crept terrified into the garret and died for love of me!" Idealist Gregers Werle views Hedvig's death as a concrete validation of his mission in life. "Hedvig has not died in vain," he pontificates to Dr. Relling. "Did you not see how sorrow set free what is noble in him [Hjalmar]?" Relling scoffs at this. He tries to warn Gregers that even Hedvig's suicide will not change Hjalmar's inherent selfishness, but Gregers refuses to believe it. "If you are right and I am wrong," he replies, "then life is not worth living." But Relling, the *raissoneur*, sees things more clearly if not skeptically. He recognizes that Hedvig's death has become for Hjalmar nothing more than an opportunity for extravagant declamation, self-admiration, and self-pity. In addition, he knows that Hedvig would not have died if Gregers hadn't misled Hjalmar with his foolish notions of "the claim of the ideal."

The death of an innocent child should be a heartbreaking event. It should bring out feelings of genuine sorrow and remorse in the characters. The family picture Ibsen illustrates at the climax of *The Wild Duck*, however, is one of drunkenness, petty vanity, and thoughtless insensitivity. Gregers had hoped to inspire Hjalmar with passionate idealism; instead, he has had the opposite effect. This climax shows in concrete form that Gregers is a failed idealist. Although Relling provides a few spoken comments on the situation, Ibsen has chosen to express the idea of the play indirectly through the actions and attitudes of the characters. Studying the climax closely like this can help to show how idea really works in plays. This is how to understand that idea in drama is not an abstract concept but rather the philosophy of the play in action.

THE MAIN IDEA

Some readers think it is necessary to see a play in concrete physical terms then rise above it somehow into an abstract world of meaning. Dramatic ideas, however, are too complicated to be expressed by abstract thinking alone. Rather by using selection and compression, playwrights transform ideas into concrete physical experience. They do this by putting audiences through a carefully controlled series of emotional adventures intended to make them feel exactly as the characters do toward life. Every word in the play exists for this reason, and every detail and incident has been prepared with this goal in view. The result is that, even though the dramatist isn't there in person, the main idea is understood by the audience as an obvious conclusion. This main idea is a result of the entire presented experience of the play. Incidentally the main idea should not be confused with the production concept. The main idea is an issue that relates to the written script. The production concept, on the other hand, is an original idea, design, or plan for producing a play. Of course, a production concept should be based on a sound understanding of a play's main idea, but unfortunately this does not always happen.

To be studied in itself, the main idea must be changed from its original concrete expression in the play into literary form. This is accomplished by applying a process of radical reduction to the entire play to disclose its basic form. An automobile, for example, stripped to its bare frame is still an automobile; though most of the details have been removed, it still retains its basic form. The other parts are extensions and elaborations of the basic framework. Similarly the main idea represents the basic framework of the play that unites all the details—the *inner structure* or *second plan* of the play. This process of extreme reduction is not merely instructive, it is essential. Only by stating the idea in condensed, simplified form does it remain close to its original unified illustration in the play. As soon as secondary qualifications are added, information enters that may obscure the idea's basic unity. Moreover whenever the formulation of the main idea is confused or contains too many qualifications, there is a strong chance that some basic misunderstanding exists about the play.

Of course, radical reduction comes after the fact, that is, after the play has already been written. Obviously most playwrights don't actually create their works backward in this way; that is, they don't begin with an intellectual conception of the play's meaning then work backward to the finished play. Usually in the initial stages of work at least, they have little concrete understanding of what it is they've written in terms of its intellectual expression. Nonetheless this fact doesn't mean their plays lack coherent main ideas, nor does it lessen the importance of the main idea for the artistic needs of actors, directors, and designers.

Although there are no fixed rules governing how to state the main idea in reduced form, it can ordinarily be expressed in one of four ways: (1) superobjective, (2) action summary, (3) thesis sentence, or (4) theme. No single method has any particular advantage over the others, and any or all of them may be used for just about any play.

The superobjective (some writers say *spine*) is Stanislavski's method of describing the main idea. It seems to be the form most widely in use, even by those who are not influenced by Stanislavski. Therefore we'll devote more time to it. Since we already know about character objectives, the principle is not that difficult to understand. According to Stanislavski, all of the individual minor and major character objectives in a play should come together under the command of a single, comprehensive objective called, appropriately enough, the superobjective. We might think of the relation between the superobjective and all the supporting objectives as the popular Russian nesting dolls (*matrushka* dolls), each of which is found to contain a smaller one.

Recall that the through-line of the character is Stanislavski's description of the controlled process that relates the character's secondary objectives together under the control of the main objective. The through-line of the play works similarly to relate the main and secondary objectives of all the characters to the superobjective for the entire play. Naturally, like other objectives, the superobjective is not ordinarily directly observable in the play but must be deduced from the action. It's the reader's responsibility to search for the through-line that frames all the character objectives to relate them to the superobjective. Any character objective, no matter how small, that does not clearly relate to the superobjective is considered incorrect or at least inappropriate. To repeat an earlier discussion, it is important to choose an infinitive form of an active, concrete verb for character objectives to energize the action in the right direction. The same principle applies in the formulation of a superobjective.

How does the entire process work? To produce *Hamlet,* for example, the superobjective of the play might be to search for a father's murderer in order to revenge his death. It is possible to imagine how all the character objectives can relate to this choice because a great deal of information in the play will support it. Strictly speaking, however, the through-line is incomplete. The problem is that, by treating the play chiefly as a revenge drama, the other ideas found in it will have only accidental importance. The play's profound social, political, moral, and religious ideas will only be afterthoughts. If the superobjective were to search for the murder of the king in order to preserve the state of Denmark, the through-line would be more developed. Hamlet's love for his fellow citizens and his country would receive the emphasis. The social ideas would also grow in importance, giving the whole play larger social and political significance. The play can be enriched still further if the superobjective is to carry out one's duty in order to discover the meaning of life. This is a paraphrase of the formulation Edward Gordon Craig and Stanislavski devised for their production at the Moscow Art Theatre in 1924. It proved to be an effective through-line for them because it successfully related the character objectives together under an appropriate commanding idea without omitting anything important in the play. Hamlet's goals became greater, and the whole play became less personal than it was when he was occupied with only his father or his country. The implications behind this superobjective are no longer overtly social or political but rather universal in scope. Moreover the poetic dimensions of the play now take on enormous significance, an important issue for Craig because of his affection for symbolic design elements.

We can see that the superobjectives were described in three stages: (1) personal (to search for a father's murderer), (2) social and political (to search for a king's murderer), and (3) universal (to search for the meaning of life). Each choice clearly had a great deal in the play to support it, but each was also progressively broader in scope and added potentially more meaning to the play. In the classroom, the exact wording of the superobjective is up to the individual reader exclusively. In production, however, the director is ultimately responsible for communicating the statement of the superobjective to the production team. The scope of the superobjective can be within any range of meaning the director desires—whether personal, sociopolitical, or universal—as long as the choice is firmly supported by sufficient information in the play itself.

The same two-step procedure can be used to develop the other types of statements that describe the central idea. First develop a concise literary description that adequately describes the important aspects of the play. Then present all the information in the play so that it is understood in a manner that clearly relates to that description. In some plays, readers may choose to state the main idea as an action summary without bothering about Stanislavski's verbal nuances. Actor Laurence Olivier used this approach when he described his film version of *Hamlet* as "the story of a man who could not make up his mind." Olivier's choice highlights the philosophical dimensions of the play with particular emphasis on its moments of existential anguish. Readers who are more socially or politically inclined may choose to express the main idea as a *thesis sentence*, a single declarative sentence that asserts a lesson about the subject of the play forcefully. For example, Ibsen may have written *The Wild Duck* to prove that impractical idealists always go wrong, or Brecht may have written *Mother Courage* to prove that capitalism destroys human feeling. Both examples show that a thesis sentence is often useful for highlighting social or political issues. In contrast to a thesis sentence, a *theme* is normally not an arguable message but rather an expression of the main idea in more universal terms. For example, the theme of *The Hairy Ape* might be *the struggle for identity* or that of *Oedipus Rex, the quest for truth*. Theme statements seem to work best when they are expressing the broad philosophical and poetic aspects of a play.

All these formulations are legitimate appraisals of the main idea for their respective plays. The logic behind them should be clear. The statement of the main idea is an effort to describe in condensed literary form the basic conflict at the heart of the play. Regardless of the formulation, the cardinal principle is to state the main idea in a single declarative statement. Main ideas stated as questions ("Is idealism worthwhile?") or calls to action ("Let's fight to preserve our ideals.") can obscure the issue. They have a reluctant or ambivalent feeling about them. The main idea will be expressed clearly and strongly if the statement firmly asserts or denies something about the meaning of the play.

Developing a statement of the main idea tests artistic awareness because it forces the artistic team to determine at the beginning of the play just what it is they want to say. There is also a good possibility that it will stimulate suggestions about acting, directing, or design.

Often it takes considerable practice before a reader acquires the skill to define the main idea accurately. The growth of this skill can be nurtured by making it a habit to define the main idea for any plays. As was seen earlier in this chapter, sometimes the playwright helps by stating the main idea somewhere in the dialogue. The task is to find that statement. In most cases, the main idea is not stated directly anywhere and so must be abstrated from the action of the whole play. The ability to draw out implications this way is usually one of the last skills acquired in learning how to analyze a play. If actors, directors, and designers can't abstract the main idea in some convincing way, it is unlikely they will be consistently successful in their artistic work.

SUMMARY
This chapter concerned itself with some of the ways in which the main idea may be expressed in plays. It takes considerable experience to develop the ability to understand and describe a play's idea with clarity and simplicity. Nevertheless it is a skill that should be acquired if students expect to communicate successfully with others involved in the artistic process not to mention the audience. Sometimes the clearest understanding of the main idea may not occur until late in the process of analysis or even during rehearsals. Sometimes the main idea does not become clear until after the play has opened, and it can at last be comprehended whole as it was originally intended. What's more, most of

the audience will never judge the play on the basis of its idea but rather as drama and feeling. But one way or another, for reasons already discussed, the main idea must motivate actors, directors, and designers. The main idea gives each play its unique identity. It is the starting point and focusing device that propels the artistic team toward its final result. Regardless of whether a particular statement about the idea is definitive, the practice of determining the main idea is one of the major goals of play analysis.

QUESTIONS

Words: Does the title reflect the meaning? If so, does it do so directly, indirectly, or ironically? Any discussions about ideas in the dialogue? If so, who is involved? What specific ideas are discussed? Are there any examples of epigrams? If so, who speaks them? What ideas do they illustrate? Any literary, religious, or cultural allusions? If so, who speaks them? What are the sources? What ideas do they illustrate? Any long, uninterrupted speeches that point out specific ideas (set speeches)? If so, who says them? What ideas do they involve? Are there any persistent literary images or intentional symbols in the dialogue? If so, what are they? What ideas do they suggest? Is there a prologue or an epilogue? If so, how does it illustrate the main idea of the play?

Characters: Is there a narrator or chorus? If so, when and how do they express the main idea? Is there a skeptical character who offers advice or tries to reason with others *(raisonneur)*? If so, how does the character express the main idea? Is there someone to whom the leading character can confide private feelings (confidant[e])? If so, how does that character relate to the main idea? In a comedy, is there an important character who has successfully adjusted to the behavioral code of the world of the play (norm character)? If so, how does that character express the main idea?

Plot: Are there any characters or situations that repeat or highlight others (parallelisms)? If so, how do they relate to the main idea? Are there any intellectual conflicts involving the existing social order, destiny, or the forces of nature? Can any intentional symbolism be found in the dialogue or action? If so, how does it relate to the central idea? How do the most intense emotional scenes (climaxes) reflect the central idea?

Statement of the main idea: What is the main idea of the play? Frame the description in the form of an action summary, a superobjective, a thesis sentence, or a thematic statement. Justify the response with detailed information from the play itself.

7

· · · · · · · ·

Dialogue

Dialogue consists of the passages of talk in the play. It is composed of all the conversations, monologues, soliloquies, narration, choral odes, songs, and anything else spoken by the actors. It obviously does not include stage directions. Enough has already been said in earlier chapters to show how important it is to study the dialogue for information about the given circumstances, background story, plot, character, and idea. Yet even when the dialogue is clear about all this information, it still deserves to be studied for its own self. In addition to being the play's primary means of communication, dialogue is also the playwright's sole means of creative expression. It can be merely workmanlike or it can display a high degree of virtuosity.

Although most readers don't pay much attention to the language in a play, it does exert a subtle influence. The language may evoke comments like

> The dialogue is easy to understand.
> The words come from the characters naturally.
> He uses lots of short words.
> I was so bored by the long and complicated sentences that I skipped
>   whole passages.

Most of these opinions are too general to be genuinely useful. Analysis needs to be more specific in order to teach anything that can be helpful in the rehearsal hall. When critics use the term diction, they mean the technical and artistic qualities of language, the selection and arrangement of words, phrases, sentences, lines, and speeches. This chapter treats dialogue as diction, starting with the basic building blocks and progressing to more creative qualities. Some features are relative and opinions about them vary, but most dialogue can be studied in the same open-minded way already recommended in this book.

Often the analysis of dialogue uncovers a hidden complication. Readers cannot hope to understand the language in a play if they have not mastered the basics of grammar, syntax, punctuation, sentences, paragraphs, and so forth. They should know before starting to work whether they need to review the fundamentals. Although the rules of diction are subtle and complex, their subtlety and complexity occurs in the way dramatists stretch the rules. Readers should know immediately which rules are being stretched and why. It's not a good idea to worry about these issues in a script analysis textbook. Script analysis is challenging enough without also having to worry about the fundamentals of English. Fortunately, the subject is not that difficult. Any serious student can cover the basics with a good guidebook and a little help from the right tutor. Two such books are *The Elements of Grammar* by Margaret D. Shertzer and *The Elements of Style* by William Strunk, Jr., and E.B. White. Both are short, accurate, practical, and available.

WORDS

There may be many characters in a play, and they may speak in various ways, but each normally preserves a certain manner of speech identified as that character's own and no one else's. Since characters speak in their own voices, the words they use potentially tell a great deal about them. This is achieved partly by choice of words; characters can be measured partly by certain features of their words.

Abstract and Concrete

One of the first values to search for in words is the quality of abstraction or concreteness. Abstract words name qualities, concepts, or ideas—things that cannot be perceived by the senses such as love, honor, experience, dimension, or materialism. Creon in *Oedipus Rex* and Cleante in *Tartuffe* use words like *power, knowledge, justice, hypocrisy,* and *self-sacrifice.* Characters who use a surplus of words describing intellectual concepts like these often appear reserved, aloof, or affected. By contrast, concrete words describe things that can be seen and touched like flowers, smiles, thumbtacks, or hammers. They are vivid and emphatic, and the characters who use them display analogous personality traits. Oedipus and Orgon speak in specific terms like this. They express their hasty judgments and rash decrees using strong, concrete language that differs considerably from Creon's and Cleante's cautious abstractions.

Formal and Informal

Another value in conversational speech is the level of formality or informality of the words. Formal speech makes generous use of elevated words of the kind often found in scholarly books—mediocrity, ubiquitous, Weltanschauung, verisimilitude—also literary words—however, nonetheless, consequently, moreover. Formal language aims at precision, but in doing so it deliberately restricts feeling. Simple language, for many sorts of characters, can be more effective. Comparing the words of Joseph Surface with those of his brother Charles in *The School for Scandal* we can see an illustration of these principles. Joseph's frequent use of *indeed, certainly,* and *however* and similarly formal wording tells us that he puts literary style first. By contrast, his brother Charles' *bumper, blockhead,* and *wench* and similar kinds of humble, everyday words grow unaffectedly out of his feelings. He doesn't worry about how he sounds to others.

Closely affiliated with formal and informal qualities is the syllabic composition of words. Polysyllabic words frequently stem from Latin, traditionally the language of scholars. Joseph Asagai is the Nigerian exchange student who is Beneatha Younger's boyfriend in *A Raisin in the Sun*. He enjoys display-ing his new American education with polysyllabic words like *mutilated, accom-modate,* and *assimilate.* On the other hand, the uneducated characters in Brecht's *Mother Courage* frequently speak in short, abrupt sentences (in translation): "Halt, you scum!" "He's pulled a black cross. He's through." "You've left your hat." Broadly speaking, formal, multisyllabic words tend to be associated with emotional restraint while short, informal words imply emotional freedom.

Jargon and Slang

Jargon (professionals' specialized vocabulary) and *slang* (nonstandard everyday speech) have special appeal in dramatic dialogue because they sound unusual, vivid, and colorful. Our recognition of such language as unusual is just as important as is the plausibility it lends to certain situations. *Mother Courage* and *Streamers* acquire some of their appeal from the liberal use of military jargon and everyday slang. They employ *good-bad speech,* bad speech that is intention-ally written to achieve certain expressive effects. Characters in *The Hairy Ape* speak the jargon of life at sea, and in *A Raisin in the Sun,* they often speak in the slang of Afro-American folk culture. Our national culture is enriched by jargon and slang from these social groups and from many more besides. On stage, jargon and slang help identify characters within a particular social context.

Connotation

Recall from the Introduction that to connote is to suggest or convey associations in addition to the explicit (denoted), dictionary meaning. Connota-tive words, therefore, are words that convey more than their literal meaning. For example, the simple sentence, "There's a spider," will often cause a shiver of disgust, whereas the statement, "There is an insect," may not. This happens because for many people *spider* is automatically associated with creepy feelings of disgust. Dramatists like to use connotative words because they add more emotion to the dialogue without adding more words.

Some words are almost purely connotative, having little or no objective meaning at all. Linguists describe them as *snarl* and *purr* words. They may look like normal words, but their literal meanings are often of only secondary importance. Words like *damn!* or *ouch!* are little more than noises that express pure feelings. Since emotion plays such a large part in dramatic dialogue, play readers should always be alert for the connotative as well as the literal meanings of words.

For example, the abusive language in *Streamers* may offend some readers, but it is actually very effective connotative dialogue. It may not seem especially dramatic, but no one will deny that it expresses thoughts and feelings impressively. It shocks, but it communicates, too. Many of Winnie's and Willie's words in *Happy Days* are richly connotative. In the right context, simple, isolated expressions like *what, no, yes,* or *God* suggest surprisingly rich and complex feelings. When Winnie discovers an ant carrying a little white ball (that is, an egg), her subsequent dialogue of six simple words with Willie forms an ironic play on words involving sex, biology, entomology, and philosophy.

SENTENCES

The next rhetorical device is the sentence, the primary tool of the play. Some very interesting observations can be made about a play by studying various features of the sentences. Literary examination can reveal dramatic possibilities that are particularly useful for actors and directors.

Length

Sentence length reveals useful information about character. Readers can begin to arrive at some legitimate understanding of an author's or character's sentence length simply by counting the words and sentences in a continuous portion of the play and then dividing the total number of words by the number of sentences. After estimating the average number of words for each sentence, more important considerations can be pursued, namely, what is the relation between sentence length, dramatic context, and character?

An illustration of the value of sentence length for character analysis occurs in the scene between Polonius and Reynaldo in Act I, Scene 2, of *Hamlet* in which Polonius is directing Reynaldo to keep an eye on Laertes while he is in France. In this short scene, Polonius speaks seven times as many words as Reynaldo; his sentences are over four times longer; and he uses a large number of abstract words. Of course, we would expect Polonius to say more in this scene because he is giving the instructions, but even so, the calculations tell us that Polonius talks too much in a misplaced attempt to sound important. Reynaldo speaks in short sentences, trying to bring the frustrating conversation to a rapid conclusion.

In *Streamers,* sentence length offers some clues for playable dramatic values. Martin, Richie, Carlyle, Billy, and Roger appear in the first informal scene of Act I. The average sentence length for all the characters in the scene is only six words. True in modern plays, characters generally say what must be said using the fewest words possible. These sentences, however, are much shorter than we might expect even for a modern play. What's more, many of them are only fragments. This might indicate a low level of formal education and strong emotion. Together with the army jargon, frequent use of abusive slang, and numerous connotative words, the short length of the sentences highlights the highly charged emotional quality of this savage play.

Long sentences may be carried along by hysterical emotion or reflect a halting, insecure feeling of anxiety. They may also be sustained by the complexity of their thought or the richness of their images as in the case of Shakespeare. Short sentences and sentence fragments can create different effects. They can be tough, penetrating, and incisive, or they can suggest weariness or dullness. Readers should learn to recognize both extremes and all the variations in between.

Kinds

Sentences can be grammatically simple, compound, complex, or compound-complex; rhetorically loose, periodic, balanced, or antithetical; or functionally statements, questions, commands, or exclamations. The kinds of sentences used in a play and the proportions of the various kinds to one another can reveal some potentially playable features. Dialogue in older, historical plays is often self-consciously composed like music. Sentences show noticeable patterns; they flow obviously from one point to another and are accentuated by prominent stops. There is frequently enough expressive matter in them to make up several modern sentences. By contrast, most sentences used in modern dialogue do not deliberately call attention to themselves. They are comparatively short, and they stop when the sense is complete. Yet within these two broad limits, there may still be many kinds of sentences. This is not the place for a discussion of the basics of grammar, rhetoric, or syntax, however. The lesson here is that once the kinds of sentences are defined, the associations between them can be studied. Their proportion to one another as well as their relationship to the dramatic context can be examined.

To illustrate this point, consider the sentences in a passage from one historical and one modern play. The first passage is from *The School for Scandal*. Rowley is attempting to persuade Sir Peter Teazle that he is mistaken in his opinions of Charles and Joseph Surface.

ROWLEY: You know, Sir Peter, I have always taken the liberty to differ with you on the subject of these two young gentlemen. I
only wish you may not be deceived in your opinion of the elder. For Charles, my life on't! he will retrieve his errors
yet. Their worthy father, once my honored master, was, at his
years, nearly as wild a spark; yet when he died, he did not
leave a more benevolent heart to lament his loss.

SIR PETER: You are wrong, Master Rowley. On their father's death,
you know, I acted as a kind of guardian to them both till
their uncle Sir Oliver's liberality gave them an early independence. Of course no person could have more opportunity of
judging their hearts, and I was never mistaken in my life.
Joseph is indeed a model for the young men of the age. He is a
man of sentiment and acts up to the sentiments he professes;
but, for the other, take my word for't, if he had any grain
of virtue by descent, he has dissipated it with the rest of
his inheritance. Ah! my old friend Sir Oliver will be deeply
mortified when he finds how part of his bounty has been
misapplied.

The modern example involves a similar situation in *The Wild Duck*. Dr. Relling is attempting to refute Gregers Werles' opinion of the character of Hjalmar Ekdal.

GREGERS: What is your explanation of the spiritual tumult that is now
going on inside Hjalmar Ekdal?

RELLING: A lot of spiritual tumult I've noticed in him.

GREGERS: What! Not at such a crisis, when his whole life has been
placed on a new foundation? How can you think that such an
individuality as Hjalmar's--

RELLING: Oh, individuality--he! If he ever had any tendency to the
abnormal developments you call individuality, I can assure you
it was rooted out of him while he was still in his teens.

GREGERS: That would be strange indeed--considering the loving care
     with which he was brought up.

RELLING: By those two high-flown, hysterical maiden aunts, you mean?

GREGERS: Let me tell you that they were women who never forgot the
     claim of the ideal--but of course you will only jeer at me
     again.

RELLING: No, I'm in no humor for that. I know all about those ladies,
     for he has ladled out no end of rhetoric on the subject of his
     "two soul mothers." But I don't think he has much to thank
     them for. Ekdal's misfortune is that in his own circle he has
     always been looked upon as a shining light.

GREGERS: Not without reason, surely. Look at the depth of his mind!

RELLING: I have never discovered it. That his father believed in it I
     don't so much wonder; the old lieutenant has been an ass all
     his days.

The passage from *The School for Scandal* contains numerous generalized or indefinite words and a variety of sentence types. The sentences are long and include an assortment of dependent and independent clauses. The tempo of the dialogue is comparatively slow and measured. In the selection from *The Wild Duck*, there is a greater percentage of concrete words, fewer different types of sentences, and shorter sentences with fewer dependent and independent clauses. The dialogue in the second passage also shows occasional broken sentences, missing links, and non-standard grammar. The characters speak rapidly, and the stresses are crowded together unevenly ("Oh, individuality—he!"). The kinds of sentences in the first passage reveal that Rowley and Sir Peter disagree in a reasonable and gentlemanly manner. The sentences in the second selection show that Gregers and Dr. Relling disagree with more emotion. Also notice that in both selections the important information normally comes at the end of a sentence. Of course here we're comparing an English play with a Norwegian play translated into English, but the practical consequences still apply. Most plays in the United States are read and performed in English. Actors obviously must attend to the features of the sentences in the English translation they are using.

Rhythm
Prose rhythm is a challenge to analyze. Although there is no reliable method for objectively measuring the rhythm of prose sentences, rhythm probably plays a large part in producing emotional effects. Scanning sentences for rhythm in the manner of poetry may not be a very valuable exercise if it is practiced for very long. The rhythmic sound of prose sentences must be heard to be appreciated. It's probably better for play readers to get into the habit of reading aloud. Oral reading allows for hearing the difference between harmonious and clashing rhythms and between agreeable and awkward sound combinations.

For illustrative purposes, try to scan the rhythm of a prose passage and compare it with the two selections just examined. Now turn to this famous prose speech from *Hamlet* that has been scanned for rhythmical accents. Stressed words are underlined and rhythmic pauses are indicated by double bars.

HAMLET: <u>Speak</u> the <u>speech,</u> // I <u>pray</u> you, // as I <u>pronounc'd</u> it to you, // <u>trippingly</u> on the tongue; // but if you <u>mouth</u> it, // as many of our <u>players</u> do, // I had as lief the <u>town crier</u> spoke my lines. // Nor do not saw the <u>air</u> too much with your <u>hand</u>, // <u>thus,</u> // but use all <u>gently</u>; // for in the very <u>torrent</u>, // <u>tempest</u>, // and, as I may say, <u>whirlwind</u> of your <u>passion</u>, // you must acquire and beget a <u>temperance</u> // that may give it <u>smoothness</u>. // O, it <u>offends</u> me to the <u>soul</u> // to hear a <u>robustious periwig-pated fellow</u> // <u>tear</u> a passion to <u>tatters</u>, // to very <u>rags</u>, // to <u>split</u> the ears of the <u>groundlings</u>, // who, // for the most part, // are capable of <u>nothing</u> // but inexplicable <u>dumb shows</u> and <u>noise</u>. // I would have such a fellow <u>whipp'd</u> for o'erdoing <u>termagent</u>; // it out-herods <u>Herod</u>. // Pray you // <u>avoid</u> it. //

For comparison, here is a prose selection from *Death of a Salesman*:

BIFF: I am not a <u>leader of men</u>, Willy, // and neither are <u>you</u>. // You were never anything but a <u>hard-working drummer</u> // who landed in the <u>ash can</u> // like all the <u>rest of them</u>! // I'm <u>one dollar an hour</u>, Willy! // I tried <u>seven states</u> // and couldn't <u>raise it</u>. // A <u>buck an hour</u>! // Do you <u>gather my meaning</u>! // I'm <u>not</u> bringing home any <u>prizes</u> anymore, // and you're going to <u>stop waiting</u> for me to <u>bring them home</u>! //

There may be other ways to scan these passages, but at least this way shows how certain important words are stressed. In this last selection, the rhythmic sound is different from the prose passages that were examined earlier. The language in *Hamlet* is formally rhetorical like that in *The School for Scandal*, but it is clearly more lyrical than its eighteenth-century counterpart. When the formal rhythms of *Hamlet* are compared to the irregular rhythms of the sentences from *Death of a Salesman*, the contrast is even more striking. The sentences in all three speeches require a precise sense of rhythm from the actors to express their musical potential completely.

SPEECHES

Routine stage speech uses short, simple sentences, sometimes broken or telegraphic, but the extra expressiveness required when speaking about misfortunes, adversities, or key ideas demands longer strings of sentences. Dramatic dialogue becomes more intense when certain crucial questions are discussed. Accordingly dramatic speeches must be treated carefully. Their punctuation, linking, internal organization, and relationship to adjacent dialogue can communicate meaning almost as powerfully do the words themselves. Despite appearances, stage speeches are not just pure emotional expression but instead purposely orchestrated to achieve dramatic effects.

Punctuation

Each punctuation mark has distinctive suggestions requiring for correct interpretation both comprehension from readers and special intonations from actors. Periods, commas, exclamation and question marks, ellipses, and single and double dashes all have distinctive meanings. The vocal drop which normally accompanies a period indicates the end of a thought or feeling. The vocal rise of a question mark demands a reply. Commas and semicolons are warnings that call for pauses of certain durations. A colon demands our attention to what follows it. An exclamation mark signals approval or disagreement. Dashes indicate an interrupted thought. Ellipses hint at something left unsaid. Director and Shakespeare scholar B. Iden Payne often reminded students that punctuation in dramatic dialogue was not only grammatical, but also *dramatical*. By this he meant that playwrights employ punctuation not solely for reasons of good grammar but also to signal dramatic action. Notice the difference, for example, between the punctuation in Shakespeare's original quartos and the later editions compiled by scholars. The emotional connotations related to punctuation are meant to help actors feel the texture of the dialogue more vividly.

We might study this passage from *A Raisin in the Sun* for a profitable illustration of the expressive use of punctuation. Readers will recall that Walter Younger is bitter over his friend Willy's theft of the $10,000 in insurance money Walter was planning to use to buy a liquor store. In an effort to replace the money, Walter has cynically agreed to accept a payoff to keep his family from moving into a white neighborhood. This deeply humiliates both Walter and his family.

WALTER: What's the matter with you all! I didn't make this world! It was give to me this way! Hell, yes, I want me some yachts someday! Yes, I want to hang some real pearls 'round my wife's neck. Ain't she supposed to wear pearls? Somebody tell me--, who decides which women is suppose to wear pearls in this world. I tell you I am a man--and I think my wife should wear pearls in this world!

MAMA: Baby, how you going to feel on the inside?

WALTER: Fine! . . . Going to feel fine . . . a man . . .

MAMA: You won't have nothing left then, Walter Lee.

WALTER: I'm going to feel fine, Mama. I'm going to look that son-of-a-bitch in the eyes and say--and say, "All right, Mr. Lindner --that's your neighborhood out there. You got the right to keep it like you want. You got the right to have it like you want. Just write the check and--the house is yours." And, and I am going to say--And you--you people just put the money in my hand and you won't have to live next to this bunch of stinking niggers! . . . Maybe--maybe I'll just get down on my black knees . . . Captain, Mistuh, Bossman. A-hee-hee-hee! Yassssuh! Great White Father, just gi' ussen de money, fo' God's sake, and we's ain't gwine come out deh and dirty up yo' white folks neighborhood . . .

To point up the emotion in this passage, Lorraine Hansberry has used exclamation points, commas, ellipses, and dashes (plus folk speech and prose rhythm) in highly dramatic fashion. As Walter reveals more and more of his deepest feelings, each punctuation mark becomes more meaningful. The exclamation points in the first line indicate his open anger. At the word *man,* he begins to hesitate, and his speech becomes increasingly halting and agitated. He falters several times during the last speech as the profound humiliation of his decision settles into his consciousness. His voice breaks, he stumbles and falls to his knees. Then he completely breaks down. The speech ends with an embarrassing silence. Hansberry has provided expressive punctuation in the dialogue to emphasize the stages in the progression of Walter's thoughts and feelings.

Linking

The idea of linking comes naturally after sentences and punctuation. We know from composition classes that linking in prose is performed by antecedents and tenses, phrases and clauses, and other forms of backward and forward reference to knit sentences firmly together. Linking is a basic principle of prose writing. When there is no linking or when it is poorly done, meaning falters. Linking is also an important feature of dramatic dialogue because it helps maintain the feeling of forward motion necessary for good dramatic structure. Moreover dialogue linking is one of the basic principles of line-to-line communication between characters, which some writers call *reciprocation* or *communion.*

Dramatic dialogue generally uses distinctive thoughts or words to link the lines together. Ordinarily, the method is one complete idea to a line or speech with the last thought of one line suggesting the first one for the next line. This is not a rigid rule, but whenever something intrudes to break the connection, it will ordinarily have a special dramatic purpose. The following excerpt shows effective dialogue linking in *The School for Scandal.* In this scene, Snake has just reported to Lady Sneerwell that he successfully managed to place scandalous reports about Charles Surface in the newspapers. Lady Sneerwell and Charles were once lovers. Now she wishes to win Charles back by discrediting him with the woman he currently loves. Charles' brother, Joseph Surface, joins the scene. Careful reading will show how the final words in each line suggest the initial words in the succeeding line.

JOSEPH SURFACE: My dear Lady Sneerwell, how do you do today? Mr.
        Snake, your most obedient.

LADY SNEERWELL: Snake has just been teasing me on our mutual attach-
        ment; but I have informed him of our real views. You know how
        useful he has been to us; and believe me, the confidence is
        not ill placed.

JOSEPH SURFACE: Madam, it is impossible for me to suspect a man of
        Mr. Snake's sensibility and discernment.

LADY SNEERWELL: Well, well, no compliments now; but tell me when you
        saw your mistress, Maria--or, what is more material to me,
        your brother.

JOSEPH SURFACE: I have not seen either since I left you; but I can inform you that they never meet. Some of your stories have taken good effect on Maria.

LADY SNEERWELL: Ah, my dear Snake! the merit of this belongs to you. But do your brother's distresses increase?

JOSEPH SURFACE: Every hour. I am told he has had another summons from the court yesterday. In short, his dissipation and extravagance exceed anything I have ever heard of.

LADY SNEERWELL: Poor Charles!

JOSEPH SURFACE: True, madam; notwithstanding his vices one can't help feeling for him. Poor Charles! I'm sure I wish it were in my power to be of any essential service to him; for the man who does not share in the distresses of a brother, even though merited by his own misconduct, serves--

LADY SNEERWELL: O Lud! you are going to be moral and forget that you are among friends.

JOSEPH SURFACE: Egad, that's true! I'll keep that sentiment till I see Sir Peter. However, it is certainly a charity to rescue Maria from such a libertine, who, if he is to be reclaimed, can be so only by a person of your ladyship's superior accomplishments and understanding.

SNAKE: I believe, Lady Sneerwell, here's company coming. I'll go and copy the letter I mentioned to you. Mr. Surface, your most obedient.

JOSEPH SURFACE: Sir, your very devoted.

It will be worth the effort to study this excerpt closely. Sheridan's dialogue is a model of skillful conventional linking. Each line connects firmly but inconspicuously with the line before and the line following. The conversation progresses smoothly from one topic to the next without any breaks in logic or feeling. The two lines that show no verbal links are linked by non-verbal means. Lady Sneerwell's expression—"Poor Charles!"—seems to end her line abruptly before furnishing a link with Joseph Surface's next line. The two lines are actually bound together by the unspoken thought of Lady Sneerwell's love for Charles. The dramatist expects the actors to provide a facial expression, gesture, or stage business to fill the pause. At first glance, Snake's line announcing the arrival of visitors also seems unlinked; however, the off-stage sounds of guests approaching provides the link here.

We have seen that linking isn't always expressed verbally in the dialogue. This is particularly true in modern plays where verbal expression is frequently less important than physical expression of feelings. Much of the dialogue in *Streamers,* for example, seems to skip from one line to another in an unlinked fashion. In performance, the dramatist expects actors and directors to search the given circumstances for appropriate physical action to provide the links.

Internal Arrangement

Just as dramatists orchestrate complications and crises leading to a climax so also they arrange the internal dynamics of speeches to achieve the strongest effects. Most speeches build toward a climax; they may do so, however, in different ways. The start may be bold, as in the previous example from *A Raisin in the Sun,* or the beginning may be a low-conflict point of departure. A resting point often occurs somewhere in the middle of a long speech, followed by the final progression to the climax at the end. Sometimes the climax may be followed by a simple, quiet close. Of course, the actor's interpretation can never be overlooked, but in any event, the inner orchestration of a speech is chiefly governed by writing considerations.

Arthur Miller arranged Linda's final speech by Willy's gravesite at the close of *Death of a Salesman* in skillful climactic fashion. The speech intensifies as it builds toward the end.

```
LINDA:  Forgive me, dear, I can't cry. I don't know what it is, but I
        can't cry. I don't understand it. Why did you ever do that?
        Help me, Willy, I can't cry. It seems to me that you're just
        on another trip. I keep expecting you. Willy, dear, I can't
        cry. Why did you do it? I search and search and I search, and
        I can't understand it, Willy. I made the last payment on the
        house today. Today, dear. And there'll be nobody home. (A sob
        rises in her throat.) We're free and clear. (sobbing more
        fully, released) We're free. (BIFF comes slowly toward her.)
        We're free . . . We're free . . .
```

Linda's speech begins quietly, then builds to a small crest ("Willy, dear, I can't cry"). After a brief emotional rest, the intensity builds once again to a final peak of emotion ("We're free and clear"), then it ends with a simple, quiet close ("We're free . . .").

External Arrangement

Chapter 3 explained how scenes are types of dramatic progressions that are structured like miniature plays. Now let's analyze the inner workings of a scene to learn how the speeches themselves also build to peaks of emotional intensity. The climax of *Death of a Salesman* is the confrontation between Willy and Biff that occurs near the end of the play. In this scene, Biff finally summons the courage to challenge his father's opinion of him. This is the *obligatory scene* that the entire play prepared us to expect. Prior to this moment, the dramatist already stockpiled a large inventory of dramatic tension in the earlier scenes. He created the necessary suspense by revealing information about Willy and Biff's relationship in small increments and by inserting scenes involving the other characters.

The scene begins when Biff comes into the backyard and informs Willy that he is leaving home for good. Biff is trying to appear calm, but he is withholding his real feelings because he doesn't want another argument with his father. Willy is preoccupied at this point and doesn't fully understand what Biff is saying anyway. The tension accumulates in the next unit. They go into the house together, and Biff tells his mother of his plans in the same controlled manner. Then Biff extends his hand to Willy to say goodbye, and the first emotional eruption occurs as Willy refuses to acknowledge Biff's gesture. When Linda tries to intervene, Willy curses Biff and refuses to accept any personal blame for his son's failure. At this point, Biff can't hold back his feelings any longer, and he decides to challenge Willy openly: "All right, phony! Then let's lay it on the line." Then Biff shows the rubber hose that Willy planned to use to commit suicide by connecting it to the gas line from the water heater. This is the second emotional eruption in the scene. When Happy tries to stop him, Biff turns on his brother, mocking his dream of becoming a successful businessman. As Willy grows more disturbed and Happy and Linda begin to panic, suddenly Biff turns on Willy and savagely denounces him: "I never got anywhere because you blew me so full of hot air I could never stand taking orders from anybody!" When Willy still doesn't understand what is happening, Biff explodes into a long speech of self-reproach. It almost seems as if Biff is going to attack Willy: "Pop, I'm nothing! I'm nothing, Pop!" but then he collapses against his father and completely breaks down. This is the major climax of the play. Finally, Willy begins to understand: "What're you doing? Why is he crying?" Biff struggles to contain himself, pulls away, and moves to the stairs. "I'll go in the morning" he says to Linda, "Put him—put him to bed," and he goes to his room. After a long pause, Willy says quietly "Isn't that—isn't that remarkable? Biff likes me!"

Of course this is only one example of how a very good playwright orchestrates the emotional peaks and valleys in one scene to build a climax. Others arrange the climaxes in their plays in different ways to suit their own characters and situations. Moreover readers should never overlook the important interpretive contributions to a scene that the actors, director, and designers can make. Studying the orchestrated arrangement of speeches in climactic scenes can provide practical artistic information about playable values.

SPECIAL QUALITIES

From the preceding discussion it should be obvious that understanding theatrical dialogue involves meticulous attention to words, sentences, and speeches. Appreciation is increased further when we can also recognize whether the dialogue has special literary beauties of its own. Dialogue that inconspicuously states the facts of the plot, characters, and idea may be no more than workmanlike and agreeable. Playwrights who feel strongly about this issue have always tried to make their dialogue attractive in itself. Some have tried to superimpose appealing qualities onto their dialogue like frosting on a cake. Occasionally they have succeeded, at least for their immediate audiences. Mostly they have failed because the added qualities did not arise logically from the characters and situations. Many dramatists are artists in words as well as actions and characters. They have a strong love for the subtleties of language.

To understand how dialogue can be inherently attractive, consider the following questions. Is the dialogue poetic? Does it simply reveal the basic facts in a practical way, or does it also display a distinctive literary style? Does the dialogue contain colorful idiomatic speech? Not every analysis needs to deal extensively with these topics, but most plays require at least some understanding of the potential literary appeal of the dialogue.

Poetry

Anyone who is serious about the theatre can't help being interested in the dramatic possibilities of poetry. Since most of us are not used to reading poetic dialogue, however, many of its dramatic possibilities tend to be overlooked. Prose dialogue, for all its potential intricacy, runs primarily straight ahead. Poetry, on the other hand, is always calling up associations from within itself, a practice that complicates and enriches its pattern of sound and meaning. Moreover prose dialogue chiefly reveals plot, character, and idea, while in poetic plays, there is additional pleasure in the dialogue as literature. It simply sounds pleasant. There is no need to spend time here discussing the long catalog of literary devices that can be found in poetry. Play readers should at least be aware that poetic dialogue has many more expressive resources at its command than does unadorned prose.

Theoretically poetic plays should be potentially more exciting than are their prose counterparts. Their emotional peaks and valleys are more vivid, and they contain more obvious rhythmic feelings. This is true for poetic dialogue as well as for poetic plays as a whole. Short extracts from two plays will illustrate this. One is formally poetic, the other written in poetic prose. The first selection is from Act IV, Scene 7, of *Hamlet*. King Claudius and Laertes have just been plotting to murder Hamlet when Queen Gertrude enters with news of Ophelia's suicide. We'll explain in a moment why the plot lines are in bold print.

```
QUEEN:    One woe doth tread upon another's heel.
          So fast they follow.
                    Your sister's drown'd, Laertes.

LAERTES:  Drown'd?
                    O, where?

QUEEN:    There is a willow grows ascant the brook
          That shows his hoar leaves in the glassy stream;
          Therewith fantastic garlands did she make
          Of cornflowers, nettles, daisies, and long purples
          That liberal shepherds give a grosser name,
          But our cold maids do dead men's fingers call them.

          There, on the pendant boughs her cornet weeds
          Clamb'ring to hang, an envious sliver broke;
          When down her weedy trophies and herself
          Fell in the weeping brook.

                    Her clothes spread wide,
          And, mermaid-like, awhile they bore her up;
          Which time she chanted snatches of old lauds,
          As one incapable of her own distress,
          Or like a creature native and imbued
          Unto that element;
                         but long it could not be
          Till that her garments, heavy with their drink,
          Pull'd the poor wretch from her melodious lay
          To muddy death.

LAERTES:  Alas, then she is drown'd!

QUEEN:    Drown'd, drown'd.
```

The passage develops in seven stages: (1) the Queen's distress, (2) the news of Ophelia's death, (3) where it happened and what she was doing there, (4) her collapse into the water, (5) how she sang as her clothes held her up, (6) how she finally drowned, and (7) Laertes' emphatic grief. As the bold print shows, the bare plot information could have been conveyed using only 40 words, yet Shakespeare has provided over 100 additional words to convey the feelings and thoughts that Ophelia's suicide calls up in the characters. We could further analyze the literary features of this passage, but no written description can do justice to its lyrical beauty. For complete expression, it must be performed by an actress who has a sense of its music as well as its drama. Incidentally although this passage contains highly polished and refined poetry, the same literary principles pertain to poetry that is intentionally poor. Doggerel or negligent grammar or syntax can be as dramatically revealing in poetry as is the good-bad prose speech we discussed earlier.

The tradition of poetry has not completely disappeared from the modern theatre. In the last 100 years, individual playwrights have repeatedly made attempts to achieve in the theatre the expressive feelings of which poetry is capable. Some authors, like William Butler Yeats, T.S. Elliot, and Maxwell Anderson, returned to writing explicitly poetic dialogue. Others, like August Strindberg, Eugene O'Neill, Tennessee Williams, Samuel Beckett, and Sam Shepard have written prose that can be as expressive as poetry. Modern poetic prose dialogue doesn't conform to historical rules; its poetic flavor is exclusively its own. It is poetic in the sense of how it is used in the play and from its context, not necessarily from its content or form.

A few lines from *Happy Days* will illustrate. Throughout the play Winnie is physically entrapped in a wasteland, isolated from human contact. She passes the time mainly with trivial activities in the hope that her life will somehow improve. Among the objects in her handbag is a revolver. This is how an excerpt early in the play is printed in the script:

```
WINNIE: But something tells me, do not overdo the bag, Winnie, make
        use of it of course, let it help you . . . along when stuck,
        by all means, but cast your mind forward, something tells me,
        cast your mind forward, Winnie, to the time when words must
        fail--(Pause. She turns to look at the bag.)--and do not
        overdo the bag.
```

Winnie, of course, is elliptically debating her own suicide. In view of the dramatic context, her everyday words, her pantomime, even her imperfect grammar and syntax, can all reveal important meanings in this passage. In fact, it would be instructive to recast it as a free verse poem about the futility of hope.

```
But something tells me,
Do not overdo the bag, Winnie,
Make use of it, of course,
Let it help you . . . along,
When stuck,
By all means,

But cast your mind forward,
```

```
Something tells me,
Cast your mind forward, Winnie,
To the time when words must fail--
And do not overdo the bag.
```

One of the distinctive rhythmical features of this passage is Beckett's way of repeating a simple phrase, bouncing it in the air like a ball. Besides repetition, the speech also employs a large number of other formal literary devices. This points up once again the difficulty of dealing with poetic speech of any kind in the modern theatre. We understand that dialogue should never be considered exclusively as literature, yet in many cases it is written as much for sound as it is for sense.

Charm

Still another value of dialogue is its inherent capacity to please through wit, irony, gracefulness, or surprise. For lack of a better term, we might call these qualities collectively *charm*. The prose dialogue of many dramatists appeals to the imagination, the appreciation of beauty, and the sense of humor in this way. Some of the most attractive qualities of *The School for Scandal*, for example, are the clever remarks and graceful turns of phrase made by the characters. The large measure of ironic humor in *The Wild Duck* is one reason this early realistic play sustains its appeal for contemporary audiences. Brecht may be a social dramatist, but the surprising literary inversions ("How can you have morality without a war?") and musical interludes found in *Mother Courage* are very important parts of its continued appeal. We remember the words as well as the characters and situations in these plays partly because of the charming qualities of the dialogue.

Dialects and Accents

Dialects have similar theatrical appeal. The regional and folk dialects of Brooklyn, the South, New England, and Appalachia, as well as those of various ethnic cultures, have all enriched our American language. The accents of native Germans, Swedes, Italians, Russians, Latin Americans, French, Japanese, Chinese, and recently various Asians and Africans are also attractive to the ear. The theatrical appeal of these dialects and accents comes from our musical appreciation of their colorful pronunciations, imaginative word choices, and affecting speech rhythms. Playwrights Eugene O'Neill, Bertolt Brecht, Arthur Miller, Tennessee Williams, Lorraine Hansberry, and David Rabe, to name only a few, have shown skill in using these speech qualities. Dialects and accents enhance plausibility, aid in rapid recognition of given circumstances, and provide additional opportunities for emotional expression.

THEATRICALITY

Besides strictly literary features, dialogue also possesses theatrical qualities. This doesn't imply the sensational, the melodramatic, or the artificial, it refers to those effects that are achieved only through the actors and the production values. Any reader with average intelligence can find literary meanings on a printed page, but it takes a special kind of experience to perceive the latent action, emotion, and subtext that is present in dramatic dialogue. This kind of perception depends on dramatic as well as literary imagination.

Action

It's hard to think of dialogue without also considering physical action as an expressive aid. As was explained earlier, an important quality of dialogue is its ability to convey stage or indigenous business. Lorraine Hansberry has provided a great deal of such business directly in the dialogue of *A Raisin in the Sun*. Mama's first appearance in Act I offers a good illustration. The scene is morning; everyone is getting ready for the day's activities.

MAMA: Who that 'round here slamming doors at this hour.

RUTH: That was Walter Lee. He and Bennie was at it again.

MAMA: My children and they tempers. Lord, if this little old plant don't get some more sun than it's been getting it ain't never going to see spring again. What's the matter with you this morning, Ruth? You looks right peaked. You aiming to iron all them things? Leave some for me. I'll get to 'em this after-noon. Bennie, honey, it's too drafty for you to be sitting around half dressed. Where's your robe?

BENEATHA: In the cleaners.

MAMA: Well, go and get mine and put it on.

BENEATHA: I'm not cold, Mama, honest.

MAMA: I know--but you so thin . . .

BENEATHA: Mama, I'm not cold.

MAMA: (*Seeing the make-down sofa-bed as young TRAVIS has left it.*) Lord have mercy, look at that poor bed. Bless his heart--he tries, don't he.

RUTH: No--he don't half try at all 'cause he knows you going to come along behind him and fix everything.

The author has provided a busy round of activities for Mama in this short selection of dialogue. During these ten lines, Mama briskly enters the room to begin her daily chores: she waters the plant in the kitchen, she moves to help Ruth with her ironing, she crosses to Bennie at the table and fusses over her clothing. Then she closes the window, moves to the sofa bed and begins straightening the covers. These activities quickly characterize Mama as an energetic, hard-working person who always thinks of others first. Some of the actions are directly stated, others implied. Alert readers can probably recognize additional illustrative actions in her lines.

Pantomime like we have just seen has become increasingly important in modern drama. Much of Winnie's role in *Happy Days* consists of pantomime that Beckett orchestrated with considerable care. Since Winnie herself hardly moves in the entire play, her pantomime with the small objects becomes an important expressive accompaniment to her dialogue. Some professional actors, directors, and designers possess astonishing skill in discovering appropriate interpretive action to accompany the dialogue. Readers should be alert for any opportunities for intensifying the dialogue by use of direct or latent illustrative action.

We already know that action in dramatic dialogue also means something more than physical activity. In the following selection from *Tartuffe*, there is no obvious physical action stated or implied, but the moment is comical in performance because of the contrasting patterns of dramatic actions or behavioral tactics. Orgon has just returned from a visit to the country. He interrogates the servant Dorine about Tartuffe's welfare while he was away.

ORGON: Has everything gone well the few days I've been away? What have you been doing? How is everyone?

DORINE: The day before yesterday the mistress was feverish all day. She had a dreadful headache.

ORGON: And Tartuffe?

DORINE: Tartuffe? He's very well: hale and hearty; in the pink.

ORGON: Poor fellow!

DORINE: In the evening she felt faint and couldn't touch anything, her headache was so bad.

ORGON: And Tartuffe?

DORINE: He supped with her. She ate nothing but he very devoutly devoured a couple of partridges and half a hashed leg of mutton.

ORGON: Poor fellow!

DORINE: She never closed her eyes all through the night. She was too feverish to sleep and we had to sit up with her until morning.

ORGON: And Tartuffe?

DORINE: Feeling pleasantly drowsy, he went straight to his room, jumped into a nice warm bed, and slept like a top until morning.

ORGON: Poor fellow!

DORINE: Eventually she yielded to our persuasions, allowed herself to be bled, and soon felt much relieved.

ORGON: And Tartuffe?

DORINE: He dutifully kept up his spirits, and took three or four good swigs of wine at breakfast to fortify himself against the worst that might happen and to make up for the blood the mistress had lost.

ORGON: Poor fellow!

This moment requires a certain amount of simple staging as Orgon takes off his coat and hat, sets down his traveling bag, and pursues Dorine around the stage with his questions. The physical action would probably not generate much interest, however, without Orgon's continuous questions about the welfare of Tartuffe. They are as comically unexpected as they are persistent.

Emotion

Another important function of dialogue is the expression of emotion. Characters don't just state the facts; they also express their feelings toward conditions they feel strongly about. The most highly emotional dialogue is often a free release of feelings stemming from an open clash of wills. Molière has provided a tense emotional encounter like this between Orgon and his son Damis in *Tartuffe*. Damis has discovered Tartuffe seducing Elmire. He thinks his father will renounce Tartuffe when he finds out, but Tartuffe outwits him. By frankly admitting the charge, Tartuffe appears to Orgon to be selflessly taking the blame for Damis' slander. Thus Orgon misinterprets Damis' accusation and turns his anger on his son instead.

ORGON: (*to DAMIS*) Doesn't your heart relent, you dog!

DAMIS: What! Can what he says so far prevail with you that . . .

ORGON: Silence, you scoundrel! (*raising up TARTUFFE*) Rise, brother--I beg you. (*to his son*) You scoundrel!

DAMIS: He may--

ORGON: Silence!

DAMIS: This is beyond bearing! What! I'm to . . .

ORGON: Say another word and I'll break every bone in your body!

TARTUFFE: In God's name, brother, calm yourself. I would rather suffer any punishment than he should receive the slightest scratch on my account.

ORGON: (*to his son*) Ungrateful wretch!

TARTUFFE: Leave him in peace! If need be, I'll ask your pardon for him on my knees . . .

ORGON: (*to TARTUFFE*) Alas! What are you thinking of? (*to his son*) See how good he is to you, you dog!

DAMIS: Then I . . .

ORGON: Enough!

DAMIS: What! Can't I . . .

ORGON: Enough, I say!

Tartuffe, Orgon, and Damis come into open conflict at this moment. They almost get into a brawl, yet their apparent loss of self-control is very deliberately orchestrated for them in the dialogue. Molière has skillfully written accusations and counter-accusations, epithets, connotative words, and broken sentences to accent their strong feelings.

We explained before how dialogue can narrate and explain ideas. Characters under stress, however, rarely stop to describe and analyze their thoughts and feelings. Such dialogue is seldom a cool academic debate. Instead it must reveal the strong emotions the characters feel for the practical outcome of their ideas. In *The Wild Duck* when Dr. Relling scoffs at Gregers Werle's idealistic image of Hjalmar Ekdal, he does so with feeling. He believes Gregers is ruining other people's lives with his meddlesome brand of idealism. Relling is not just debating abstract ideas here, he's talking about the welfare of his own friends.

GREGERS: (*indignantly*) Is it Hjalmar Ekdal you are talking about in this strain?

RELLING: Yes, with your permission; I am simply giving you an inside view of the idol you are groveling before.

GREGERS: I should hardly have thought I was quite stone-blind.

RELLING: Yes, you are--or not far from it. You are a sick man, too, you see.

GREGERS: You are right there.

RELLING: Yes. Yours is a complicated case. First of all, there is that plague of integrity fever, and then--what's worse--you are always in a delirium of hero worship; you must always have something to adore, outside yourself.

GREGERS: Yes, I must certainly seek it outside myself.

RELLING: But you make such a shocking mistake about every new phoenix you think you have discovered.

. . .

GREGERS: If you don't think better than that of Hjalmar Ekdal, what pleasure can you find in being everlastingly with him?

RELLING: Well, you see, I'm supposed to be a sort of a doctor--God help me! I have to give a hand to the poor sick people who live under the same roof with me.

Relling may be an intellectual, but he is not the coldhearted cynic Gregers thinks he is. He originally chose to be a doctor because he wanted to help people in a practical way. His sympathy for the suffering of others shows in the strong emotions of this passage. For Dr. Relling as for other characters who speak about their most cherished beliefs, ideas have practical consequences.

Subtext

Some plays reveal plot, character, and idea mainly through their words. Much of their beauty can be found in their *texts,* the actual structure of words in the dialogue. The words provide most of the thoughts the author considers necessary for the characters. The acting, directing, and design are bonded to the text, and the basis of their theatrical effectiveness is largely contained in it. Many of these are excellent plays, yet in the theatre, the spoken word is not always as valuable in itself. Sometimes it is the unspoken *subtext* that is the primary basis of theatricality.

Subtext consists of the unspoken words that run directly beneath the dialogue. It is one of Stanislavski's most widely honored contributions to the study of plays, and it stems from two basic premises. First characters actually speak only a small percentage of what they are thinking. Second a point-to-point correspondence exists between what the characters are saying and what they are thinking. Subtext is much more than simply reading between the lines; it is a carefully defined technical feature. In many plays, it is not enough to study the dialogue alone; knowledge of the specific subtext is necessary to energize the dialogue and make it theatrical. Success depends on the vocal intonations, facial expressions, gestures, and illustrative actions that can only be provided by acting the subtext along with the text. One of the reader's serious tasks is to define the subtext with certainty so that it may take explicit form in production.

Certain writers extend the definition of subtext to include all the thoughts and feelings not expressed in the dialogue as well as the shape of the plot and the patterns of the imagery—in other words the entire inner life of the play. Chapter 6 referred to this concept as the second plan or inner structure. There is no need to impose a standard vocabulary, but knowing the distinction can be useful sometimes in the rehearsal hall.

Subtext plays an important role in *The Wild Duck*. Not much of a physical nature happens in the play. There are none of the big scenes we traditionally associate with the stage. The major confrontations between Gregers and his father, Hjalmar and Gina, and Gregers and Relling are brief and relatively subdued, not climactic in the usual sense. Even Hedvig's death occurs off stage; we only see its effects on the characters afterward. The real drama is expressed chiefly through acting the subtext. Uncovering the subtext means close reading for all evidence of conflicts, in this case those conflicts involving Gregers and Hjalmar. It's particularly important to understand Gregers' relationship with his father, who he believes was responsible for his mother's death. A large part of Gregers' so-called mission in life is to punish his father for this. Most of the information comes out frankly in the background story, which Ibsen scholar P.D.F. Tennant has shown to be among the most intricate in all of the dramatist's plays. *The Wild Duck* becomes truly dramatic, however, only when its subtext is fully expressed by the actors.

Subtext is not restricted to modern plays. An enlightening example is provided by Stanislavski himself from the production of Tartuffe described in Toporkov's *Stanislavski in Rehearsal*. The passage happens to be the same one between Orgon and Dorine used earlier in this chapter in the discussion of action. It won't be reproduced here, but readers can consult Toporkov's book if they wish. In the context of a rehearsal, Stanislavski furnishes fresh and imaginative subtext for each line to help the actors find and express the latent humor. Actors and directors will find his comments about subtext worth their attention.

SUMMARY

Dramatic dialogue is a very austere form of writing. Normally it is denied any type of expressiveness that is not exclusively devoted to the practical workings of the play. Even when dialogue employs special literary qualities of its own, they cannot appear to be artificially applied. From beginning to end, good dialogue is crafted so that each line advances the action, adding to the harmony and strength of the whole play.

Readers can be very successful at detailed analysis of dialogue because *at the table* there is enough time and concentration available to do so. Closely studying the nature of dramatic dialogue, however, should not be cause to overlook its fundamental role. Drama is in danger when too much theoretical interest is taken in language or when language becomes a constant subject of meditation. If theatre is really to happen, language must be an integral part of it, not independent from it. It is important to understand the dialogue, but it is necessary to guard against thinking too much about it. Dramatists are generally more concerned with what they have to say than with the way they say it.

QUESTIONS

Words: Does the dialogue frequently employ abstract words? Concrete words? Formal words? Informal words? Do any of the characters specifically do so? Are there any examples of professional jargon or slang? Are there a large number of words that convey more than their dictionary meanings (connotations)? If so, who speaks them? What associations do the words suggest?

Sentences: How long is the average sentence in the play? Does anyone speak sentences that are obviously longer or shorter than the average? What types of sentences are represented? Are the types of sentences generally similar, or is there a variety of sentence types? Do any characters speak in distinctive types of sentences? What do the sentences in the play sound like? Is their rhythm special or unusual in any way?

Speeches: Is punctuation strictly grammatical, or is it also used for dramatic purposes? Can examples of dramatic punctuation be cited? How are the speeches linked to one another? By words? Thoughts? Is verbal linking present in all the lines? Are there any examples of dialogue linking by means of action? How are the sentences dramatically arranged within the longer speeches? How are the speeches dramatically orchestrated within units and scenes?

Special qualities: Is the dialogue written in verse? If so, what types of verse are represented? Is the dialogue obviously written in carefully composed prose? If so, what makes it special or unusual? Is the dialogue appealing in any other way? If so, how? Are there any examples of dialects or accents? If so, what kinds?

Theatricality: Does the dialogue express physical or psychological action? Is the dialogue highly emotional? If so, how is emotion expressed? Does the dialogue contain a great deal of unspoken inner tension (subtext)? If so, how is it meant to be expressed?

8

· · · · · · · · · ·

Tempo, Rhythm, and Mood

The words tempo, rhythm, and mood are used here to describe a feature Aristotle originally called *music*. Greek tragedies were written in verse, and critics believe that Aristotle's term referred to the metrical cadences of the poetry. He observed that rhythm was capable of projecting feelings, and he concluded that these feelings added to the emotional effect of plays. From this, he deduced that "the music of the language" should be considered one of the six basic elements of drama.

Although not many plays use verse today, they do employ tempos, rhythms, and moods to communicate feelings just as verse and music do. Rhythmical cadences can stimulate overt emotional responses such as laughter, tears, and applause. They can also stimulate more subtle physical responses like breathing, heartbeat, blood pressure, and muscular tension, which we normally associate with the emotions. Whether they acquire their powers from poetry, music, or nature, the features of tempo, rhythm, and mood undoubtedly can convey authentic feelings.

Some might argue that these features cannot be empirically observed in a playscript. They would say that these are metaphysical dimensions that do not represent actual material reality. Others disagree. Psychologist William James maintained that there is no reason to call emotional sensations unreal just because they may be largely unseen. If something produces real effects (and most people would argue that feelings are real), it must be a reality itself. Stanislavski read William James' *Principles of Psychology* and seems to have agreed with him. In his book *Building a Character,* Stanislavski devoted two chapters to defining these features and explaining their importance for actors. Richard Boleslavsky, Georgi Tovstonogov, Alexander Dean, Lawrence Carra, F. Cowles Strickland, F. Curtis Canfield, and Francis Hodge have also written about the empirical aspects of tempo, rhythm, and mood. Apparently there are some objective, teachable elements involved. They are subtle and complex but need to be understood because they help to shape the emotional experience of a play.

Understanding tempo, rhythm, and mood requires wide experience in play reading and production. That's why analyzing them is one of the last stages of table work. Even then a reader will probably not be able to perceive them with much clarity before rehearsals begin. During the preliminary reading phase, tempo, rhythm, and mood may be only minimally there and sometimes only as educated guesswork. It is almost impossible to plan them in advance authoritatively. The production will express these features, but they may emerge very differently in practice than they did at the table. Nevertheless analysis is needed to remove as many confusions as possible and to clarify thinking before rehearsals begin.

TEMPO

First some definitions and distinctions are needed. Timing, speed, pace, tempo, and rhythm are five different but related concepts. They have no precise definitions in the theatre, however, the definitions stated here are for use in this book. *Timing* means the temporal relationship between one spoken word and another or between a spoken word and a physical action. *Speed* is the measurable rate of movement or speech in real time, and *pace* means the spectator's or director's subjective perception of speed emotionally. These three terms deal principally with aspects of time during a live performance. This section and the next concern tempo and rhythm because they stem initially from the script itself.

As has been discussed in earlier chapters, every moment in a good play is aimed at expressing the plot, character, and idea. How these features emerge from within the script has also been examined. *Tempo* refers to how often information about plot, character, and idea occurs in the dialogue, the frequency of information. In this special context, tempo is not related to the usual meanings of velocity or measurable speed but is actually closer to the concept of texture or density. When a sequence of dialogue is crowded with information about plot, character, or idea, the inner tempo is slow because there is a large quantity of information to express. When such information is scarce, the content is thinner (less dense) and the inner tempo is swift because there is less for the mind to dwell on. The questions to ask are, When does the author present important dramatic information? What kind of information is it? Plot? Character? Idea? How much information is there? The answers to these questions according to the definition, describe tempo. Rhythm and its features will be defined later. Now the sources of tempo and tempo patterns are most relevant.

In the Plot

When trying to determine the tempo of the plot, it is instructive to recall that plot unfolds gradually in progressions and that the smallest progressions are called beats. Each beat is devoted to the development of a single limited topic. Ibsen was an excellent craftsman when it came to writing dialogue that expresses the plot in comprehensible beats. In the scene between Gregers and his father near the end of the first act of *The Wild Duck*, the chief dramatic interest is plot. Although revealing a little about the characters through what they talk about and how they treat each other, very few lines express character as such. Only one line in the scene relates candidly to the idea of the play. None contain any special literary qualities (in the English translation at least), and there is very little physical action to speak of.

The scene occurs on stage while the dinner party continues in the background off stage. The plot advances in four stages: (1) Gregers admonishes his father for the decline of the Ekdal family; (2) Gregers threatens to reveal his father's sexual affair with their former housemaid who is now Hjalmar Ekdal's wife; (3) Werle informs Gregers of his engagement to Mrs. Sorby; and (4) Gregers condemns his father and announces his intention to leave home and embark on his life's mission.

The first beat (six lines) establishes Gregers' urgent wish to speak to his father privately.

GREGERS: Father, won't you stay a moment?

WERLE: (*stops*) What is it?

GREGERS: I must have a word with you.

WERLE: Can't it wait until we are alone?

GREGERS: No, it can't, for perhaps we shall never be alone together.

WERLE: (*drawing nearer*) What do you mean by that?

Notice the suspenseful link to the following beat in the last line. Next is a beat of 12 lines, six questions or accusations by Gregers and six reactions or replies by Mr. Werle. We might even call these reactions and replies *sub-beats* because each clearly adds its own small piece of new information about the plot. The entire beat deals with the illegal timber incident, but seven related topics are also treated, each expressed in two or three crisply written lines of dialogue: (1) the decline in the fortunes of the Ekdals, (2) the former friendship between Lieutenant Ekdal and Mr. Werle, (3) their mutual participation in the illegal timber-cutting affair, (4) Ekdal's responsibility in drawing up the fraudulent boundary map, (5) Ekdal's illegal cutting of the timber, (6) Werle's alleged ignorance of Ekdal's actions, and (7) the guilty verdict handed down against Ekdal together with the acquittal of Mr. Werle for lack of evidence. Sub-beats, or conversational topics, are delineated here by a double bar for clarity.

GREGERS: How has that family been allowed to go so miserably to the wall?

WERLE: You mean the Ekdals, I suppose?

GREGERS: Yes, I mean the Ekdals. // Lieutenant Ekdal was once so closely associated with you.

WERLE: Much too closely; I have felt that to my cost for many years. It is thanks to him that I--yes I--have had a kind of slur cast upon my reputation. //

GREGERS: (*softly*) Are you sure that he alone was to blame?

WERLE: Who else do you suppose?

GREGERS: You and he acted together in that affair of the forests--//

WERLE: But was it not Ekdal that drew the map of the tracts we had bought--that fraudulent map! // It was he who felled all the timber illegally on government property. In fact the whole management was in his hands. // I was quite in the dark as to what Lieutenant Ekdal was doing.

GREGERS: Lieutenant Ekdal himself seems to have been very much in the dark as to what he was doing.

WERLE: That may be. // But the fact remains that he was found guilty and I was acquitted.

GREGERS: Yes, I know that nothing was proved against you.

WERLE: Acquittal is acquittal.

Mr. Werle takes the offensive in the next beat. It consists of four new topics expressed in two or three lines each, totaling nine lines: (1) Werle's wish to put the timber affair behind him once and for all, (2) Ekdal's emotional collapse after his release from prison, (3) Werle's attempt to assist Ekdal with money and a job, and (4) Werle's decision not to record this generosity officially in his financial accounts.

WERLE (*continued*): Why do you rake up these old miseries that turned my hair gray before its time? Is that the sort of thing you have been brooding over up there all these years? I can assure you, Gregers, here in the town the whole story has been forgotten long ago--as far as I am concerned. //

GREGERS: But that unhappy Ekdal family--

WERLE: What would you have me do for those people? When Ekdal came out of prison he was a broken man, past all help. There are people in the world who dive to the bottom the moment they get a couple of slugs in their body and never come to the surface again. // You may take my word for it, Gregers, I have done all I could without positively laying myself open to all sorts of suspicion and gossip.

GREGERS: Suspicion? Oh, I see.

WERLE: I have given Ekdal copying work to do for the office, and I pay him far, far more than his work is worth.

GREGERS: (*without looking at him*) H'm; that I don't doubt.

WERLE: You laugh? Do you think I'm not telling you the truth? // Well, I certainly can't refer you to my books, for I never enter payments of that sort.

GREGERS: (*smiles coldly*) No, there are certain payments it is best to keep no account of.

The first unit ends here. In the remainder of the scene, Gregers presses Werle to admit he paid for Hjalmar Ekdal's photography training and helped to set him up in business; Gregers accuses Werle of having an affair with their former housemaid and then conveniently arranging her marriage to Hjalmar Ekdal; Werle accuses Gregers and his deceased mother of neurotically conspiring against him; Werle informs Gregers of his illness and his forthcoming marriage to Mrs. Sorby; Werle offers Gregers a partnership in his firm; Gregers condemns his father's amoral behavior; Gregers announces he has found his mission in life and departs. Because Ibsen's dialogue in this scene is densely packed with detailed plot information, the internal tempo of the plot is slow. It unfolds gradually, piece by piece in very small increments, and each piece adds a little more to understanding the play.

Under most conditions, the tempo of the plot in the script logically determines the *speed* with which the scene is performed. According to this way of thinking, this scene would be performed slowly and deliberately with the actors carefully accentuating everything they say. It is also quite possible, however, that the plot may not need as much emphasis in a modern performance as this early realistic play seems to indicate. After many years of experience with realism, audiences have been conditioned to routinely deal with the complicated background material that is a hallmark of realistic style. This being the case, in the contemporary theatre the scene might be performed faster than it was in the past. Perhaps there would be more emphasis on the tense emotional relationship between Gregers and Werle, possibly building to a climax at the end of the act. Of course, this is a matter of interpretation. Beats that are too long can oversell a topic and weaken the tension. They may have to be performed rapidly to sustain the level of conflict. Beats that are too short may have to be expanded in performance with illustrative action. In either case, the tempo of the plot in the script would remain unchanged.

Compare this scene with the climax of *Death of a Salesman* that was treated in Chapter 8. In that scene, except for Biff's announcement of his intention to leave home for good, neither Biff nor Willy furnish any new information about the plot. Essentially, they repeat in more forceful terms information that each of them expressed earlier in the play in different contexts. The inner tempo of the plot is fast because most of the plot information is already known. Once again, however, the speed of the actual performance will depend on the interpretive considerations of the actors and directors involved.

In the Characters

As seen earlier in this book, many scenes contain material the dramatist has introduced primarily to express character. The key issue for the reader in these situations is whether the dialogue expresses character, and if so, what aspects of character are being presented? Scenes containing considerable character information normally occur near the beginning of a play or when a new and important character first appears.

The dialogue in Sophocles' *Oedipus Rex* presents an instructive example of character tempo in an older historical play. Creon's first appearance occurs in Episode 2. In that scene, Oedipus wishes to learn if Teiresias originally accused him of being Laius' murderer when it was first discovered that Laius was killed many years ago. Most of the scene, however, is devoted to presenting the characters of Creon and Oedipus in contrast with one another. In the first beat, Creon confirms that Oedipus accused him of treason. He explains that the accusation is particularly offensive because he values honor and loyalty above everything else. Character lines are in bold type.

```
CREON:  Men of Thebes:
        I am told that heavy accusations
        Have been brought against me by King Oedipus.
        I am not the kind of man to bear this tamely.

        If in these present difficulties
        He holds me accountable for any harm to him
        Through anything I have said or done--why, then,
        I do not value life in this dishonor.
        It is not as though this rumor touched upon
        Some private indiscretion. The matter is grave.
        The fact is that I am being called disloyal
        To the State, to my fellow citizens, to my friends.
```

In the next beat the Choragos attempts to persuade Creon that Oedipus didn't really mean what he said. He's implying that Oedipus is impetuous and hot-tempered. He's reluctant to say so, however, and this makes Creon impatient. The excuses the Choragos offers to explain Oedipus' behavior reveal as much about his own character as they do about Oedipus.

```
CHORAGOS:  He may have spoken in anger, not from his mind.

CREON:  But did you not hear him say that I was the one
        Who seduced the old prophet into lying?

CHORAGOS:  The thing was said; I do not know how seriously.

CREON:  But you were watching him! Were his eyes steady?
        Did he look like a man in his right mind?

CHORAGOS:                   I do not know.
        I cannot judge the behavior of great men.
```

Oedipus enters in the next unit, whose first beat contains eight balanced lines of dialogue. Oedipus' first five poetic lines simply restate what is already known about the plot. The remainder of the beat is devoted to the expression of character. We see Oedipus' bullheaded pride contrasted with Creon's determination to be reasonable. In the final four lines of dialogue, Oedipus mocks Creon's educated style of speech.

```
OEDIPUS:                  So you dared come back.
        Why? How brazen of you to come to my house,
        You murderer!
                         Do you think I do not know
        That you plotted to kill me, plotted to steal my throne?
        Tell me, in God's name, am I a coward, a fool,
        That you should dream you could accomplish this?
        A fool who could not see your slippery game?
        A coward, not to fight back when I saw it?
        You are the fool, Creon, are you not? hoping
        Without support or friends to get a throne?
        Thrones may be won or bought: you could do neither.

CREON:  Now listen to me. You have talked; let me talk, too.
        You can not judge unless you know the facts.
```

```
OEDIPUS: You speak well: there is one fact; but I find it hard
         To learn from the deadliest enemy I have.

CREON:   That above all I must dispute with you.

OEDIPUS: That above all I will not hear you deny.

CREON:   If you think there is anything good in being stubborn
         Against all reason, then I say you are wrong.

OEDIPUS: If you think a man can sin against his own kind
         And not be punished for it, I say you are mad.

CREON:   I agree.
```

The beat that follows reinforces plot information initially revealed in the previous scene with Teiresias. The next beat returns to character expression. It contains a long speech in which Creon defends himself by explaining his values. Readers should note how he uses carefully arranged rhetorical speech and supports his arguments with epigrams. The final beat is devoted to an exchange of short lines that vividly contrast the two characters.

```
CREON:   But now it is my turn to question you.

OEDIPUS: Put your questions. I am no murderer.

CREON:   First, then: you married my sister?

OEDIPUS:                 I married your sister.

CREON:   And you rule the kingdom equally with her?

OEDIPUS: Everything that she wants she has from me.

CREON:   And am I the third, equal to both of you?

OEDIPUS: That is why I call you a bad friend.

CREON:   No. Reason it out, as I have done.
         Think of this first: Would any sane man prefer
         Power, with all a king's anxieties,
         To that same power and the grace of sleep?
         Certainly not I.
         I have never longed for the king's power--only his rights.
         Would any wise man differ from me in this?
         As matters stand, I have my way in everything
         With your consent, and no responsibilities.
         If I were king, I should be a slave to policy.

         How could I desire a scepter more
         Than what is now mine--untroubled influence?
         No, I have not gone mad; I need no honors,
         Except those with the perquisites I have now.
         I am welcome everywhere; every man salutes me.
         And those who want your favor seek my ear,
         Since I know how to manage what they ask.
         Should I exchange this ease for that anxiety?
         Besides, no sober mind is treasonable.
```

I hate anarchy
And never would deal with any man who likes it.

Test what I have said. Go to the priestess
At Delphi, ask if I quoted her correctly.
And as for this other thing: If I am found
Guilty of treason with Teiresias,
Then sentence me to death! You have my word
It is a sentence I should cast my vote for--
But not without evidence!
                    You do wrong
When you take good men for bad, bad men for good.
A true friend thrown aside--why, life itself
Is not more precious!
                    In time, you will know this well:
For time, and time alone, will show the just man,
Though scoundrels are discovered in a day.

CHORAGOS: This is well said, and a prudent man would ponder it.

OEDIPUS: But is he not quick in his duplicity?
        And shall I not be quick to parry him?
        Would you have me stand still, hold my peace, and let
        This man win everything, through my inaction?

CREON: And you want--what is it, then? To banish me?

OEDIPUS: No, not exile. It is your death I want.
        So that all the world may see what treason means.

CREON: You will persist, then? You will not believe me?

OEDIPUS: How can I believe you?

CREON: Then you are a fool.

OEDIPUS: To save myself?

CREON: In justice, think of me.

OEDIPUS: You are evil incarnate.

CREON: But suppose that you are wrong?

OEDIPUS: Still I must rule.

CREON: But not if you rule badly.

OEDIPUS: O city, city!

CREON: It is my city, too!

The plot tempo in this unit is moderately fast because little is said about the plot that is not already known. The character tempo is slow, however, because so much of the dialogue is devoted to its expression. The stately character tempo and reliance on words instead of illustrative actions are standard playwriting techniques in older period plays. When speaking formally in public or in a court of law, classical conventions often required speakers to establish their credibility by declaring family lineage and personal values. If the beats revealing character seem too long for modern tastes, they might be speeded up and illustrative character business added to supplement the dialogue.

When modern dramatists write dialogue primarily devoted to character expression, they usually do it in short passages. They are also inclined to supplement the dialogue with opportunities for character business. The first entrance of Anna Fierling in *Mother Courage* is a representative case. The plot at this point in the play involves the recruiting sergeant's demand for identity papers, but he has to wait while Anna (Mother Courage) chatters about herself throughout the entire unit. In the first beat, she makes wisecracks about how she got her nickname. In the second one, she jokes about the useless collection of official papers she has accumulated over the years. She also defends her reputation for honest dealing. All this talk is a pure expression of her character. In fact, she reveals almost everything about her character in these 13 lines. Brecht has deliberately created a slow character tempo at this point expressly to introduce this character. He has also provided plenty of opportunities in the dialogue for illustrative actions with props to embellish her character.

In the Idea

When dramatists choose to express idea frankly in words, the tempo slows to conform to the quality and amount of intellectual information being presented. Probably the slowest tempos arising from idea are found in historical plays. In them, it was often the custom to present ideas in long speeches arranged according to classical rhetorical principles. Cleante's initial scene with Orgon in the first act of *Tartuffe*, for example, includes two very long idea speeches (set speeches). Together they contain a total of 25 sentences averaging over 25 words each. Close analysis reveals them to be skillfully written expressions of the central intellectual issues at stake. Whatever the tempos may be elsewhere in the play, the tempo of the idea is slow and deliberate throughout these particular speeches.

Modern dramatists are inclined to integrate talk about ideas more realistically within the character and situation. In *Death of a Salesman*, Miller demonstrates considerable skill at directly presenting ideas in the dialogue without obviously appearing to do so. Occasionally his characters present ideas in the form of epigrams that sound like casual expressions of personal values. Willy offers instructions to his sons: "The man who makes an appearance in the business world, the man who creates personal interest, is the man who gets ahead. Be liked and you will never want." "Start big , and you'll end big." Ben advises Willy: "Never fight fair with a stranger. . . . You'll never get out of the jungle that way." Linda admonishes Biff: "A small man can be just as exhausted as a great man." Charley warns Willy: "When a deposit bottle is broken, you don't get your nickel back." These simple homely expressions aren't meant to slow the tempo of the idea to a halt like Cleante's long speeches. Instead they should slow the tempo only for a moment, like brief retards in music, while they harmonize or counterpoint the central idea of the play.

Chapter 6 showed that epilogues traditionally provide opportunities for the characters to speak candidly about the ideas in the play. Arthur Miller uses an epilogue in *Death of a Salesman* although he calls it a "Requiem." He also provides a funeral to give the scene the plausibility that realistic conventions require. Biff reflects bitterly about his father, "He had all the wrong dreams. All, all, wrong." Then Charley admonishes him for dishonoring Willy's memory.

CHARLEY: Nobody dast blame this man. You don't understand. Willy was
        a salesman. And for a salesman, there is no rock bottom to
        life. He don't put a bolt to a nut, he don't tell you the law
        or give you medicine. He's a man way out there in the blue,
        riding on a smile and a shoeshine. And when they start not
        smiling back--that's an earthquake. And then you get yourself
        a couple of spots on your hat, and you're finished. Nobody
        dast blame this man. A salesman got to dream, boy. It comes
        with the territory.

The way the dramatist expresses idea in this passage is characteristic of modern playwrights. Biff's line is plainly a statement about idea, but within the context of the situation, it sounds like a spontaneous emotional outburst. Charley's speech is also an extended expression of idea, technically similar to Cleante's in *Tartuffe*. The tempo of his dialogue is slow because the speech is comparatively long, also like Cleante's. Charley's speech, however, sounds realistically believable because Miller has placed it in a solemn situation and divided it into 11 short sentences averaging only nine words each. The skillfully selected dramatic context plus the halting emotional progression of the words conceal the intellectual content of the speech and make it sound like an expression of character and feeling.

RHYTHM

Rhythm is the pattern of changing tensions in the beats, units, scenes, and acts, a pulsing feeling that is experienced when the dramatic impressions build up and are released in each dramatic progression. Broadly speaking, rhythm operates the same way in drama as it does in metrical poetry. It uses recurring stresses and variations in the placement of accents to stimulate feelings and associations that enhance the meaning. Rhythm assists progressions in establishing interest, maintaining suspense, developing the theme logically, and concluding interest in the work. Dramatic rhythm does not rely exclusively on regular metrical pulses, however, like those normally found in poetry or music. As already seen, there is a large variety in the speed with which tensions are built up and released within progressions. With tempo, rhythm is the second element of drama capable of directly representing human feelings. Because it is based in natural human instincts, rhythm induces feelings effortlessly. Most of us are constitutionally inclined to accept its emotional effects without even thinking about them.

In the Plot

Almost any good play will exemplify most of the devices dramatists use to create plot rhythm. The difficulty is that skillful dramatists use rhythm so inconspicuously that its features hardly show to the inexperienced observer. This is where close analysis becomes helpful once again. To some extent, rhythm was already dealt with while considering Freytag's principles of dramatic technique. Recall in Chapter 4 his point that a plot is not a flat, featureless composition. It consists of complications and climaxes orchestrated to convey the meaning desired by the dramatist. Freytag's equilateral pyramid was an attempt to describe an idealized structural arrangement of these features. But in doing so, he also provided a picture of how dramatic rhythm operates. By visualizing the maximum and minimum tensions (crises and climaxes) and the length of the intervals between them, a pyramid like Freytag's can give a total rhythmic picture of a play. Of course, Freytag's approach is not the only way to study rhythm. Readers could also use the simple method of noting the stresses or major emotional impressions within a series of dramatic actions like scanning verse. Collecting the stressed and unstressed impressions into coherent groups can furnish a narrative description of the rhythm. In any case, what we are attempting to find is how the dramatic tensions collect and develop to create plot rhythm in a play.

Studying how an individual dramatist uses rhythm will help to account for how it produces its effects. Referring to *The Wild Duck*, remember that Act I occurs in Haakon Werle's study. As the play opens, a dinner party is underway off stage, and the servants are putting the study in order. Pettersen lights a lamp on the mantle of the fireplace and says resentfully, "Listen to them, Jensen!" Then there is a whispered conversation about Mr. Werle and his son, Gregers. During the conversation, the other hired waiters can be seen busily at work through the doorway upstage. While they are moving about and arranging things, there is conversation and laughter coming from the guests in the dining room. As the two servants continue speaking, the side door opens and Old Ekdal bursts in, drunk. Horrified, Pettersen says, "Good Lord!—what do you want here?" and Ekdal asks to be allowed into the office to pick up his salary. After Ekdal goes into the office, Jensen asks skeptically "Is he one of the office people?" Then there is a secretive conversation about Ekdal. As the two servants are speaking, Pettersen hears the dinner party breaking up in the dining room. He suddenly warns Jensen, "Sh! They're leaving the table." The double doors are thrown wide open, and Mrs. Sorby enters. The two servants instantly stop their conversation and hurry on to perform their duties.

The rhythm in this scene is controlled by (1) the immediate tension underlying the first whispered conversation about Werle and Gregers, (2) the abrupt increase in suspense accompanying Ekdal's surprise appearance, (3) the escalated tension of the second whispered conversation about Ekdal, and (4) the sudden interruption of the conversation when Mrs. Sorby appears. The accumulated tension is held in check during the next unit. It is a transitional moment consisting of nine lines during which Mrs. Sorby and several guests engage in cheerful small talk as they pass through the study on their way to another room. Gregers and Hjalmar are then left alone on stage.

The scene between Gregers and Hjalmar contains seven short units crowded with enticing fragments of background story. There is immediate suspense when Hjalmar begins by responding to a caustic remark made by one of the guests about his presence at the dinner party, "You ought not to have invited me, Gregers." After Gregers reassures him, they talk about their school days together, their subsequent separation for 17 years, Old Ekdal's imprisonment, Hjalmar's photography career, the Ekdal family's separation from their previous circle of friends, Hjalmar's intervening marriage to Gina, and Werle's secret financial backing of Hjalmar's photography business. As Gregers is about to ask more about his father, Mrs. Sorby enters again and again brings the conversation on stage to an abrupt halt. Each of these topics is rapidly introduced then just as quickly interrupted by the introduction of the next topic. Although each topic clearly means a great deal to both characters, the suspense continues to build in the scene because nothing is fully explained.

Director Tyrone Guthrie believed that anyone who wishes to know a play well, as actors, directors, and designers should, ought to be able to observe the rhythmic performance like a graph similar to a patient's hospital chart or a company's sales statistics. In other words, from the description the reader should see the emotional peaks and valleys and be able to picture the shape of the scene in a graphic form that helps to make the scene more understandable. Graphing can also help in understanding the neighboring scenes better. Ideally, each scene should have its own small graph and correspondingly, a graph of each act should be developed from these. It is possible in this way to arrive at a complete understanding of the rhythmic peaks and valleys of the entire play.

This view of the rhythm arises mainly from the words of the play. All the sounds and movements, however, as well as the visual aspects of scenery, lighting, and costume contribute to the rhythm and should become part of that rhythm in production. In *The Wild Duck,* these elements are composed of, but not limited to, the sounds of the dinner party off stage and the piano music, the entrances and exits of the characters and the sounds of their footsteps, the movements of Pettersen and Jensen and the other servants, and even the pauses in the dialogue. In production, everything is ultimately part of the rhythm, including the speed and intensity of the light changes and the fast or slow curtains or blackouts between acts. Although awareness of rhythm begins with understanding what's going on in the script, it also demands sensitivity to the contributions made by all the production elements involved with the performance.

In the Characters
The frequency and amount of change shown by the characters marks their rhythm. How much change occurs in the characters from beginning to end? How much from one entrance to the next? In his useful handbook, *Acting: The First Six Lessons,* Richard Boleslavsky offered the following practical explanation for character rhythm. He and his student took the elevator to the top of New York's Empire State Building to illustrate the point. Boleslavsky maintains that the reason they were exhilarated by the view from the 102d floor is because it is so radically different from the view at street level. He said that if, instead of taking the elevator, they had ascended one floor at a time, they would still know intellectually where they were and how high. They would continue to realize the change, but there would be very little of the earlier

feeling because the view from one floor to the next would not alter very much. The final view would be the same in the end, but the gradual, step-by-step manner of getting there would make it feel different.

The emotional exhilaration they experienced after taking the elevator to the top floor was the result of several combined features: (1) the sudden shutting-out of the complex sights and sounds at street level when they stepped into the elevator, (2) the silent, accelerated ascent through space, and (3) the infinite expanse of open space that suddenly greeted them as they emerged onto the viewing deck. They were instantly transported from a noisy, restrictive world of chaotic impressions and thrust into a new world of openness, freedom, and silence.

Boleslavsky's lesson illustrates how rhythm operates in the expression of character. Hamlet's character is considerably different at the end of the play, for example, than it was at the beginning. We won't argue whether he has truly been transformed or has only revealed traits that used to be hidden. The point is that however changes occur, the alterations in Hamlet have occurred almost imperceptibly in small increments one scene at a time. The rhythm of Hamlet's character development is comparatively slow and steady, and the final effect is cumulative rather than surprising. Character development is also patterned like this in *Death of a Salesman* and *Streamers*. On the other hand, Oedipus descends from an arrogant dictator to a blind outcast in five enormous leaps. His personality is appreciably altered in each succeeding episode, and the emotional impact of his final appearance is that much greater because of the rapid, lurching rhythm of the changes. A similar style of rhythmical development is employed in *Tartuffe* and *A Raisin in the Sun*. Readers should understand that the manner dramatists choose for developing character rhythmically is an important feature in communicating the meaning of a play to the audience.

MOOD

Everyone agrees that successful plays evoke strong moods in both performers and audiences. Mood doesn't mean moodiness, the condition of being gloomy or sullen. In drama, mood is a particular state of persistent emotion that includes the whole range of possible human feelings. Acting teacher Mikhail Chekhov and his adherents refer to this as the play's "atmosphere." Some of these states lie exclusively within the play; others refer to a world outside the play. Although both frequently coexist in a play, the main concern here is the moods that arise from within the closed context of the play itself.

The given circumstances of time, locale, season, and social conditions can be effective sources of mood. Plot can elicit mood through tension, suspense, climax, and release. Moods can be activated by the mental states and emotions of the characters and the things they do, and in certain plays, connotations associated with the central idea can induce moods as well as intellectual awareness. Dialogue can also evoke moods by means of word choices, rhythms, imagery, and sound. In short, every play has the potential for creating moods in a variety of ways. Normally there will be one dominant mood that functions as a dominant musical chord, then from this controlling mood anything which evokes feelings can offer additional shadings and contrasts.

In the Given Circumstances

Although the general function of the given circumstances is to provide the temporal, spatial, and social context of the play, mood can be a by-product of those elements. Seventeenth-century, war-torn eastern Europe creates a pervasive tone of hopelessness in *Mother Courage*. The late seasons (fall and winter) and the desolate locales (a highway, outside a half-demolished presbytery, an army camp, and so on) contribute to the oppressiveness. The barren emotionless economy of a military cadre room like the one in *Streamers* can establish an ironic background mood for the highly-charged feelings expressed in a play.

A dinner party at the home of a successful businessman (the bustle of servants, sparkling candles, a comfortable fire in the fireplace, genial piano music, luxurious furnishings, and expensive decorations) produces an ironically pleasant emotional background mood for the first act of *The Wild Duck*, which is packed with tense personal conflicts. Compare this to the mood created by the given circumstances of the rest of the play, which takes place in Hjalmar Ekdal's flat. Instead of luxury, happiness, and warmth there is a cramped tenement with snow coming in through the broken windows whenever someone enters through the front door. These are only a few examples of how playwrights use moods created by the given circumstances to strengthen the emotional impact of the other dramatic elements in a play.

In the Plot

Among the easiest kinds of moods to recognize are those created by the emotional dynamics found in the plot. Murder mysteries offer some of the best examples of this principle. The moods created by the tensions, suspense, and surprises in mystery plots are a major part of their popular appeal. Though character is probably the dominant element in *Hamlet*, the magnificent scope of its plot has an emotional impact as well. It contains scenes of mystery, political intrigue, delicate lyricism, boisterous good humor, supernatural horror, pomp and circumstance, bitter irony, and sinister conspiracy and concludes with savage multiple killings and a stately military procession. Eugene O'Neill's drama *The Hairy Ape* provides another example of energetic plot dynamics. Some playwrights take the opposite approach. The sharply sardonic mood created by the deliberately flat plot dynamics of Beckett's *Happy Days* is a key to that drama's unusual brand of theatricality. In these plays and many others, the forces released or withheld in the plot can contribute strongly to the creation of mood.

In the Characters

Characters themselves can create mood through their actions, desires, and behavioral mannerisms. Molière's characters are excellent examples. Tartuffe's audacious and clever hypocrisy, Dorine's merry rebelliousness,

Mariane's childishly romantic affection, and Orgon's impulsive temperament contribute strong mood values to *Tartuffe*. The characters in *A Raisin in the Sun* create moods both individually and as a group. Each brings a special feeling to the total mood of the play: Mama's quiet moral strength, Walter's desperate longing, Ruth's sturdy forbearance, Asagai's stimulating optimism, and Beneatha's youthful exuberance. Individual character moods also contribute significantly to the total mood appeal of *Mother Courage, Streamers,* and *Death of a Salesman.*

Some characters are so effectively written and compelling that their moods determine the controlling mood for the entire play. The characters of Oedipus and Hamlet, for example, tower over everyone else. They define the dominant moods of their respective plays regardless of whether they are on stage. In monodramas, the leading character must be so interesting that the character's moods replace those normally provided by plot, characters, and idea in multicharacter plays. Winnie in *Happy Days* is an example. Similarly Yank's moods both dominate and characterize *The Hairy Ape,* which is almost a monodrama in production.

In the Idea

Depending on what's going on in the mind of the observer and in the everyday world outside the play, idea can sometimes generate strong moods. Spirited feelings can arise when ideas in the play make direct contact with controversial real world ideas about politics, economics, science, religion, or art. The politics in *Mother Courage,* for example, were initially so provocative that its productions in this country enraged some people as late as the 1950s. When *Death of a Salesman* was originally produced in 1949, it was not unusual for fathers in the audience to weep openly. Its intellectual issues were relevant and affecting during the post-World War II economic boom. The anticapitalist implications of *Death of a Salesman* were also a subject of debate in the press. David Rabe's 1976 play *Streamers* is another instance. Today the play seems to be a compassionate plea for human understanding. In 1976, however, the Vietnam War and intense social upheaval were the immediate background. The incidental motifs of homosexuality and the brutality of war incited audiences and at the same time made them think. As was discussed in Chapter 6, dramatists write idea into their plays in the firm belief that they will excite our feelings. Readers can probably provide many other examples of plays in which ideas strongly excite the emotions.

SUMMARY

Tempo, rhythm, and mood are empirical human experiences, just as thinking, feeling, and behavior are. This chapter showed that plays depend for much of their appeal on these emotional experiences that normally lie hidden beneath plot, character, idea, and dialogue. The patterns formed of these experiences are not formal; they tend to be irregular and free. In a production, it is normally the director who deals with the issues of tempo, rhythm, and mood. It helps, however, if the entire artistic team at least understands these features and knows how they can influence a play. In this way, everyone will be capable of comprehending what the dramatic effects are and how they operate. Equally important, everyone will understand how moods can actually be accomplished. Of course, there is always the possibility of confusing internal tempo, rhythm, and mood with their actual external achievement in performance. It is important to remember that analysis is only part of what needs to be done to understand them. It is a way of helping to define goals and making the most of inspiration.

QUESTIONS

Tempo: Studying the beats and units, how often is information presented about plot? About character? About idea? Is the play crowded with such information? What kind of information appears most often? Or is there comparatively little information? Where is most of this information presented? Which characters express these elements most?

Rhythm: How do the emotional tensions collect and develop during each scene? Each act? The entire play? Can the rhythmical patterns of tensions be narratively described? Graphically represented? How much, if at all, do the leading characters change or develop from one scene to the next? From the beginning of the play to the end?

Mood: Are there any strong feelings associated with the year in which the play is set? The season? The time of day? The locale? Any strong feelings associated with the social groups? Are the characters distinguished by their own special kinds of feelings? Any strong feelings associated with the specific characters selected? Any strong feelings associated with the major or minor ideas? What has stimulated the ideas in the play to create strong moods?

9
. . . .

The Style
of the Play

The previous chapters were about the basic elements of a play and how they work their effects. The final stage of formalist analysis is about how the dramatist selects and arranges those elements to fashion a unique, imaginative creation. Every dramatist has a special individual style and can also be influenced by contemporary writing practices, but it is still worthwhile to analyze the style of each play. This is particularly true if the dramatist is known for exploring different styles as is the case with Ibsen and O'Neill, for instance. Analyzing the separate technical details of the play and their relationships to each other will reveal the most important impressions the dramatist wishes to convey.

Style may come from the dominance of certain elements in a play. In *A Raisin in the Sun*, for example, it is the element of character that makes the strongest impression. The play expresses itself primarily through the attitudes, ideas, and actions of the characters, and the dramatist has fashioned the play mainly for them. Plainly the main idea is also important. The situations in which the characters are involved reflect some of the most important social concerns of modern Afro-American culture. But even though idea helps to give the play significance and scope, it is not as important as are the characters themselves. The most vivid impressions are of Mama, Walter, Beneatha, and Ruth, as well as the other memorable characters in the play.

In *Mother Courage*, on the other hand, the dominant element is idea. Brecht attempts to present the life of Anna Fierling and her children as documentary evidence of the immoral effects of a certain brand of capitalism. Certainly Anna and the other characters are interesting in themselves, but their significance stems primarily from their relation to the idea expressed by the play. The elements of plot and dialogue plus a whole range of other theatrical and journalistic devices serve to keep attention focused strictly on the intellectual issues.

Style may also be categorized by the degree to which a play reflects reality. At one end of the scale are plays that are as close to reality as possible. *The Wild Duck, A Raisin in the Sun,* and *Streamers* are in this group as is any other play that presents a consistently plausible picture of everyday life. At the other end of the scale are plays that purposely don't refer to real-life situations such as *Happy Days* and August Strindberg's *The Ghost Sonata*. Between these poles are plays that sometimes reflect reality and sometimes don't. *Hamlet, Tartuffe, The School for Scandal*, and *Death of a Salesman* belong to this group. The task here is to consider the technical functions of the elements in plays from these three groups. As the level of reality changes, so also the principles behind their use may change. In the choice and arrangement of given circumstances, background story, plot, and character, a stylistic principle may be at work.

This chapter will return to the basic building blocks of drama and reconsider them individually. This time, however, the concentration will be on how they are fashioned and how they relate to each other and to the entire play. The division of analysis into factual and stylistic phases involves some repetition, but it is the only way to understand these broad dimensions. In addition to learning about the play's style, this will make possible the evaluation of the appropriateness of the technical features to the play's content. It's important to determine whether dramatic emphasis is being achieved by technical means, by the content, or by both.

GIVEN CIRCUMSTANCES

Time

Any feature that strays from conventional expectations has the potential of becoming a style feature. The treatment of time is no exception. For example, dramatic time in *Death of a Salesman* is unusual because it exists in several dimensions at once. In addition to the customary forward progress of time in the main plot, there are also Willy's many flashbacks. In his imagined or recollected reveries, dramatic time seems to go backward. Furthermore there are no realistic transition scenes to make clear the switching between present and past. The time changes occur almost imperceptibly, creating the impression of seamless continuity. The dramatist wrote in this unusual manner so he wouldn't have to devote valuable stage time to formal connecting scenes and scenes that allowed enough time for events to happen realistically. He chose instead to write only scenes that revealed the real meaning of the play. He wanted to emphasize that essence and restrict himself to it.

Dramatic time in Beckett's *Happy Days* literally stands still throughout the entire play. The harsh bright stage light never changes as there is no passage of time. A loud bell located somewhere off stage is the only signal for Winnie to wake and sleep. Winnie often speaks about time, but when she does, it only emphasizes the fact that time in the traditional sense no longer exists for her.

In these two plays, the treatment of dramatic time is meant to be distinctive because it intentionally deviates from conventional, realistic expectations.

Place

To answer the question, "Can place be stylistically important in the play?" it is helpful to learn if one of the chief interests in the play is its general or its specific locale. The attic in *The Wild Duck* is a useful example. Ibsen describes it in elaborate detail. It contains mysterious *"odd nooks and corners, stovepipes running through it from the rooms below, . . .* [and] *a skylight through which clear moonbeams shine in."* Inside it are doves flying around, hens cackling, rabbits and other small animals, assorted small trees, and of course the wild duck. Access is through a sliding door in the back wall of the studio and through a specially-constructed curtain, *"the lower part consisting of a piece of old sailcloth, the upper part of a stretched fishing net."* Throughout the play, much dialogue, action, visual interest, and sound effects are related specifically to this locale. Old Ekdal treats the attic almost as if it were a shrine; Hjalmar uses it as a hideaway; and Hedvig eventually kills herself there. In *The Wild Duck,* the attic assumes almost symbolic importance, and its design and use should be carefully considered in any production.

Beyond unusual individual locales, dramatic interest can also be found in the use of multiple locales or complex changes of locale. Initially the Loman house in *Death of a Salesman* must evoke a realistic sense of place, but it must also provide enough scenic flexibility to permit the fluid expression of time in the play. This calls for the complex and distinctive scenery and costuming that has become one of the hallmarks of this play. How, for example, do the characters manage to change their costumes when they appear in adjacent scenes in different time frames? How are the lighting changes handled? These will be important stylistic features for any production.

The multiple locales in *Mother Courage* also contribute to the style of that play. The action roams all over central Europe, yet the consistent presence of the canteen wagon adds a note of poetic timelessness to the scenic transitions.

The multiple locales in *The Hairy Ape* are as uncommon as they are varied. They consist of the fireman's forecastle, the promenade deck, the stokehole of an ocean liner, a corner on Fifth Avenue in New York City, a prison on Blackwell's Island, a union hall, and the monkey house at a zoo. The dizzying succession of unusual locales, each different from the other, contributes to the feeling of disorientation in the play and highlights Yank's conflict. The emotional impact of locales—individually, sequentially, and collectively—can add an extra measure of expressiveness to a play.

Society
Some very provocative observations can be made about a play's style and a playwright's thinking by studying the social features of the given circumstances. In *Mimesis,* for instance, Erich Auerbach has discussed the meaning of Shakespeare's persistent attention to the aristocratic classes of society. He points out that when members of the middle or lower classes appear, they almost always speak and behave in a comic, or at least an unserious, fashion. Aristocratic characters may frequently lapse into a familiar manner of expression or behavior, but the reverse rarely happens. Auerbach contends that this is evidence of the authoritarian, aristocratic values implicitly conveyed in Shakespeare's plays. The plays of Sophocles and Molière show similar tendencies. On the other hand, the plays of Sheridan, Miller, Brecht, and Hansberry suggest a fundamental mistrust of accepted social values; the

middle- and lower-class characters that comprise the dominant social groups in plays by these playwrights consistently speak and behave in serious, meaningful ways. It is the wealthy, upper-class, or conventionally bourgeois, characters who talk and act in comic, satiric, or unserious ways. In a way, this stylistic feature can be understood as a subtle critique of wealthy, or at least of bourgeois, society.

In contrast to the drama of earlier centuries, modern drama is generally characterized by its preoccupation with middle- and lower-class working society, but there are still variations in the social groups even in modern plays. Eugene O'Neill's plays are among the most widely produced American plays worldwide. We can arrive at some useful observations about the universal appeal of his style by examining the social groupings in *The Hairy Ape*. The basic social group consists of working-class seamen, but within this broad category are found stokers, engineers, and mates and Irishmen, Germans, Cockney, Frenchmen, Scandinavians, Chinese, Dutch, and Italians. Also present are marxists, capitalists, policemen, criminals, prison guards, trade unionists, and anarchists. There is variety even among the wealthy classes represented, including industrialists, robber barons, high society, religious leaders, and politicians. Apes and monkeys have their day, too. The remarkable number and variety of social groups lead to the feeling of seeing the whole world spread out and contribute a sense of universality to Yank's plight.

The choice of fashionable social groups or fashionable values may also lead to some helpful stylistic insights that may have been overlooked or at least underexpressed in earlier interpretations. *The School for Scandal* is a satire about a small circle of comically malicious characters who entertain themselves by destroying the reputations of other people. One of these characters is Joseph Surface, whom Sheridan has singled out for special comic disapproval. Joseph admits to being a "sentimentalist." The sentimentalists were a fashionable social group current in eighteenth century London. They were distinguished by their obvious aristocratic class consciousness, their flamboyant moral self-righteousness, and their habit of sprinkling conversations with clever epigrams drawn from popular sentimentalist literature. Joseph displays all these traits. Against Joseph and his sentimentalists, Sheridan places Charles Surface and his egalitarian circle of friends, who condemn class distinctions and sentimental cant and espouse democratic ideals. Sheridan's style in this play is marked by the contrast between these distinctive social groups.

Other Stylistic Considerations

A close study of other given circumstances can uncover further theatrical values that contribute to a play's appeal. Under the category of intellect (science and technology), for example, there are intriguing historical details about a late nineteenth century photography studio elaborately described in *The Wild Duck*. Scattered around Hjalmar's studio are *"photographic instruments and apparatus of different kinds, boxes and bottles of chemicals, instruments, tools, photographs and small articles, such as camel's-hair pencils, paper, and so forth."* Act III opens with Hjalmar colorizing and retouching photographs. At the beginning of Act IV, Gina has just finished a photographic sitting. She's shown "*with a little box and a wet glass plate in her hand,*" and later she "*slips the plate into the box and puts it into the covered camera.*" Hjalmar's photography business is a plot motif that runs throughout the play.

A little supplementary study reveals that Ibsen has accurately described the practice of *wet plate* photography that was used during the period. Historians of photography also suggest that, in its infant stages at least, photography was popularly admired as a shortcut for artists so that they could avoid the necessity of learning basic drawing and painting techniques. With a little imagination, readers should recognize the potential theatrical appeal of these unusual technological and historical details. Photography was still relatively novel in 1884, and Hjalmar's studio may have been one of the first in his city. He would naturally be proud of that. The fact that photography was considered by some to be a shortcut to art logically calls to mind Hjalmar's desire to be treated as an artist without having to do the actual hard work of making art. He maintained this illusion about himself partly by leaving to Gina the messy work of taking pictures and developing them while reserving for himself the artistic work of touching up and adding color to the final results. The scientific dimension of photography also provided him with public proof of his desire to be thought an inventor, another illusion of his. The fact that in this play about sexual infidelity Hjalmar specializes in wedding pictures is a delicate little example of Ibsen's wry sense of humor. The given circumstances connected with photography highlight many interesting features of Hjalmar's character when they are closely examined.

BACKGROUND STORY

Dramatists treat background story carefully because they know that it will provide at least as much dramatic potential as the on-stage action. They carefully break lengthy narration into parts and interrupt it with other speeches, permit other characters to underscore the speaker's feelings by intruding with their own comments, and arrange all the pieces skillfully in a climactic pattern. Because background story is often as complicated as is the on-stage plot, its treatment can be an important feature of a play's special uniqueness.

Nature

Apart from having occurred in the past, what kind of information is expressed in the background story? Ordinarily it consists of events. Early in *Streamers,* for instance, Roger informs Billy about Sergeant Rooney's military specialty when he was fighting in Vietnam, "You know what's the ole boy's MOS? His Military Occupation Speciality? Demolitions, baby. Expert is his name." He also reveals Rooney's experience in World War II: "Ole Sarge was over in Europe in the big one, Billy. Did all kinds a bad things." Background story, however, can also contain other kinds of information besides events. Again in *Streamers,* Billy asks about Rooney's personal feelings when he learned he had been reassigned back to Vietnam, "Was he drinkin' since he got the word?" Roger uses a sensory response about the past to imply that Rooney was clearly frightened, "Was he breathin', Billy, was he breathin'?" As their conversation continues, they discuss events, feelings, and sensory responses from their own pasts. In Roger's portrayal of the NCO, there are also examples of background story containing character descriptions. Past events in themselves play a relatively minor role in *Streamers*; past feelings, character descriptions, and sensory responses, however, are important features of style in the background story.

Quality
How the background story is disclosed is another revealing feature. As already discussed, playwrights use various methods also used by other kinds of writers. In older period plays, the practice was frequently to tell the background story as sustained direct narration presented somewhere near the beginning of the play. Used effectively by early dramatists, the direct narrative persisted through the eighteenth century and in some cases still exists. David Rabe's *Streamers* is justly admired for its realism, but in the handling of background story, Rabe relies on the tested method of prolonged direct narration. Billy's speech at the end of Act I is a good demonstration. Its function is mainly character description enhanced with assorted other types of events and feelings. Even though Billy's story is 457 words long, Rabe has insured that the uninterrupted presentation remains realistically plausible. The situation establishes that the characters are in their bunks about to go to sleep for the night. It is dark and quiet. The striking events of the previous scene have stirred the characters' feelings. Billy dreamily reflects on the experiences of a boyhood friend or maybe of Billy himself. His sentences are short, and the grammar and syntax are irregular. In this context, the length and placement of Billy's story does not appear improbable.

Modern background story technique, influenced largely by realism, develops in fragments retrospectively. The chapter devoted to background story already discussed the enterprising ways in which Ibsen and others treated background story. It also described the contemporary practice of purposely withholding, concealing, or even ignoring background information to achieve dramatic effects. Samuel Beckett has done this so artistically that it has become one of the chief stylistic features of his plays. A great deal of the background story in *Happy Days*, for instance, is either carefully hidden within elliptical suggestions and accidental remarks or else it has been deliberately eliminated. Beckett's background story style has theatrical appeal. It's part of the play's overall style. It evokes ambiguity, ominous forebodings, and, most important, the quality of universality.

Premises for Disclosure
One difficulty with realistic dramaturgy is the time and effort needed to establish believability. Apart from the visual considerations, characters must be occupied continuously doing plausible actions and speaking in believable ways. They must observe all the details of ordinary life that have no other purpose on stage than to make what is going on seem real. This is particularly true for background story. It takes a great deal of time and extraordinary skill to

incorporate technical devices into a plot to justify the disclosure of the past by the characters. This means that, besides the nature and quality of background story, there is also the possibility of style in the premises used for its disclosure. Tennant's study, *Ibsen's Dramatic Technique,* provides useful insights into the development of Ibsen's background story technique. He explains how Ibsen sustains realistic believability in disclosing the background story by using the conventions of confidants, the meetings of old friends, inquiring strangers, *raissoneurs,* and written correspondence. Ibsen's methods worked so well that they have become the model for realistic dramatists.

In *Death of a Salesman,* Arthur Miller shows that he is one of the principal beneficiaries of Ibsen's artistry. Miller repeatedly uses the conventional devices of returning characters and confidants to justify the disclosure of the past realistically. In the opening scene of the play, Willy's surprise return from a sales trip provides a plausible reason for him to explain why he came back. Willy also talks about Biff's recent return home after a long absence. In the next scene, Biff's return furnishes the chance for him to talk about his childhood with Happy and also about what has happened during the intervening years. Later in the act, a confidant appears in the form of Charley, the Lomans' next door neighbor. Charley's encouraging questions permit Willy to unburden himself about Biff's return and other related information. Ben's appearance in a memory flashback scene supplies the justification for him and Willy to discuss their pasts. The frequent use of returning characters and confidants to justify disclosure of the background story realistically is an important feature of this play's style.

Historical authors and some modern authors as well do not bother so much about surface plausibility. They dispense background story as swiftly as possible, often in great, long passages. This does not mean the background story is handled clumsily. It means that it is disclosed speedily in order to devote more attention to plot, character, and meaning. The conventional, nonrealistic devices for narrating the background story in nonrealistic plays are asides, prologues, choruses, messengers, soliloquies, and dumb shows (plays-within-plays). Many of these devices are used in *Mother Courage.*

PLOT

Nature
That there is a need for understanding the genre or collective emotional spirit of a play is clear. This book, however, is not directly concerned with the theoretical definitions of tragedy, comedy, melodrama, and farce (see Appendix B). The purpose behind studying the spirit of a play's actions is not to comply with theoretical categories; rather it is to understand the emotional feel of a play as the basis for an approach to acting, directing, or designing. For the time being, it is enough to recognize that in comedies unhappy situations are prevented from becoming too serious so that they will not break the comic mood, and in tragedies, these situations develop to the fullest possible extent.

The difference is more of degree than it is of kind. In the technical treatment of plot, character, idea, dialogue, and other features, all dramatic genres are essentially alike.

The nature of the actions in a play can tell a great deal about its emotional spirit, which can be a key feature of its theatrical appeal. In the past, the actions expressed in plays tended to be consistent with classical conventions. Comedies like *The School for Scandal* contained primarily cheerful incidents and happy endings. Tragedies like *Oedipus Rex* involved essentially serious incidents and unhappy endings. Enforced uniformity, however, was never completely popular. In even the earliest plays, comic or at least lighthearted actions were found even within the most serious of plays and vice versa. One of the major characteristics of Shakespeare's style and his point of departure from previous writers was his simultaneous mixture of comic and serious actions. For example, although most of the incidents in *Hamlet* are serious, nevertheless comic or ironic moments continually intrude. This is true in single speeches, within individual characters, in scenes, and throughout the entire play. To a lesser extent, Molière's plays show similar tendencies. *Tartuffe* is mainly cheerful in spirit although some scenes, notably those between Elmire and Tartuffe, contain moments of genuine seriousness. To maintain dramatic focus, some plays try to sustain a consistent general mood even though they may contain contrasting actions. Arthur Miller's *Death of a Salesman,* for example, contains some comic and ironic moments, but its dominant mood is serious.

There are also modern plays that combine serious with not-so-serious actions to a much greater extent. In the final scene of *The Wild Duck,* Hedvig's heartbreaking suicide shares the stage with the drunkenness of Ekdal and Reverend Molvik and the egotistical bombast of Hjalmar's sentimental self-admiration and self-pity. The simultaneous combination of contrasting actions is as shockingly incongruous as it is unique.

At the end of *The Hairy Ape,* Yank encounters an ape at the zoo. In any other context, the combination of characters would be funny, but O'Neill has chosen to draw a parallel between Yank's psychological alienation from society and the ape's enforced isolation from his natural environment. The result is a unique dramatic conclusion. The ending of *Streamers* also displays simultaneous contrasting actions. After a horribly violent scene in which two characters are slashed to death graphically, Sergeant Cokes sits on a footlocker and serenely sings a ballad to the tune of "Beautiful Dreamer." Mixing incongruous actions is intentionally discomforting and an important stylistic statement. Few plays today maintain the kind of consistent emotional mood once found in historical dramas. Instead, like *The Hairy Ape* and *Streamers,* they tend to emphasize unusual combinations of actions and the uncomfortable feelings that arise from them as part of their style.

Organization
Most dramas are organized by cause and effect. They lead through a series of consecutive, apparently inevitable events without anything missing or out of place, from an initial situation to its logical conclusion. The chain of events and consequences is the essence of causally organized dramas such as

Tartuffe, The School for Scandal, The Wild Duck, Death of a Salesman, and *A Raisin in the Sun.* Starting immediately with the opening lines, questions, forebodings, and possibilities are raised that carry our interest from unit to unit and act to act to a logical conclusion.

Cause and effect is among the most common organizing principles of plays, but to be effective in performance, it needs to be seen at work in a play. Think of *The School for Scandal.* Although plot summaries usually overlook the influence of Lady Sneerwell in the play, the germ of the entire tangled story is her strong wish to destroy the love between Charles Surface and Maria. Unless her objective has a probable and satisfactory cause, however, she is not a credible character, and the play becomes little more than a collection of jokes and high jinks. Several things could account for her objective: malice, hatred, spite, envy, revenge, and even entertainment. The task is to determine which cause, from all the possible and probable causes, is the one that motivates her.

The answer is in the opening scene. Lady Sneerwell was herself the victim of scandal once, stemming from a love affair she had with none other than Charles Surface. What made the scandal particularly malicious was the class distinction between her and Charles and rumors of an illegitimate child. Now to revenge her misfortune and regain Charles, she says she would "sacrifice everything." This important information is disclosed almost accidentally in a short conversation with Mr. Snake, but undoubtedly it is the root of her main objective. It is logical enough and it certainly is adequate to explain the extreme nature of its consequences. For the cause-and-effect sequence to work right, Lady Sneerwell must disclose her motive in a way that clearly emphasizes its relationship to her objective. This sets off the chain of events and consequences that ultimately leads to the conclusion.

Cause-and-effect principles like those just studied in connection with Lady Sneerwell are normally treated in a logic class. Nonetheless, actors, directors, and designers need to be aware of them too and should recognize how they work in a play. The questions to ask are: (1) Which cause, out of all the possible and probable causes, is the one that activates the effect? (2) Can that cause plausibly produce that particular effect? (3) How is cause and effect disclosed? As the example from *The School for Scandal* shows, readers should be careful dealing with cause and effect in plays having complicated plots.

Not all plays are organized by cause and effect. Although this has historically been the dominant principle, many plays use other methods. *Oedipus Rex* is interrupted by improbable choral interludes. The stream of action in *Hamlet* often comes to a complete standstill while the leading character reveals his most intimate thoughts. The scenic development in *Mother Courage* is punctuated by signs, songs, and other journalistic and cabaret devices. *The Hairy Ape* and *Happy Days* have no causally related chains of events; they move ahead not by dramatized actions but rather by varieties of set speeches.

Some unconventional plays work by abstract logic, not causation. Take *Happy Days*. The play is presented in two sections. In the first, Winnie has sunk up to her waist in the earth. In the second, she's in it up to her neck. The second section develops causally from the first but only by accident. The real organizing principle is abstract, not dramatic in the ordinary sense. Winnie exists as the ironic symbol of humanity scuttled in a universe that has no answers, only dilemmas. She's a pathetic victim, and the earth in which she's embedded is the malfunctioning universe.

This play is plainly not organized by cause and effect. It's a self-conscious demonstration of the relationship between human nature and the universe, attempting to show Winnie as humanity at its most pathetic. Of course the play does more than this, but at least it is organized as a demonstration, not as a conventional cause-and-effect dramatization. Its parts exist mainly for the sake of illustrating an abstract idea that in turn must be reasoned out from the situation being demonstrated. *The Hairy Ape* and *Mother Courage* are organized along similarly unconventional lines. Some readers find this kind of thing unsettling, and they should; but there have been an increasing number of examples since World War II so it would be worthwhile to understand how it works.

Simple and Complex Plots

Whether the plot is technically simple or complex is another important stylistic consideration. Chapter 4 explained that a complex plot contains a profound reversal in the fortunes of the leading character and a change in that character's self-understanding. Think for a moment of *Tartuffe* and note immediately that the plot is technically complex. At the moment Orgon understands how misplaced his devotion to Tartuffe has been, he endures the loss of his personal fortune and reputation, not to mention the respect of his family. The plot of *Death of a Salesman* also presents interesting considerations. The playwright says that Willy Loman comes to a profound understanding of his situation. This means the plot is technically complex and Willy is elevated to the stature of a tragic hero. Critic Francis Fergusson contends in *The Idea of a Theatre*, however, that the plot is technically simple. It is not clear to Fergusson that Willy passes from ignorance to knowledge. The key to the dilemma lies in the scenes where Willy is planting in his garden. Does Willy attach any particular significance to his actions in these scenes? Does he associate the garden symbolically with his role as a father? Is the garden emblematic of the future or of posterity? If the answer to these questions is yes, the play could be a tragedy; if it is no, then it probably is not one. As this example shows, the issue of complex or simple plots is more than theoretical. It has practical implications because it involves specific actions in the play and how they are interpreted by actors and directors. Stylistically, the play may depend for its effects strongly on the emotional dynamics inherent in simple or complex plotting.

In a simple plot, there is no significant reversal either in the nature of the situation or in the understanding of the leading character. *The Wild Duck* is an example of a play with a simple plot. Hedvig's death is arguably a major change of fortune for Hjalmar and Gregers. Ibsen cleverly points out the error of this impression, however. When Gregers insists that Hedvig's suicide has improved Hjalmar's character, Dr. Relling carefully corrects his sentimental interpretation, "Before a year is over, little Hedvig will be nothing to him but a pretty theme for declamation," nor does Gregers give any indication that Hedvig's death has had any serious effect on his arrogant brand of idealism.

Censured by Relling for perpetually interfering in other people's lives, Gregers replies: "I am glad that my destiny is what it is. . . . To be thirteenth at table." The stylistic feature that lies behind Ibsen's use of a simple plot in this play is his determined skepticism and avoidance of traditional climactic endings. By declining to provide a conventional resolution of the situation, the action of the play underscores the attitude that people simply don't change, no matter how badly others may want them to. Other plays that effectively use simple plots are *Mother Courage* and *Happy Days*. Things grow from bad to worse in simple plots, but no one is any the wiser for it. To express the meaning of the play as it was originally intended by the author, it's important to express the simple or complex nature of the plot as clearly as possible. It could be a stylistic disaster to interpret simple plots as complex or vice versa.

Scenic Linking

Chapter 7 treated linking as one of the basic operations of dialogue. As parts of a whole, actions are also required to be linked together. Their connections prepare logically for the sequence of events and help to form a coherent world within the play. Actions are linked in practical terms by the repetition of selected features from one scene to the next throughout the entire play. The ways in which plot, character, dialogue, and idea accomplish the linking determine the stylistic feature that should be emphasized. In many historical plays, scenes are linked by direct statements placed emphatically at the ends and beginnings of scenes. The last topic in one scene forms the first topic in the next. Key issues are also briefly repeated within each scene. In *Oedipus Rex*, the scenic linking operates frankly in this way. Moreover important plot issues like the murder of Laius, Oedipus' past, and the prophecies of the oracles are also directly restated within each scene as linking devices.

Understandably linking actions is subtler in realistic plays. Tennant has shown in *Ibsen's Dramatic Technique* that the linking in *The Wild Duck* consists of repeated hints about certain fatal objects, words, and actions. Close analysis reveals continuous accenting of carefully selected plot incidents—specifically Hjalmar's youth, Ekdal's and Werle's pasts, Gina's past, Hjalmar's marriage, Hedvig's birthday, Werle's and Hedvig's weak eyesight, the wild duck, and the fatal pistol. The links are all united in the final misfortune of Hedvig's suicide. Ibsen's style of linking depends largely on allusions, direct and indirect statements, and inadvertent remarks.

Linking in drama is more than literary foreshadowing to arrange events and information so that later events are prepared for audiences beforehand. By intentional repetition, linking underscores the main idea and provides artistic coherence and completeness to the play.

Scenic Openings and Closings

In older plays, a scene was usually identified with the introduction and development of a single complete topic. New scenes opened either with the entrance of new characters or with the reappearance of earlier characters conveying fresh information. They closed after the information was developed and concluded. A quick review of *Hamlet*, *Tartuffe*, or *The School for Scandal* will show that this is their pattern. The scenic openings and closings are motivated chiefly by practical considerations, but they are believable in a live performance because other features distract attention from whatever structural improbabilities they might possess. Equally utilitarian openings and closings are also used in modern plays. The openings and closings in *A Raisin in the Sun* are governed chiefly by the necessities of the plot. Yet the emotional impact of the performance permits the improbabilities of the openings and closings to go unnoticed. The same considerations hold true for the openings and closings in almost every drama on television and in films. Theatre directors and actors can learn useful lessons from closely observing how scenic openings and closings are handled in these other mediums.

The appearance of the modern realistic style of playwriting altered this pattern significantly. In modern realism, characters are frequently introduced not to present new information but rather to interrupt conversations before they are fully developed. This practice intentionally creates suspense by delaying the full disclosure of information until later. This can be seen in *Streamers*. In Act I, Carlyle's arrival interrupts the conversation just when Richie is trying to find a way to conceal Martin's attempted suicide from the military authorities. Then Billy comes in and interrupts Carlyle just as he is about to release his aggression on Martin and Richie. Not until much later in the act does Carlyle reappear and furnish more complete information about himself. In *Death of a Salesman*, the action is repeatedly interrupted by the flashbacks and the appearances of Uncle Ben. The flashbacks in turn are interrupted by a return to the main action. In this way, the real reason why Biff didn't graduate from high school is not completely disclosed until late in Act II just before the final build toward the climax. These openings and closings are plausibly motivated according to realistic conventions. Characters do not turn up or depart on demand as they frequently do in older plays. The realistic style of interruption requires that the utmost tension and suspense should be expressed in these openings and closings.

CHARACTERS

Objectives
Theatrical appeal is often created by what characters want and by the nature of the forces that oppose them. Oedipus strives for self-knowledge in direct opposition to the will of the gods. Although he eventually loses on the physical level, he nonetheless achieves tragic stature spiritually by a heroic exertion of his will. By contrast, both Willy Loman and Walter Younger seek to defend their ideals against those of a world dominated by outmoded social conventions. Willy becomes a victim (perhaps), but Walter clearly overcomes and leads his family to a new beginning. Anna Fierling and Yank also try to defend their ideals in a hostile world, but in their cases, they are only pawns in a societal struggle far beyond their understanding or control. Stylistic appeal in all these plays results from the nature of the characters' goals, from what opposes them—whether fate, personal ideals, or socioeconomic forces—and from their final victory or defeat.

Values

In the past, established standards of right and wrong were more widely accepted. Consequently there was little attempt on the part of dramatists to use their plays to challenge the values of their times. On the contrary, dramatists generally endorsed the established social interpretations of good and evil. Hamlet and Orgon exist within societies where specific standards of virtue and vice were largely acknowledged as true. Their personal challenges consisted of striving to understand and conform to normal values.

Modern dramatists, on the other hand, repeatedly challenge accepted notions of right and wrong. This is not the place to consider the historical circumstances that led to such a radical shift in the general view of the world. Whatever the reasons, the results are there for everyone to see. The aim of many modern dramatists is to replace accepted values with new ones based on the conditions of life as they currently understand them. Plays such as *The Wild Duck, Death of a Salesman, Mother Courage,* and *Streamers* attempt to reveal the motives allegedly hidden behind existing standards of good and evil. In doing so, traditional values are frequently turned upside down. What was originally considered good becomes evil, and what was evil becomes fundamentally good. The clash of old versus new values forms a major part of the stylistic attractiveness of these plays.

Depiction

Characters may be revealed through either narration or action. The relative balance between the two methods is part of a play's style. That two of the major restrictions of playwriting are time and proportion has already been shown. Since most plays are written to conform to a two-and-a-half-hour playing limit, attention must be focused tightly on the most important elements of a character. Most of the play must be devoted to showing the actions of the leading character. Supporting characters have to be presented as economically as possible, often through narration. This fact is apparent every time the secondary characters in a play are analyzed.

When narration furnishes the majority of the information about major characters, however, the reasons may be other than practical. George Pierce Baker pointed out that the essential distinction between character drawing in drama and fiction is precisely the difference between action and narration. A corollary to this is that narrated characters are by definition more literary than they are dramatic. Certain major characters in *Mother Courage, A Raisin in the Sun,* and *Streamers* fall into this category. Whether these are dramatic necessity or lapses in technique is a matter for the reader to decide after studying the other features in the plays.

One major character who is almost completely narrated for sound dramatic reasons is Haakon Werle, Gregers' father and the alleged father of Hedvig in *The Wild Duck.* The paradoxes of his personality are disclosed mainly through the opinions of Gregers, Hjalmar, Gina, and Mrs. Sorby, all of whom seem to have differing, if not conflicting, opinions of him. The only substantial actions he performs on stage are the announcement to Gregers of his engagement to Mrs. Sorby in Act I and his visit to the Ekdals' flat to offer Gregers a position in the firm in Act III. Virtually everything else known about him comes from others. Of course, Ibsen's use of narration in this case should not be attributed to faulty writing. He carefully avoided showing too much of Werle's real character in order to leave an ambiguous impression of him. Werle's character is a diversionary tactic. What he did in the past matters little to the outcome of the play. The key issue is precisely what others think of him, specifically what Gregers and Hjalmar think of him. Ibsen's choice of a narrative style of disclosure for Werle is in harmony with the main idea of the entire play.

In older plays, it was often the stylistic practice to present certain major characters through a balanced combination of narration and action. Notable among them is Tartuffe. He forms the chief topic of conversation in Acts I and II of Molière's play. By the time of his first appearance in Act III, a very considerable amount is known through other people's opinions of him. Unlike Haakon Werle, however, throughout the remainder of the play, Tartuffe's personality is revealed frankly through his own words and actions. The audience has ample opportunity to test the impressions of the other characters by actually witnessing Tartuffe seduce Elmire and swindle Orgon out of his financial assets.

Narration defines Werle, and a balance of narration and action does the same for Tartuffe, but action is the chief method of presenting most major characters. It is by their actions that it is possible to understand the most celebrated figures in dramatic literature such as Oedipus, Hamlet, Orgon in *Tartuffe,* Gregers Werle and Hjalmar Ekdal in *The Wild Duck*, Willy Loman in *Death of a Salesman*, and Winnie in *Happy Days*. The way narration or action is used for presenting character is an important element of a play's style. Of course, regardless of the final balance in the script, the performer's responsibility remains unchanged. Both narrated and illustrated characters must always be acted to the fullest extent possible. The difference is that for narrated characters the actors should discover illustrative actions on their own without the direct aid of the playwright.

IDEA

The dramatist decides the meaning to convey and selects and arranges everything in the play to express it with maximum effectiveness. It follows naturally that the ideas that playwrights choose to present are important features of a play's style. Ordinarily in scrutinizing ideas in a play, the principles of logic help. Plays are chiefly emotional experiences, however, and the value of an idea as scientific truth is always less important in plays than is its emotional value. In art, the word *truth* has a broader meaning. It means not that the play is logically accurate but rather that we agree with it or that the feelings it evokes will lead to better human understanding.

Persuasiveness

The ideas in a play arise from the actions and characters created by the playwright. The credibility of the playwright's ideas stem from their suitability to the actions and characters and from how they stand up to examination. But psychological consistency is not the only reason an idea can be persuasive. Sometimes ideas may be compelling for conventional theatrical reasons. The extravagant ideas presented in comedies, for instance, are acceptable even though they will usually not withstand close logical examination. Comic ideas usually have only momentary appeal as entertaining premises for the plot, though they must be at least internally consistent. The religious hypocrisy in *Tartuffe* is as easy to accept as is the ruthless materialism in *Death of a Salesman*. They persuade because they arise logically from their contexts. On the other hand, certain readers may not completely believe in the kind of economic determinism presented in *Mother Courage* or the scientific materialism in *Happy Days*. They may feel that these ideas have not been adequately justified by the actions and characters. Some plays tax credibility despite the best efforts of dramatists. In any case, the persuasive power or lack of it in the central idea are important stylistic considerations.

Scope

The extent of the idea's application to life is another part of its style. Many dramas attempt to deal with universal artistic truths. These are feelings or understandings that are valuable to society under all circumstances. Solving important political, social, or moral questions is not part of the style of these plays. Although social and political ideas are certainly present in *Oedipus Rex*, Sophocles does not try to judge his characters on this basis exclusively. Most readers would also agree that even though Shakespeare deals with ideas about society and politics in *Hamlet*, he is more concerned with the characters trying to solve their own problems than with solving them himself. These dramatists observe, select, and combine ideas primarily for the sake of art. Their styles are based on the assumption that theatre is chiefly an entertaining experience, and interpreting their plays otherwise is a hazardous exercise.

The compelling question for other playwrights is whether such universal artistic understanding stands the test of time. The world has changed, they argue. The stylistic theory of *art for art's sake* may be a noble ideal, but it leaves much to be desired under current social and political conditions. Consequently, some writers feel they should make a stand in their plays on the important social and political questions of the day. Dramatists from Ibsen to the present have come out on one side or another of important moral and political issues. The ideas in *The Wild Duck, Mother Courage,* and *Streamers,* for example, attempt to contribute toward the creation of a new social order that is radically different from the prevailing one. The style of these ideas suggests dislike for, or at least dissatisfaction with, values that may be perceived as unhealthy for our society. Ideas are critical in these plays, and audiences look forward to being challenged intellectually by the productions.

But there are questions with this stylistic approach, too. George Bernard Shaw was probably one of the most articulate representatives among the socially responsible playwrights. Yet even Shaw (in an essay entitled "The Problem Play," reprinted in *Dramatic Theory and Criticism* by Bernard F. Dukore) expressed concern about the authority of the playwright to pronounce judgment on social or political issues, his own plays notwithstanding. He pointed out that dramatists tend to lead literary lives. They dwell for the most part in the world of the imagination instead of the world of politics, business, and law. Shaw argued that although such authors may seek to raise social issues in their plays, some of them remain surprisingly unaware of real life as it is lived by ordinary people. Few would disagree with Shaw on this point. Many modern playwrights present moral and political ideas with exceptionally high degrees of imagination and sharp senses of observation, but the key issue for readers here is more than one of technical skill. It is necessary to judge whether authors have enough wisdom to make the ideas presented in their plays both desirable and practical.

DIALOGUE

Since dialogue is the most obvious part of a play, it certainly is an important component of the play's style. The large assortment of potentially interesting features can appeal to audiences as strongly as does any other element in the play. Apart from its literary aspects, however, dialogue also functions as the container for the plot, character, and idea. These theatrical operations may be less obvious to an untrained observer, but they are no less important in determining style.

Literary Features

Literary style in the dialogue includes all of those features studied in Chapter 7, including verse forms, rhetorical or telegraphic or emotional speech, imagery and formal symbolism, songs, jokes, colorful and unusual words, idiomatic phrases, dialects, and anything that calls attention to the dialogue strictly as dialogue. There are many examples of plays that contain these features. *Oedipus Rex, Hamlet,* and *Tartuffe* contain many different verse forms as well as rhetorical speech, epigrams, and purely historical charm. These literary devices indicate that, even though the chief technical features in these plays are character and idea, dialogue is still extremely important in achieving the total effect.

The expectation of everyday talk in modern plays may lead some readers to find little literary appeal in realistic speech. Many modern realistic dramatists, however, also use literary features though less obviously than their nonrealistic counterparts. Arthur Miller's dramatic language in *Death of a Salesman,* as was mentioned earlier, contains pronounced rhythms, colorful words and phrases, and emotional speeches that contribute strongly to its total appeal. Dialogue is one of the main stylistic attractions of Brecht's plays—almost as much so as it is in older or so-called *stylized* dramas although with Brecht the language has a more surprising effect because of its contrast with the homeliness of the characters. O'Neill's use of dialects, imagery, and rhythms is not as important as is character revelation and idea in *The Hairy Ape,* yet the dialogue appeals strongly to the ear as José Quintero's recent radio production confirmed. Both historical and modern playwrights have used a rich variety of literary stylistic devices to focus attention on their language.

Text and Subtext

The question of speech rhythm brings up consideration of another element of style found in dialogue. One of the chief differences between older and modern dialogue is compactness. Modern plays tend to use language economically. They dispense with the traditional, elaborate modes of expression and cut out everything that is not absolutely essential. This radical reduction of the number of words in modern plays has had important stylistic results. Chiefly it has caused a corresponding enlargement of unspoken inner tensions. Stanislavski called these inner tensions the *subtext,* the unspoken words behind the text.

An important question for Stanislavski was how to determine for performance the relative dramatic balance between words on the one hand and subtext on the other. Literary dialogue places more emphasis on spoken words, less on subtext. In contrast, economical modern dialogue capitalizes strongly on subtext to express character, feelings, and ideas. Thus some realistic dialogue may sound conversational, but in reality, it may be far different from relaxed, everyday speech. Forceful subtext revealed through vocal rhythms and word choices energizes the dialogue and makes it dramatic in a modern way. In the plays of Ibsen, Miller, and Beckett, for instance, characters say what they mean using the fewest possible words, yet they seem to understand subtle hints and veiled allusions almost at first hearing. When this occurs frequently in the play, it is for a conscious purpose, and it is a sure sign that subtext is a prominent element of the play's style.

MOOD

Once again, mood does not mean moodiness. Mood in drama is a particular state of sustained emotion that includes the whole range of possible human feelings. Production values contribute strongly to mood, but to be truly effective, mood values should develop in harmony with other values already present in the script. Mood is an important stylistic factor in the play when the persistent feelings generated by the plot, the characters, or the idea are potent enough to be memorable in themselves. As the chief element of dramatic interest, however, a unified persistent mood is important in only a few selected plays, mainly in the works of the symbolists. Although the ideas in symbolist plays are important as well, the semiconscious dreamlike atmosphere that suffuses the entire action is the outstanding stylistic feature. It had better be conspicuously there in production, or the play will surely suffer.

There are a number of modern plays in which persistent mood plays at least a minor role. The plays of Anton Chekhov, William Saroyan, and Tennessee Williams are valued partly for their sustained feelings of nostalgic charm. The moods in these plays are unique, but they seldom overpower the principal interest in character. Fantasy plays like James Barrie's *Peter Pan* or Jean Giraudoux's *The Madwoman of Chaillot* also emphasize sustained mood. Even though mood is not their dominant appeal, their atmosphere of make-believe must be understood if they are to be successfully produced. Not least important among the list of plays in which mood is stylistically important are comedies, especially romantic comedies, and satires. In such plays, the influence of sustained moods of cheerfulness, romance, or irony are, or should be, fundamental parts of their appeal.

A FINAL WORD

This is the end of a long, close look at the complex subject of script analysis. Yet one of the difficulties with analytical principles when they are defined and explained in a textbook is that they can remain inactive on the printed page. When this happens readers will remain just as mystified about how plays work as they may have been before they read the book, despite the best efforts of author and teachers. One remedy is to consider that the principles might work better as questions that encourage a search for answers. The questions at the end of each chapter should be a guide to what is included in basic script analysis. They are meant to encourage as much familiarity as possible with all the facets of plays and all the possible relationships among them. Equally important, the questions encourage examination of the facts behind the assumptions the reader considers important in a play. They also reinforce the practice of systematic inquiry, which after all will be conducted ordinarily without the benefit of an expert guide.

Even though not all of the topics will be equally helpful all the time, readers should determine for themselves which ones are more valuable and which ones less so for each individual play. This means answering, or attempting to answer, completely all the questions. It means thinking out the most subtle implications of what the characters say and do and what the play intends. By the same token, script analysis should never be allowed to become fussy or overwrought. The ultimate goal is to stir up the imagination and to provide suggestions for acting, directing, and design. As much as possible, this objective should be foremost in the students' minds, and other considerations should be kept in the background.

SUMMARY

The assumption underlying this chapter is that playwrights are self-conscious artists. They know what they want to do and have the skills to achieve their dramatic goals using the most effective means possible. Playwrights fashion plot, character, idea, and dialogue as well as tempo, rhythm, and mood to concentrate attention on certain important features in their plays. In many plays, the dominant stylistic attraction might be character with supporting interests in idea, plot, or dialogue. In others, the main appeal might be idea with characters, dialogue, and plot occupying strong supporting positions. In still other plays, the plot might be the center of attention, and "what's going to happen next?" becomes more important than who the characters are, what they're saying, or even what it all means in the end. In a few plays, the primary technical features appeal so powerfully that the subsidiary elements may have almost no intrinsic interest.

Playwrights make the stylistic values of their plays apparent in various ways. The length and number of scenes devoted to a particular feature, the qualities of thoroughness and detail, and the spirit of the main idea all contribute to stylistic focus. Studying the artistic reasons behind these choices may seem abstract and theoretical compared to the crisp kind of analysis presented in the earlier chapters, but it is necessary for the discovery of still more playable values. Each reader will form personal stylistic impressions, of course, but they can never be totally separated from the elements within the play itself.

QUESTIONS

Given circumstances: How is time handled? Is it continuous or interrupted? Does it flow logically from beginning to end, or is there another pattern? How is continuity of time maintained? Is there anything special about the geographical locale? The specific locale? How many specific locales are presented? How is continuity of place maintained? What social groups are presented? What is the point of view expressed toward them by the play as a whole? Are any unusual or uncelebrated social groups presented? Anything special about the economic circumstances? Political and legal circumstances? Intellectual and cultural circumstances? Religious circumstances? Any special scientific or technological details in the plot? Any unusual social or professional practices?

Background story: What does the background story mainly consist of? Events? Character descriptions? Feelings? Sense impressions? Is the background story disclosed in large pieces? Retrospectively? Is it frankly stated, or does it consist of subtle hints and veiled allusions? What situations in the play are used to justify disclosure of the past? Who discloses most of the background story?

Plot: What kinds of dramatic action are represented? Are the actions predominantly serious? Comic? Ironic? Why? Are different kinds of actions presented simultaneously? How is the introductory portion of the play managed? How is the main subject introduced at the beginning of the play? What is the play's point of view to its subject? Serious? Comic? Ironic? Critical? How is the point of view introduced? How are the incidents arranged? Through cause and effect? Chronologically? In progressively more intensive scenes? From familiar to unfamiliar? How is the conclusion managed? Restatement? Amplification? Emotional call-to-arms? Upbeat? Does the plot contain a serious reversal of fortune for the leading character? Does the leading character come to a new understanding of the situation? How are the scenes linked? How are the openings and closings of scenes managed? Is the story in each scene completed? Interrupted? How are the curtain scenes managed? How are the act endings handled?

Character: What do the characters want out of life? Power? Knowledge? Love? Wealth? Fame? Spiritual fulfillment? What do the characters consider to be good or evil in the world of the play? How completely are the characters depicted in the script? Are the characters revealed through action? Narration? Both?

Idea: What ideas are dealt with in the play? Why? How are they related to one another? Is the main idea persuasive? How credible is the author's authority to speak about the idea? Is the central idea artistic? Practical? Moralistic?

Dialogue: Is the dialogue predominantly literary? If so, what are its main literary features? Is the dialogue predominantly conversational? If so, what are its main conversational features? How important is the text as compared to the subtext? Why? What is their relative balance in performance?

Mood: Is there a single predominant mood sustained throughout the play? If so, what is it? What features create the mood? Any shorter sequences of unusual, interesting, or effective moods? If so, what are they? Any seriously contrasting moods within the same or adjacent scenes? Are the moods independent of one another? Are they mixed?

Statement of playscript style: What is the single most important dramatic element in the play? Plot? Character? Idea? Dialogue? Mood? Why? What are the secondary dramatic elements? Why?

Appendix A

. . . .

Supplementary Topics for Script Analysis

Throughout the book a play is treated as an independent object with its own self-contained context. A good play becomes even better, however, when its external connections as well as its internal features are understood. If analyzing the play reveals associations with the life of the author, other plays, and the world at large, then the characters become more interesting, the plot thickens, and the whole play seems to expand. It becomes part of something on a scale greater than itself. In other words, while basic analysis can reveal the internal qualities of a play, outside information is necessary for a complete artistic understanding.

Questions to guide this process are provided below, but a word of caution should be added. Theoretical statements, the biography of the author, the historical or social context, the history of the play, variations of the text, and so forth—evidence that goes beyond the play—can only offer hints about the meaning. External information should always be considered supplementary evidence and its results confirmed by close study of the play itself. It must be tested against internal analysis in order to be acceptable.

BIOGRAPHICAL CONTEXT

Sources: What were the possible sources of inspiration for the plot? The characters? The idea?

Ideas: What ideas has the playwright been continuously concerned with, and how are they shown in other works by the same playwright? In the work under study?

Writing: How did the play come to be written in the first place? How does the play fit into the entire canon of the author's works (particularly in relation to those written immediately before and after the play under study)? What are the author's characteristic writing techniques within the play, and how do they relate to the author's other works?

ARTISTIC CONTEXT
Form and style: What is the dramatic form of the play? Why? What historical or artistic style is associated with the play? Why? (See Appendix B.)

Views of the play: What were the circumstances surrounding the play's premiere? How was it received by audiences and critics? Any other major professional productions? What were the major productions like? Was the emphasis on acting? Directing? Scenery and costumes? Which characters dominated? What did later critics and audiences have to say about it?

Translations or editions: If the play was originally written in another language, what translations are available, and what are their respective advantages and disadvantages? If more than one edition has been published, what are the advantages and disadvantages of each?

HISTORICAL CONTEXT
Theatre history: What was the artistic world of the theatre like at the time the play was written? Describe the acting, staging, theatre architecture, scenery, costume, lighting, makeup, and social composition of the audiences. How has the artistic world of the theatre changed since the play was originally produced? Will any of these changes affect a new production in any significant way?

Society and politics: What important social and political features characterized society and politics when the play was written? Can any direct or indirect connections be made between the play and its original social and political world? Are these connections accidental or intentionally point-to-point in the play? How has society changed since the play was originally produced? Will the changes affect a new production in any significant way?

Appendix B

• • • • • • • • •

Introduction to Genres and Styles of Drama

The topics of genre and style have traditionally provided the basis for courses in dramatic literature and criticism. They have also been the subjects of countless books and articles. A direct outcome of all this attention is that many terms and definitions are available for inspection. In the interests of brevity, however, this appendix treats only major genres and styles and mainstream viewpoints. The main purpose is simply to review the range of genres and styles that actors, directors, and designers must convert into theatrical form and to understand some of their major features. Genre and style are complicated but important subjects. Readers are strongly encouraged to consult some of the specialized writing listed in the bibliography before attempting to arrive at anything like a complete artistic understanding. Georgi Tovstonogov's essay, "Genre," in *The Profession of the Stage Director* is a particularly lucid and practical introduction for theatre students.

GENRES

The word *genre* was adopted from the Latin words for *genus* and *gender*. Broadly speaking, it refers to a kind or type of object, usually concerning works of literature. Dramatic genres are distinguished by the nature of a play's content, that is, by the ideas, feelings, events, and characters of which the play is composed. In classical drama, the original genres were tragedy, comedy, and farce, to which melodrama, or (serious) drama was added. From the Italian Renaissance through the eighteenth century in Europe dramatic genres were painstakingly defined, and authors were obliged to adhere to the rules prescribed for them. Later the notion of *purity of genre* grew less important as authors began to mix contrasting moods within their plays and otherwise create single works containing multiple points of view.

Genre is a theoretical and historical concept, but the need for actors, directors, and designers to understand it is just as important as it is for critics and historians to do so. Classification by genre is an attempt to define the play's point of view toward the world. In a play, life may be viewed as tragic, comic, or farcical; it may change from one attitude to another during the course of the action; or it may even mix viewpoints simultaneously to produce a feeling of absurdity or insanity. Consequently, in practical artistic terms, genre sets the tone for the production approach. It controls the general mood or spirit as well as the emotional rhythm of the play. By guiding the play in this way, genre helps to unify all the elements of production into a single harmonious totality.

Tragedy

Tragedy means literally the song of the goat, referring probably to a sacrificial animal (scapegoat) used in certain religious rituals of preclassical Greece. Classical Greek tragedy emerged from a form of ritualistic sacrifice accompanied by choral songs performed in honor of Dionysus, the Greek god of fields and vineyards. Today, a tragedy may be any deeply serious play with a profoundly unhappy or disastrous ending brought about by the leading character who is compelled by fate, moral weakness, or more recently by psychological maladjustment or social pressures. It is impossible to arrive at a more precise definition because the term has widely different meanings in various theoretical schemes. Broken down to its simplest terms, however, tragedy contains a powerful force, a victim aware of his condition, and the strong will of the victim to struggle against the force and overcome it.

In tragedies, serious events are carried to their extreme psychological and physical limits. The plots are usually complex in the technical sense, containing a psychological realization on the part of the leading character (*anagnorisis*), together with a major reversal of fortune from good to bad (*peripeteia*). It is crucial that the reversal is accompanied by physical and emotional violence, which often, though not always, leads to death. Tragedies are dominated by a central character who possesses psychological stature either of an historically majestic kind or that of a modern ordinary person. In either case, the character possesses a will at least strong enough to confront the major opposing force on relatively equal terms. The value system espoused by the leading character is said to contain a serious personal misjudgment or *tragic flaw* (*hamartia*) that forms the basis of the realization at the climax of the play. In a successful tragedy, the universal importance of the subject can lead to both sympathy for the tragic hero and apprehension for his plight—so-called *pity and fear*. This combination of feelings creates a social bond between the drama and its audience that is unique to tragedy. According to Aristotle, pity and fear combine to produce a therapeutic release of tensions in the audience that is known as *catharsis*. Minor genres of tragedy include domestic, heroic, modern, neoclassical, and revenge tragedies and tragicomedy.

Melodrama

Although melodramatic plays have existed throughout history, melodrama as a distinct genre is believed to have originated toward the end of the eighteenth century in France. The main features included a deliberately sensational plot with songs and musical accompaniment. Hence the French source for the composite term, *melo* (music) plus *drame* (drama). Its leading characters were plainly either virtuous or evil, and its endings were invariably life affirming. This was the original form, but melodrama did not remain fixed in this state for long. Dramatists soon began to combine melodramatic techniques with the techniques found in the more subtle and dignified genre of tragedy.

Today the term melodrama may refer to any serious play with thrilling, often violent, actions and strong emotions. Sometimes modern melodrama can be as serious as tragedy, but still retaining the life-affirming ending of its eighteenth-century ancestor. Historical and modern melodramas continue to share a major emphasis on plot, on "What's going to happen next?" They also share the same intention of attracting wide audiences by means of exciting scenes, tense suspense, and strong conflicts. (In France, the term *drame* was originally given by Diderot to a type of eighteenth-century play that was neither tragedy nor comedy but rather a serious play that fell somewhere in between the two. Diderot's definition is now more accurately applied to *sentimental comedy*, a minor historical genre. Today, the Anglicized term *drama* is used by critics to refer to modern serious melodrama to distinguish it from historical melodrama.)

The basic plot premise of melodrama tends to be exaggerated, but not enough to make it too hard for the audience to accept. Individual scenes are often completely dramatic in themselves, and the social circumstances generally play an unusually important role. Scenes are marked by sudden changes in incident and mood and linked by taut suspense with contrast customarily provided by comic scenes or characters. In modern melodramas, there is a clear hierarchy of character depiction with the major characters much more fully written (sometimes with the most up-to-date neuroses) than are the supporting characters. Melodramatic dialogue tends to swing from exaggerated to under-stated emotion with sharply defined spoken rhythms to strengthen mood. Socially relevant central ideas that point to a clear moral are another major characteristic of modern melodramas.

Comedy

Comedy can be traced to classical Greek source words for *banquet* and *song*. Much like tragedy, the earliest examples of comedy were related to fertility rituals and the worship of the god Dionysus. Gradually the early folk practices became formalized, and since the fifth century BC in Athens comedy has been associated with drama. Aristotle distinguished comedy from tragedy by pointing out that it deals in an amusing way with ordinary characters in everyday situations, and although comedy has passed through many different historical stages, the basic intention has always remained essentially the same—to portray human behavior in an amusing and playful way. Historically any play that was not tragic was considered a comedy, and for many centuries, critics expected authors to maintain the distinction between them. Although some of the thinking behind this contrast may still be valid, it was much too narrow for practical artistic purposes, and eventually it yielded to a broader understanding. Currently almost any play that deals with ordinary life in a predominantly amusing way and ends happily is called a comedy. Contemporary writers have discovered that in some situations comedy may be as serious as tragedy, and the ideas found in some contemporary comedies can be as profound as those in tragedies.

Unlike tragedy, the comic point of view is intellectual rather than emotional. Comedy is a way of looking at life coolly with the mind, and its success depends on keeping things at a distance so as not to stir up deep feelings. Of course, some emotional involvement is always necessary in the live theatre, but in general, real comedy appears only when feelings are held in check. Comic plots may arise from a variety of ordinary situations. Sometimes the release of restrictive behavior results in comedy. Incongruous contrasts, repetitions, inverted situations, mistaken identities, misunderstandings, and character automatism are other common plot premises.

Farce

Farce comes from the French term *to stuff*, as in cooking. Some say this is because early examples were used to fill in the intervals between the parts of a play; others say that it refers to vernacular passages inserted into Latin liturgical texts. Farce is a broader and simpler form of comedy in which everything is aimed at creating the utmost outright laughter. Its *slapstick* (visual and physical humor), *horseplay* (rough, noisy fun), *gags* (practical jokes with unexpected turns), *high jinks* (noisy pranks), and *jokes* (amusing tales), regardless of how artificial, are meant obviously for the sake of laughter. Since its earliest sources stemmed from an improvised folk tradition, farce hasn't left much in the way of written records. The chief historical examples were written at the beginning of the classical periods of Greece and Rome, during the Middle Ages, during the seventeenth century in Italy and France, and in the eighteenth and nineteenth centuries for English and American stages in one-act form as parts of bills with longer plays.

Except when it contains maxims, epigrams or wisecracks, as in Oscar Wilde's play *The Importance of Being Earnest*, farce generally has little literary merit. Mostly it depends on physical humor and its chief interest is to amuse by inventive plots and characters that deliberately create laughter. Even when the goal is social satire or commentary as in Alan Ayckbourn's *Bedroom Farce* or Michael Frayn's *Noises Off*, farce is still frankly contrived. But despite its exaggerated and excessive humor, farce is fun nonetheless to believe. Its strong popular entertainment value stems from its consistent internal logic and from the fact that its conflicts are resolved amicably, often with the use of surprisingly funny endings.

Farce also employs appealing leading characters written in large, bold strokes. Originally they were only stock characters drawn from stereotypes, but nowadays farces like those of Alan Ayckbourn can display more detailed character depiction. Still virtually all farcical characters are more impulsive than they are rational. They are usually gripped by a fixed idea and fail to respond to obvious clues. Reacting automatically to everything around them, they seldom learn anything and seldom even think about what is happening to them. Through their wit and cleverness, however, they easily compensate for their lack of psychological plausibility. At any rate, farce is not about character but rather about characters caught in funny predicaments.

STYLES

Genres are distinguished by their content. In contrast, style is distinguished by the form of a play, that is, by the shape and organization of the
technical components out of which the dramatist has fashioned the work. The
major historical, or period, styles are *classicism* (including neoclassicism), *Greek
and Roman comedy, morality drama,* and *romanticism.* Modern styles are classified
according to self-conscious schools and movements, or according to manners
and modes of individual artistic expression. The most widespread modern
styles are *realism* (including naturalism), *symbolism,* and *expressionism* (including
epic theatre and theatre of the absurd).

Dramatic styles originally appeared as historical expressions of
dominant points of view about the world whereas today all styles are mixed
and modified liberally—for example, *Romeo and Juliet* done in terms of modern
psychological Realism or *Tartuffe* done in terms of twentieth-century religious
skepticism. Sometimes it seems as though style may become little more than a game
of dress-up or hide-and-seek. Even though the idea of dramatic style is sometimes
misunderstood, however, the basic issues remain important. For audiences, the
play is always a single, continuous experience, but for theatre artists, style is the
distinct imaginative reality in which the story of the play takes place. Style is a
particular way of playwriting that creates its own distinctive artistic world.

Theatricalism and Illusionism

Broadly speaking, dramatic styles may be divided into two categories:
theatrical (nonrealistic or presentational) and *illusionistic* (realistic or representa-
tional). In theatrical styles, creating an impression of everyday life on stage is of
little importance. The main purpose is to express the content directly with as
little as possible coming between the play and the audience. Direct expression
may mean the use of a chorus, verse forms, candid narration, slides and film,
television, or anything else it may take to communicate effectively. A character's
inner life may be expressed openly, sung, or possibly even displayed on
photographic slides or television screens. Scenic locales may be conveyed by
narrative descriptions or perhaps not at all. In short, there will be no conscious
attempt on the part of the playwright to create the illusion of everyday life. By
far, most plays have been in this general style from classical Greek tragedies
through modern musicals. In contrast, illusionistic plays intentionally aim at
being nontheatrical. Plot, characters, and dialogue are carefully selected and
arranged to give the closest approximation to actual life.

Although the two approaches are diametrically opposed in intention, it
is a misunderstanding to think of these functional definitions as hard and fast.
As pointed out repeatedly, even in the most intensely realistic plays plot,
character, dialogue, idea, and tempo-rhythm-mood have been studiously
selected and arranged. In other words, realism is also a style although one
whose conventions require the carefully crafted illusion of daily life. Conversely
theatricalism does not exist in a pure state. Many scenes from classical Greek
tragedies, the plays of Shakespeare, or theatre of the absurd are as honest and real
as anything written by Arthur Miller or David Rabe. The use of one style does
not hinder the use of the other by the same playwright or even within the same

play. Identification of style is essentially a question of determining the relative importance or unimportance of selected dramatic features within the play.

Classicism

A *classic* is an outstanding or superior achievement which has endured in time or the peak expression of a culture or epoch. In drama, the classical period is generally considered to be the fifth and fourth centuries BC in Greece and first centuries BC and AD in Rome. Examples include the plays of Aeschylus, Sophocles, and Euripides as well as those of Seneca (read though not usually performed). Classical tragedies are characterized by compactness and single-minded, economic concentration on artistic unity. Scenic episodes separated by choral odes comprise the main structural pattern of the plays, which also contain verse recitatives, songs, and prose narration. Although they include violent physical action of the most extreme kind, such actions normally occur offstage, leaving them to be depicted more dramatically through long emotional narratives. Specific production features like masks, limitations on the number of actors, and the use of a singing and dancing chorus are unusual today but do not present too much difficulty in modern productions. In modern times, the term *classical* can refer to any play that emulates Greek and Roman models by the use of restricted plots, refined language and characters, a carefully crafted structure, emotional restraint, and economy of dramatic means.

Today classicism is sometimes mistakenly called neoclassicism; strictly speaking, however, neoclassicism means an imitation of classicism. Scholars say that in Europe the period 1650–1750 was strongly characterized by respect for classical literary tradition plus attentive study and application of its predetermined artistic principles. Neoclassical drama is primarily associated with the plays of the seventeenth-century French playwright Jean Racine. Although there is no chorus, music, or dance as was the case in the original Greek models, in other respects his plays are comparable to their historical counterparts. Neoclassical plays, however, observe the concept of artistic unity even more ardently than did the Greek plays, expanding it to include strict singleness of plot, character actions and personality traits, scenic locale, and passage of time. Such excessively academic attention to formal rules tends to render neoclassical plays exceedingly troublesome for modern readers. As a result, although neoclassical drama is still widely read in the classroom, its production is virtually extinct today in the United States.

Greek and Roman Comedy

Greek comedy was a form of rowdy, bawdy topical satire about contemporary public issues connected with politics, religion, education, and literary fashion. It employed music, dancing, and songs and was self-consciously extravagant and fantastic. Its plots were loosely linked by emotional contrasts and surprises rather than by cause and effect, and characters were broadly drawn from exaggerated types. Because the plays of Aristophanes are the only extant examples, this form is also called *Aristophanic comedy.*

Roman-style comedy actually began with the late Greek playwright Menander and continued with the Romans Plautus and Terence. It was neither lyrical, fantastic, or broadly satirical like its Greek predecessor. Its subjects were everyday domestic affairs, especially romances and family squabbles. Characters were stock types—braggarts, parasites, young lovers, aging parents, and so on. Roman comedy plots were more conventional and complicated than were their Greek predecessors. Character reactions were more down-to-earth, not as exaggerated or fantastic. The dialogue was meant to sound realistic, containing numerous colloquial expressions.

Aristophanic, or *old, comedy,* is strictly theatrical, whereas *Roman,* or *new, comedy,* was more illusionist. Roman comedy is also considered *comedy of character* because it dealt with characters caught in recognizable human conflicts and *comedy of manners* because it reflected the manners and morals of the period in which it was written. It is also *domestic comedy* because the characters and plots stem from everyday family situations. Roman-style comedy was subsequently revived in medieval farces and interludes, Renaissance *commedia dell' arte,* Elizabethan romantic comedies and comedies of humours, Molière's comedies, Restoration comedies, sentimental comedies, comedies of ideas (Shaw), and to the present in the popular comedies of theatre, film, and television. The differences are mainly questions of emphasis among technical elements.

Morality Drama

Mystery (also called *miracle*) plays were medieval dramas stemming from Christian ceremonial sources. Often performed on religious holidays, each work originally formed part of a cycle of plays based on the Christian Bible (beginning with the creation and continuing through the second coming of Jesus Christ) or on the lives of holy people. Mystery plays were simple religious stories written in the rough, direct, uncomplicated manner of folk tales. Morality plays, on the other hand, were a later and more sophisticated style. They were allegorical in nature and instructional, and their characters were personifications of abstract vices and virtues, like the characters of Good Deeds and Riches from *Everyman.* The appeal of medieval religious drama lies in its simple charm and, in the case of morality plays, its use of frankly allegorical characters. Although the original mystery and morality plays were strictly religious, later plays adapted some of their simplified techniques to suit more modern humanistic attitudes. Allegorical elements traced to medieval moral drama may be found in the plays of Eugene O'Neill (*The Hairy Ape*), Samuel Beckett (*Waiting for Godot*), Edward Albee (*Tiny Alice*), and Harold Pinter (*The Caretaker*), to name only a few.

Romanticism

Romanticism is broadly represented by the dramas of Elizabethan England (1555–1642) and the Spanish Golden Age (1575–1675) as well as by the adventure dramas of Johann Wolfgang von Goethe and Fredrich von Schiller, the plays of Victor Hugo and Edmund Rostand, and Ibsen's early verse dramas. The important stylistic motifs associated with romanticism are plots with multiple actions, scenes, and locales plus considerable freedom in the treatment of time. Political intrigues often form the background. Romanticism's major feature, though, is its liberal mixing of comedy, farce, tragedy, and melodrama, and of upper- and lower-class characters within the same plays, according to the authors' individual manners. The plays of Shakespeare, Goethe, and Schiller also contain large amounts of poetry, though not necessarily of the formal, classical variety. Romantic drama is idealized, that is, the characters speak the expressive fluent language of poets. Consequently it often uses nonillusionistic features, like soliloquies, asides, choruses, music, songs, narration, and direct address although some modern examples may still attempt to be illusionistic.

Realism

Realism has already been explained in terms of illusionism, but a few more words should be added. It is a flexible literary term whose many qualifications and equivocations can often be more trouble to understand than they are worth. What is clear, however, is that as the expression of an attitude to life, realism attempts to be scientific. It assumes that everything and everyone exist as integral parts of nature and uses illusionistic methods to convey the notion that human behavior is explained by natural (that is, material) causes, instead of supernatural or spiritual ones. Along with naturalism, its more extreme cousin, early realism was strongly influenced by Charles Darwin's biological theories and by Auguste Comte's theories about the application of scientific principles to the study of society. To this end, its artistic advocates concentrate on the depiction of social environment, particularly on the deficiencies and vices of human beings. This explains realism's major reliance on given circumstances as crucial features of its plots.

It should be noted too that strict adherence to the principles of illusionism existed only in realism's earliest stages. Later works contain numerous theatrical techniques such as multiple locales, telescoping dramatic time, allegorical characters, lengthy narratives, and direct address. A carefully crafted illusion of realistic plausibility, however, disguises them from all but the closest detection.

Symbolism

The symbolist viewpoint asserts that truth can be found only in the inner life of the human spirit, not in the realistic appearances of everyday life. The unspoken assumption is that the real world is a failure and that imagination is therefore truer and better than life. As exemplified in the plays of Belgian author Maurice Maeterlinck and Russian author Leonid Andreyev, the main characteristics of symbolism are sustained self-conscious moods of dreamy meditation. A *symbol* is something that stands for something else, and in their extreme forms, symbolist dramas contain abundant examples of formal symbols and allegorical characters. In Andreyev's *King Hunger*, for example, the intellectual idea of hunger is frankly illustrated by the allegorical figure of the King himself. But such plays also invite a large amount of informal symbolism by combining dreamy suggestiveness and carefully calculated physical actions with external reference points supplied by the audience. In Maeterlinck's *The Blind*, for instance, the sightless characters automatically conjure up images of spiritual deprivation, and the Priest becomes a representative of spiritual dogmatism. Legitimate symbolist plays require meticulous analysis to understand and deft interpretation to express their true ideas.

Less radical instances of symbolism occur in plays like *The Wild Duck, The Sea Gull, The Hairy Ape,* and *Happy Days.* In these works, all the characters are basically realistic, but certain other features are thoroughly symbolic. Symbolism is less important as a major point of style in them, but the plays would not make sense without a clear comprehension of their symbolic features and an unambiguous communication of their meaning.

Expressionism

Originally a response to excessive illusionism, expressionism was an artistic concept that developed during the early years of the twentieth century in Germany. It is the most candidly theatrical of all dramatic styles. Plot, character, dialogue, and tempo-rhythm-mood are employed frankly as artistic devices to achieve the greatest expressiveness possible for the play. Little attention is devoted to creating sustained illusionistic believability. Mixing theatricalism with illusionism is one of the main stylistic features. The beginning and end of *The Hairy Ape,* for example, are traditional illusionistic scenes while the scenes between them are highly theatricalized illustrations of the frightening social world in which Yank finds himself increasingly a stranger. Critics say that the distortion of given circumstances that normally accompanies expressionism is a reflection of the leading character's (read *author's*) state of mind. In other words, Yank's world is portrayed in distorted fashion in an attempt to communicate his personal conflicts more vividly. By the use of telegraphic speech, long narratives, asides, good-bad speech, and frequent repetitions, dialogue becomes a device to accentuate the leading character's conflicts.

One of the more important variations of expressionism is *epic theatre.* Arising in the late 1920s in Germany, it was initially the concept of director Erwin Piscator, but later it was adopted and expanded by playwright Bertolt Brecht who critics consider its greatest proponent. The term *epic* stems from Aristotle and refers to a type of plot that presents a series of incidents simply and directly without traditional cause and effect linking. The chief stylistic feature is epic theatre's frank admission of being demonstration drama for teaching purposes. The so-called *living newspapers* of America's Federal Theater Project in the 1930s deliberately employed epic theatre techniques as did Julian Beck's and Judith Malina's Living Theatre in the 1960s and 70s.

Epic theatre is somewhat different from true expressionism mainly because it employs journalistic, instead of artistic, devices to illustrate its ideas. They appear as visual projections, film, television, and placards; narrators, music, and songs; and obvious pieces of formal symbolism. Their use is understandable because the main purpose of epic theatre is to instruct rather than simply to entertain. According to Brecht, the main point is that epic theatre appeals less to the spectator's feelings than it does to his reason. For instance, in Brecht's *Mother Courage,* the main topic is economic injustice. To illustrate the theme, assorted characters perform self-contained dramatic lesson-scenes; they address the audience with narratives and songs to explain the meaning; and signs appear containing stage directions, penetrating quotations, and relevant statistics. Clearly, epic theatre potentially has a great deal of dramatic expressiveness at its disposal, but it may encounter resistance from those in the audience who disagree with the point of view it advocates.

In the 1950s, another variation of expressionism emerged, called *theatre of the absurd or absurdism*. Originally so called by critic Martin Esslin in his book, *Theatre of the Absurd*, it describes an informal group of like-minded playwrights that include Samuel Beckett and Eugene Ionesco. Absurdism is more of an attitude than it is a coherent aesthetic system. The term refers to intellectual irrationality, not necessarily to comic ridiculousness. Its point of view is that the universe is perceived as irrational (absurd) because the moral and philosophical beliefs of previous ages have all proved useless and the human race has nothing with which to replace them. Absurdism dramatizes the metaphysical anguish that results when human beings attempt to struggle with this irrational universe.

To express their highly individualistic view of the world, absurdist playwrights employ frankly theatrical devices in somewhat the same candid way as do the early expressionists. Instead of telling a story illusionistically, they tend to demonstrate a static condition from a variety of different perspectives. Traditional illusionistic plots with their logical progressions and cause-and-effect linking are routinely sacrificed in favor of plots that appear to be static and illogical. Absurdist characters are shown attempting to insulate themselves from the metaphysical mindlessness in which they find themselves trapped.

Beckett's *Happy Days* is a typical and excellent example of absurdist style. It contains little plot in the traditional illusionistic sense. In the first act, Winnie is trapped waist-deep in a mound of scorched earth; in the second act, she is in it up to her neck. She doesn't seem to struggle or attempt to escape from her strange condition. Instead she tries to make sense of her life by ceaselessly examining and reexamining the trivial objects she keeps handy in her shopping bag. The end of the play (since it's technically a simple plot, there is no climax in the orthodox sense) comes when her husband, until now virtually unseen, emerges from his hole behind the mound, crawls up within Winnie's view, and reaches for her gun, possibly to shoot himself or her. The plot (especially the detailed pantomime), dialogue, and tempo-rhythm-mood have been expressionistically selected and arranged to demonstrate the absurdity of her situation. The extremely exaggerated manner of *Happy Days*, as with other Absurdist plays, is inseparably an expression of its attitude to the world.

Selected Bibliography

• • • • • • • •

Abel, Lionel. *Metatheatre: A New View of Dramatic Form.* New York: Hill and Wang, 1963.

Albright, H.D., and Halstead, William P. *Principles of Theatre Art.* Boston: Houghton Mifflin Company, 1968.

Appia, Adolphe. *Music and the Art of the Theatre.* Trans. Robert W. Corrigan and Mary Douglas Dirks. Coral Gables, Fla.: University of Miami Press, 1962 (originally published 1899).

Archer, William. *Playmaking: A Manual of Craftsmanship.* Boston: Small Maynard & Company, 1912.

Aristotle. *Aristotle's Theory of Poetry and Fine Art.* Ed and trans. S.H. Butcher. London: Macmillan and Co., 1902.

———. *Rhetoric.* Trans. Lane Cooper. New York: Appleton-Century-Crofts, 1960.

Auerbach, Erich. *Mimesis: The Representation of Reality in Western Literature.* Trans. Willard Trask. Princeton, N.J.: Princeton University Press, 1968.

Baker, George Pierce. *Dramatic Technique.* Boston: Houghton Mifflin Company, 1919.

Ball, David. *Backwards and Forwards: A Technical Manual for Reading Plays.* Carbondale, Ill.: Southern Illinois University Press, 1983.

Ball, William. *A Sense of Direction.* New York: Drama Book Publishers, 1984.

Barrault, Jean-Louis. *Reflections on the Theatre.* Trans. Barbara Wall. London: Rockliff, 1951.

Barry, Jackson G. *Dramatic Structure: The Shaping of Experience.* Berkeley: University of California Press, 1970.

Barzun, Jacques. *The Culture We Deserve.* Middletown, Conn.: Wesleyan University Press, 1989.

———. *The Use and Abuse of Art.* Princeton, N.J.: Princeton University Press, 1974.

Beckerman, Bernard. *Dynamics of Drama.* New York: Drama Book Publishers, 1979.

Benedetti, Jean, ed. and trans. *The Moscow Art Theatre Letters.* New York: Routledge, 1991.

Bentley, Eric. *The Life of the Drama.* New York: Atheneum Press, 1964.

———. *In Search of Theatre.* New York: Vintage Books, 1956.

———. *The Play: A Critical Anthology.* Englewood Cliffs, N.J.: Prentice-Hall, 1951.

———. *The Playwright as Thinker.* New York: Harcourt, Brace & World, 1946.

Boleslavsky, Richard. *Acting: The First Six Lessons.* New York: Theatre Arts Books, 1933.

Brook, Peter. *The Empty Space.* London: MacGibbon & Kee, 1968.

Brooks, Cleanth. *Modern Rhetoric.* New York: Harcourt, Brace, 1958.

———. *Understanding Poetry.* New York: Holt, 1938.

———, and Heilman, Robert B. *Understanding Drama.* New York: Henry Holt and Company, 1948.

———, and Warren, Robert Penn. *Understanding Fiction.* New York: Appleton-Century-Crofts, 1943.

Brownstein, Oscar Lee, and Daubert, Darlene. *Analytical Sourcebook of Concepts in Dramatic Theory.* Westport, Conn.: Greenwood Press, 1981.

Busfield, Roger M. *The Playwright's Art.* New York: Harper & Row, Publishers. 1958.

Canfield, F. Curtis. *The Craft of Play Directing.* New York: Holt, Rinehart and Winston, 1963.

Carlson, Marvin. *Theories of the Theatre: A Historical and Critical Survey from the Greeks to the*

Present. Ithaca, N.Y.: Cornell University Press, 1984.

Carra, Lawrence. *Controls in Play Directing.* New York: Vantage Press, 1985.

Chekhov, Michael. *To the Director and the Playwright.* Ed. Charles Leonard. New York: Harper & Row, 1963.

⎯⎯⎯. *To the Actor: On the Technique of Acting.* New York: Harper & Row, 1953.

Clark, Barret H. *European Theories of the Drama.* New York: Crown Publishers, 1965 (revised edition).

Clay, James H., and Krempel, Daniel. *The Theatrical Image.* New York: McGraw-Hill Book Company, 1967.

Clurman, Harold. *On Directing.* New York: Macmillan, 1974.

⎯⎯⎯. *The Divine Pastime.* New York: Macmillan, 1974.

⎯⎯⎯. *The Naked Image.* New York: Macmillan, 1966.

⎯⎯⎯ *Lies Like Truth.* New York: Macmillan, 1958.

⎯⎯⎯. "The Principles of Interpretation" in *Producing the Play.* Ed. John Gassner. New York: The Dryden Press, 1941.

Cole, Toby, ed. *Acting: A Handbook of the Stanislavski Method.* New York: Bonanza Books, 1973 (originally published 1947).

Conrad, Joseph. *Joseph Conrad on Fiction.* Ed. Walter F. Wright. Lincoln: University of Nebraska Press, 1964.

Craig, Edward Gordon. *On the Art of the Theatre.* New York: Theatre Arts Books, 1956 (originally published 1911).

Daiches, David. *Critical Approaches to Literature.* Englewood Cliffs, N.J.: Prentice-Hall, 1956.

Danziger, Marlies K., and Johnson, W. Stacy. *The Study of Literature.* Boston: D.C. Heath and Co., 1965.

Dean, Alexander and Carra, Lawrence. *Fundamentals of Play Directing.* New York: Holt, Rinehart and Winston, 1974.

Dietrich, John E. *Play Direction.* Englewood Cliffs, N.J.: Prentice-Hall, 1953.

Druten, John van. *Playwright at Work.* New York: Harper & Brothers, Publishers. 1953.

Dukore, Bernard F. *Dramatic Theory and Criticism.* New York: Holt, Rinehart and Winston, 1974.

Egri, Lajos. *The Art of Dramatic Writing.* New York: Simon and Schuster, 1946.

Eliot, T.S. "The Function of Criticism," in *Selected Essays: 1917–1932.* Ed., T.S. Eliot. New York: Harcourt, Brace and Company, 1932.

Falls, Gregory A. "Intellect and the Theatre," *Educational Theatre Journal* 18, no. 1 (March 1966): 1–6.

Fergusson, Francis. *The Human Image in Dramatic Literature.* Garden City, N.Y.: Doubleday, 1957.

⎯⎯⎯. *The Idea of a Theatre.* Garden City, N.Y.: Doubleday Anchor Books, 1949.

Fogerty, Elsie. *Rhythm.* London: George Allen & Unwin, 1937.

⎯⎯⎯. *The Speaking of English Verse.* New York: E. P. Dutton & Co., 1929.

Forster, E.M. *Aspects of the Novel.* New York: Harcourt, Brace & World, 1956.

Frenz, Horst, ed. *American Playwrights on Drama.* New York: Hill and Wang, 1965.

Frye, Northrop. *Anatomy of Criticism.* Princeton, N.J.: Princeton University Press, 1957.

Gallway, Marian. *Constructing a Play.* Englewood Cliffs, N.J.: Prentice-Hall, 1950.

Gardner, John. *The Art of Fiction.* New York: Alfred A. Knopf, 1984.

Gassner, John. *Form and Idea in Modern Theatre.* New York: Dryden Press, 1956.

⎯⎯⎯. *Producing the Play.* New York: Dryden Press, 1941.

Gorchakov, Nikolai. *Stanislavsky Directs.* Trans. Miriam Goldina. New York: Minerva Press, 1954.

Granville-Barker, Harley. *On Dramatic Method.* New York: Hill and Wang, 1956.

Grebanier, Bernard. *Playwriting.* New York: Thomas Y. Crowell Company, 1961.

Gregory, W.A. *The Director: A Guide to Modern Theatre Practice.* New York: Funk & Wagnalls, 1968.

Griffiths, Stuart. *How Plays are Made: The Fundamental Elements of Play Construction.* Englewood Cliffs, N.J.: Prentice-Hall, 1982.

Gross, Roger. *Understanding Playscripts: Theory and Method.* Bowling Green, O.: Bowling Green University Press, 1974.

Grote, David. *Script Analysis: Reading and Understanding the Playscript for Production.* Belmont, Calif.: Wadsworth Publishing Company, 1985.

Guerin, Wilfred L., et. al. *A Handbook of Criticial Approaches to Literature.* New York: Harper & Row, 1966.

Hayakawa, S.I. *Language in Action: A Guide to Accurate Thinking.* New York: Harcourt, Brace and Company, 1940.

Hobgood, Burnet M. "Framework for the Study of Directing in the Theatre," *Empirical Research in Theatre* 1, no. 1 (August 1984): 1–51.

———. "Central Conceptions in Stanislavski's System," *Educational Theatre Journal* 25, no. 2 (May 1973): 147–159.

Hodge, Francis. *Play Directing: Analysis, Communication, and Style.* Englewood Cliffs, N.J.: Prentice-Hall, 1971.

Hopkins, Arthur. *How's Your Second Act?* New York: Samuel French, 1931.

Hornby, Richard. *Script into Performance: A Structuralist View of Play Production.* Austin: University of Texas Press, 1977.

Hyman, Stanley Edgar. *The Armed Vision: A Study in the Methods of Modern Literary Criticism.* New York: Vintage Books, 1955.

James, Henry. *Theory of Fiction: Henry James.* Ed. James E. Miller, Jr. Lincoln: University of Nebraska Press, 1972.

Kernan, Alvin. *The Death of Literature.* New Haven, Conn.: Yale University Press, 1990.

Knight, George Wilson. *The Wheel of Fire.* London, Eng.: Oxford University Press, 1930.

Lawson, John Howard. *Theory and Technique of Playwriting.* New York: G. P. Putnam's Sons, 1949.

Lemon, Lee T., and Reis, Marion J., ed. and trans. *Russian Formalist Criticism: Four Essays.* Lincoln: University of Nebraska Press, 1965.

Levin, Irina and Igor. *Methodology of Working on the Play and the Role.* Washington, D.C.: Ladore Press, 1990.

Lewis, Robert. *Advice to the Players.* New York: Harper & Row, Publishers, 1980.

Lynch, William F. *Christ and Apollo: The Dimensions of the Literary Imagination.* New York: Sheed and Ward, 1960.

MacGowan, Kenneth. *A Primer of Playwriting.* Garden City, N.Y.: Dolphin Books, 1962.

McMullan, Frank. *Directing Shakespeare in the Contemporary Theatre.* New York: Richards Rosen Press, 1974.

———. *The Director's Handbook.* Hamden, Conn.: The Shoestring Press, 1964.

———. *The Directorial Image.* Hamden, Conn.: The Shoestring Press, 1962.

Meyer, Leonard B. *Emotion and Meaning in Music.* Chicago: The University of Chicago Press, 1956.

Millett, Fred B. *Reading Drama.* New York: Harper & Brothers, 1950.

Nicoll, Alardyce. *The Theory of Drama.* New York: Thomas Y. Crowell, 1931.

Nietzsche, Friedrich. "The Birth of Tragedy," in *The Birth of Tragedy and The Genealogy of Morals.* Trans. Francis Golffing. New York: Anchor Press, 1956 (originally published 1870).

O'Connor, Flannery. *Mystery and Manners.* New York: Farrar, Straus and Giroux, 1962.

Pfister, Manfred. *Theory and Analysis of Drama.* Trans. John Halliday. Cambridge, Eng.:

Cambridge University Press, 1988 (originally published 1977).

Pope, Randolph H., ed. *The Analysis of Literary Texts: Current Trends in Methodology.* Ypsilanti, Mich.: Bilingual Press, 1980.

Ransom, John Crowe. *The New Criticism.* Norfolk, Conn.: New Directions, 1941.

Rowe, Kenneth Thorpe. *A Theatre in Your Head.* New York: Funk and Wagnalls, 1960.

Saint-Denis, Michel. *Theatre: The Rediscovery of Style.* New York: Theatre Arts Books, 1960.

Schechner, Richard, et. al. *Stanislavski and America.* Ed. Erika Munk. New York: Hill and Wang, 1966.

Schmid, Herta, and Van Kesteren, Aloysius, eds. *Semiotics of Drama and Theatre.* Philadelphia: John Benjamins Publishing Company, 1984.

Selden, Raman. *A Researcher's Guide to Contemporary Literary Theory.* Lexington: University Press of Kentucky, 1989.

Selden, Samuel. *An Introduction to Playwriting.* New York: F. S. Croft & Company, 1946.

Sharp, William L. *Language in Drama: Meanings for the Director and the Actor.* Scranton, Pa.: Chandler Publishing Co., 1970.

Smiley, Sam. *Playwriting: The Structure of Action.* Englewood Cliffs, N.J.: Prentice-Hall, Inc., 1971.

Spurgeon, Caroline. *Shakespeare's Imagery and What It Tells Us.* Cambridge, Eng.: Cambridge University Press, 1935.

Stanislavski, Constantin. *Selected Works.* Ed. Oksana Korneva. Moscow: Raduga Publishers, 1984.

———. *Stanislavski's Legacy.* Ed. and trans. Elizabeth Reynolds Hapgood. New York: Theatre Arts Books, 1968.

———. *An Actor's Handbook.* Ed. and trans. Elizabeth Reynolds Hapgood. New York: Theatre Arts Books, 1963.

———. *Stanislavski.* Ed. Sergei Melik-Zakharov and Shoel Bogatyrev. Trans. Vic Schneierson. Moscow: Progress Publishers, 1963.

———. *Creating a Role.* Trans. Elizabeth Reynolds Hapgood. New York: Theatre Arts Books, 1961.

———. *Stanislavsky on the Art of the Stage.* Trans. David Magarshack. New York: Hill and Wang, 1961.

———. *Building a Character.* Trans. Elizabeth Reynolds Hapgood. New York: Theatre Arts Books, 1949.

———. *An Actor Prepares.* Trans. Elizabeth Reynolds Hapgood. New York: Theatre Arts Books, 1936.

———. *My Life in Art.* Trans. G. Ivanov-Mumijev. Moscow: Foreign Languages Publishing House, 1925.

Stevens, Bonnie Klomp, and Stewart, Larry L. *A Guide to Literary Criticism and Research.* New York: Holt, Rinehart and Winston, 1987.

Strickland, F. Cowles. *The Technique of Acting.* New York: McGraw-Hill Book Company, 1956.

Styan, J.L. *The Elements of Drama.* Cambridge, Eng.: Cambridge University Press, 1960.

Tennant, P.F.D. *Ibsen's Dramatic Technique.* New York: Humanities Press, 1965 (originally published 1946).

Thompson, A.R. *The Anatomy of Drama.* Berkeley: University of California Press, 1946.

Thompson, Ewa M. *Russian Formalism and Anglo-American New Criticism.* The Hague: Mouton, 1971.

Toporkov, Vasily Osipovich. *Stanislavsky in Rehearsal.* Trans. Christine Edwards. New York: Theatre Arts Books, 1979.

Tovstonogov, Georgi. *The Profession of the Stage Director.* Moscow: Progress Publishers, 1972.

Vaughn, Jack. *Drama A to Z: A Handbook.* New York: Frederick Ungar Publishing Co., 1978.

Wimsatt, William K. *The Verbal Icon.* Lexington: University of Kentucky Press, 1954.

———, and Brooks, Cleanth. *Literary Criticism: A Short History.* New York: Alfred A. Knopf, 1965.

Young, Thomas Daniel, ed. *The New Criticism and After.* Charlottesville: University Press of Virginia, 1976.

Index

· · · · · · ·